WESTMINSTER ABBEY

OFFICIAL GUIDE

NEW AND REVISED EDITION: 1965

Printed in Great Britain by
Jarrold & Sons Limited, Norwich

CONTENTS

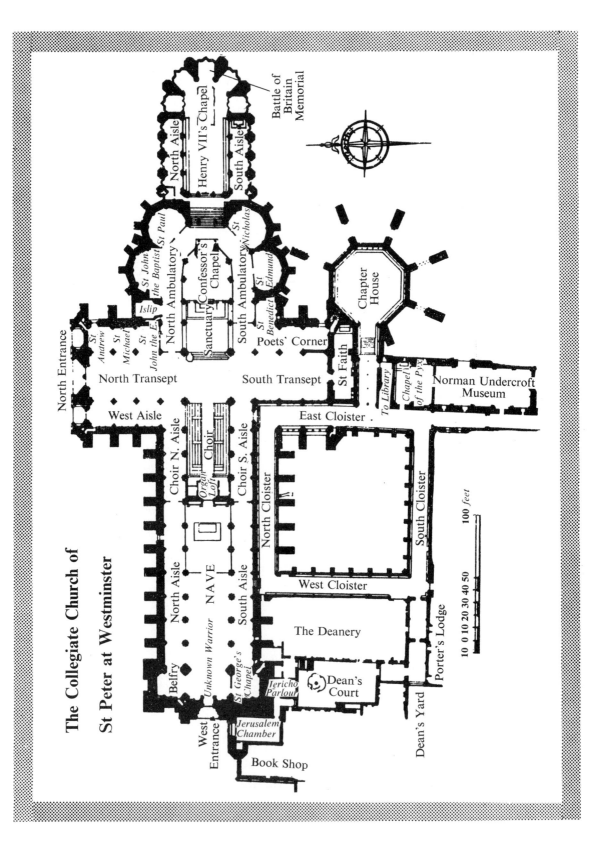

The Collegiate Church of
St Peter at Westminster

Henry VII's Chapel

North Aisle

South Aisle

Battle of
Britain
Memorial

St John
the Baptist

St Paul

St John
the E.

St Michael

St Andrew

Islip

North Ambulatory

Confessor's
Chapel

Sanctuary

South Ambulatory

St Nicholas

St Edmund

St Benedict

Poets' Corner

St Faith

Chapter
House

To Library

Chapel of the Pyx

Norman Undercroft
Museum

North Entrance

North Transept

South Transept

West Aisle

East Cloister

Choir N. Aisle

Choir

Organ
Loft

Choir S. Aisle

North Cloister

South Cloister

West Cloister

100 feet

10 0 10 20 30 40 50

North Aisle

NAVE

Unknown Warrior

South Aisle

The Deanery

Belfry

St George's Chapel

Jericho
Parlour

Dean's
Court

Porter's Lodge

Dean's Yard

West
Entrance

Jerusalem
Chamber

Book Shop

LIST OF ILLUSTRATIONS

SOME WORKS
OF REFERENCE

Camden, William	**Reges, Reginae, Nobiles et alii in Ecclesia Collegiata Beati Petri Westmonasterii sepulti**. 1600–1606. The first printed Guide.
Keepe, Henry	**Monumenta Westmonasteriensia**. 1683
Dart, John	**History and Antiquities of the Abbey Church of Westminster** (*2 vols.*). 1723
Widmore, Richard	**An History of the Church of St Peter, Westminster**. 1750. The first book based on the Abbey Muniments.
Ackermann, R.	**History of the Abbey Church of St Peter's Westminster** (*2 vols.*). 1812. With coloured plates.
Neale, John and Brayley, Edward	**History and Antiquities of the Abbey Church of St Peter, Westminster** (*2 vols.*). 1818. This is still the best authority for the monuments and epitaphs.
Scott, Sir Gilbert	**Gleanings from Westminster Abbey** (2nd ed. enlarged). 1863
Stanley, Arthur P. (Dean of Westminster)	**Historical Memorials of Westminster Abbey** (5th and best edition with the Author's final revisions, but omitting some Appendices of former editions). 1882
Bradley, E. T.	**Annals of Westminster Abbey**. 1898
Chester, J. L.	**The Marriage, Baptismal and Burial Registers** [of Westminster Abbey]. Harleian Society Publications. Vol. x. 1875–6
Lethaby, W. R.	**Westminster Abbey and the Kings' Craftsmen**. 1906 **Westminster Abbey Re-Examined**. 1925
Westlake, H. F.	**Westminster Abbey** (*2 vols.*). 1923. Based on the Abbey Muniments and very valuable for the Monastic period.
The Royal Commission on Historical Monuments (England)	**London. Vol. I: Westminster Abbey, an Inventory**. 1924
Perkins, J. H. T.	**Westminster Abbey. Its Worship and Ornaments** (*3 vols.*). Alcuin Club Collections. Vols. xxxiii, xxxiv, xxxviii. 1938–52
Tanner, L. E.	**The History and Treasures of Westminster Abbey**. 1953

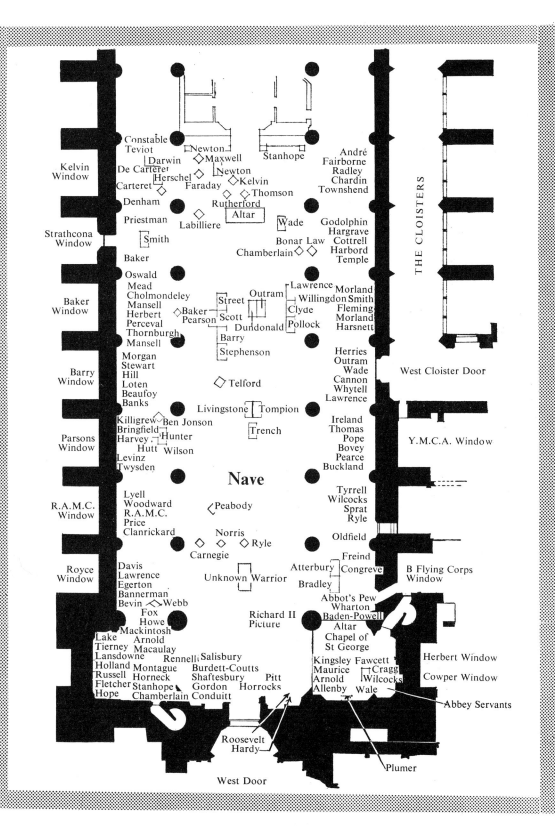

Kelvin Window

Strathcona Window

Baker Window

Barry Window

Parsons Window

R.A.M.C. Window

Royce Window

Constable
Teviot
Darwin
De Carteret
Herschel
Carteret
Denham
Priestman
Smith
Baker
Oswald
Mead
Cholmondeley
Mansell
Herbert
Perceval
Thornburgh
Mansell
Morgan
Stewart
Hill
Loten
Beaufoy
Banks
Killigrew
Bringfield
Harvey
Hutt
Levinz
Twysden

Newton
Maxwell
Newton
Faraday
Kelvin
Thomson
Rutherford
Altar
Labilliere

Stanhope

André
Fairborne
Radley
Chardin
Townshend

Wade

Godolphin
Hargrave
Cottrell
Harbord
Temple

Bonar Law
Chamberlain

Lawrence
Street
Outram
Willingdon
Scott
Clyde
Baker
Pearson
Dundonald
Pollock
Barry
Stephenson

Morland
Smith
Fleming
Morland
Harsnett

Telford

Ben Jonson
Hunter
Wilson

Livingstone
Tompion

Trench

Herries
Outram
Wade
Cannon
Whytell
Lawrence

West Cloister Door

Ireland
Thomas
Pope
Bovey
Pearce
Buckland

Y.M.C.A. Window

Nave

Lyell
Woodward
R.A.M.C.
Price
Clanrickard

Peabody

Norris
Ryle
Carnegie

Tyrrell
Wilcocks
Sprat
Ryle

Oldfield

THE CLOISTERS

Davis
Lawrence
Egerton
Bannerman
Bevin
Webb
Fox
Howe
Mackintosh
Lake
Arnold
Tierney
Macaulay
Lansdowne
Holland
Montague
Russell
Horneck
Fletcher
Stanhope
Hope
Chamberlain

Unknown Warrior

Richard II
Picture

Rennell
Salisbury
Burdett-Coutts
Shaftesbury
Pitt
Gordon
Horrocks
Conduitt

Atterbury
Bradley

Freind
Congreve

Abbot's Pew
Wharton
Baden-Powell
Altar
Chapel of
St George
Kingsley Fawcett
Maurice
Cragg
Arnold
Wilcocks
Allenby
Wale

B Flying Corps
Window

Herbert Window

Cowper Window

Abbey Servants

Roosevelt
Hardy

Plumer

West Door

LIST OF PLANS

FOREWORD

The Westminster Abbey Guide was first compiled in 1885 by two daughters of Dean Bradley (1881–1902), who afterwards became Mrs A. Murray Smith and Lady Birchenough. At that time there was no satisfactory guide to the monuments, and their work, which supplemented Dean Stanley's *Memorials of Westminster Abbey*, was of great use and value, as indeed is shown by the fact that by 1959 the Guide had reached its 34th edition. Mrs Murray Smith continued to revise and edit the Guide until her death in 1946.

It is felt, however, that the time has now come for a complete revision, and in this edition the letterpress has been largely rewritten, dates have been checked, and a more representative selection of illustrations has been added.

A VISIT TO THE ABBEY

THE INTEREST OF A visit to the Abbey will be infinitely increased by some acquaintance with its true character and history. The key to some measure of such knowledge lies in the answer to a few simple questions.

What is the nature of the church which you are about to visit? Why is it called 'Westminster Abbey'? Why not 'Westminster Cathedral'? What is its true title? How long has it stood where and as you see it? How came it to be thus crowded with royal and other monuments? How is it that it has been the scene of so many coronations, so many funerals? Whence arose its singular connexion with the whole course of English history?

The name 'Westminster Abbey' is shortened from the fuller phrase, 'Westminster Abbey Church'; the church, that is, of the Abbey of Westminster. It at once carries us back to its early history. Up to the year 1540, in the reign of Henry VIII, the 'Abbey', as we call it today, was the church of a great Benedictine monastery. These monasteries, once thickly strewn throughout England and much of Europe, were called abbeys from being ruled by abbots[1] (or *abbats*, from *abba*, Syriac for *father*), as those governed by a prior were called priories. A great society of monks lived in buildings, of which the present Deanery, the Jerusalem Chamber, the Cloisters, the Chapter House, which will be described further on, formed parts. The 'Abbey', as we call it, was the church in which these monks worshipped. Its legal title was *Ecclesia Abbatiae Westmonasteriensis*. Hence its traditional designation.

It is not a cathedral. By a cathedral we mean a church situated in a city which gives its name to an episcopal see (Fr. *siège*, 'seat'), and in which a bishop has his raised seat or throne (Gk. *kathedra*) assigned to him. St Paul's is the cathedral of London. For a brief space in its long history (A.D. 1540 to A.D. 1550) the 'Abbey' was the cathedral of a diocese of Westminster, and for a few years, under Edward VI, it was declared by Act of Parliament to be 'a Cathedral in the Diocese of London'. It suffered many losses at the time. 'Peter was robbed to pay Paul.' But with these exceptions, its entire independence of all episcopal control, the Pope alone excepted, was its most cherished prerogative in the days of its mitred abbots, and its 'extra-diocesan' character has been carefully maintained to the present date.

The 'Abbey'–that is the actual monastery–disappeared in the reign of Henry VIII. But though the name survives, its legal title is 'the Collegiate Church of St Peter in Westminster', and this designation it has borne in all legal documents since 1560, when Queen Elizabeth I (the foundress of Westminster School) replaced the abbot and monastery, which Queen Mary had restored for a time, by a dean, canons, and other officers.

How long has it stood here? Why is it called the Church of St Peter?

The church that we see today is the growth of centuries. But its main portion is the work of King Henry III. In order to do honour to the sainted King, Edward the Confessor, he demolished all the eastern portion of the Norman church which that monarch had built, and, leaving the greater part of the Nave still standing, placed the body of the Saint in the most sacred quarter of his own beautiful fabric, in the shrine where it now lies. His work was carried on by his successors, especially by Edward I, Richard II, and Henry V, and by various abbots. The western end was not entirely completed until the reign of Henry VII, and the western towers were not finished till about 1745. The present church is, therefore, the work not of one generation but of five centuries.

The church which it replaced was the work of Edward the Confessor, who died a few days after its dedication (28 December 1065). He also endowed the monastery on its south side, which from the position west of London gave its name (Westminster) to the King's palace, which lay close to its eastern end, and to the neighbouring district.

An account of this monastery, with its great possessions and manors in the metropolis, of which Covent Garden, Hyde Park, St James's Park, the greater part of Kensington and of modern Belgravia, form only a portion; with its dependent priories, such as Malvern; its estates in at least fourteen counties; its mitred and croziered abbots, members of the House of Lords, and often the trusted ministers and friends of kings, would too greatly extend the limits of the present introduction.

The Church of the Confessor was dedicated to St Peter. It is certain that an earlier church stood a few yards to the west of that which he built, and that Benedictine monks had been established there, at all events in the time of St Dunstan (about 960), endowed, if we could accept the existing charters as genuine, with large estates by King Edgar, and even earlier.

But the traditions and legends of the generations that followed the Norman Conquest pointed to a far earlier origin both of the Church of St Peter and of the name of Westminster. They told how, in the days when Augustine and his brother monks had converted the men of Kent, and founded the metropolitan See of Canterbury, Mellitus, a noble Roman, was consecrated first Bishop of London, and persuaded Sebert, King of the East Saxons,

---

[1] *Hebrew* ab, *a father; Latin* abbas.

whose tomb is still shown in the Abbey, to build a church where you now stand. The spot was called Thorneye, 'the Isle of Thorn', a thicket-grown, sandy island, enclosed between the Thames, then unembanked and spreading at high water over a marshy district now covered with human habitations, and its tributary streams, for which today you must search underground. The church, said the story, was to be dedicated to St Peter one Sunday morning (A.D. 616). On the previous night, a fisherman ferried over from the Lambeth side a stranger, who proved to be none other than St Peter himself, the fisher of the Lake of Galilee. The ferryman saw the church lighted up with a dazzling illumination, and heard the sound of choirs of angels. The apostle on his return bade him tell Mellitus that he would find all the signs of consecration already completed, and rewarded him with an enormous draught of salmon, which were never to fail himself and his successors so long as they abstained from Sunday fishing, and paid tithe of all they caught to St Peter's Church. The legend is interesting for the threefold claim which it indicates–first, to an antiquity equal to that assigned to St Paul's; secondly, to an independence of all episcopal authority other than that of St Peter, reputed the first Bishop of Rome; and thirdly, to a tithe in Thames-caught fish long claimed by the monks of Westminster. It is hardly necessary to say that the legend has no historical foundation. What we can say with absolute certainty is that the present church was opened for service in A.D. 1269, and was the successor of one which was consecrated in A.D. 1065.

But the question still remains, What is it that gives 'the Abbey' its unequalled historic interest in the eyes of all who speak our language? Why should Nelson have named 'Westminster Abbey' rather than York Minster, or Canterbury Cathedral, or St Paul's, where he was actually buried?

It arose from the following causes: Edward the Confessor's great church was close to his palace. It was designed by him for his own burial-place. He was interred before the Altar within a few days of its consecration. From that moment, Norman kings, monks, clergy, and the English people, vied with each other in honouring his name. William the Conqueror based his claim to the Crown on an alleged gift from the King, who had long lived an exile in Normandy. To the monks he was dear, not only from his munificent donations, but as being in life and character almost one of themselves. The Commons of England, groaning under a foreign yoke, looked back to the peaceful reign of the pious and gentle Confessor, the last king of the old English stock, as to a golden age. To be crowned by his graveside lent an additional sanctity to the rite, and thus from the Conqueror to the present day every sovereign has received the crown beneath this roof, within a few yards of the dust of the Confessor.

Moreover, as time went on, a swarm of traditions and legends grew up round the name of the King, who was canonized by the Pope in 1163. To be buried near those saintly ashes was a privilege that kings might covet. Accordingly, when Henry III, a sovereign in many points resembling him, had drained the resources of his kingdom to rebuild the church, palace, and monastery at Westminster, he chose his own burial-place on the north side of the stately shrine to which he had 'translated' the body of the Confessor. There in due time lay his son Edward I and his Queen; there king after king was buried; the

children, relations, ministers and standard-bearers of successive sovereigns; there the Abbots of the monastery; there lay Chaucer, who died hard by; there, nearly two centuries later, Spenser; and it is easy to understand how increasingly the feeling spread that to be laid to sleep in ground sacred with the dust of kings, warriors, churchmen, statesmen, and poets was an honour of the highest order.

Up to the time of the Reformation the 'Church of the Abbey' was also not only the scene of coronations, royal marriages and funerals, but till the reign of Henry VIII was closely identified in other ways with the history and feelings both of kings and people. The last-named king, driven by a destructive fire from Westminster Palace, established himself in White Hall or York Place, which he took from Wolsey, and in St James's Palace, which he raised on the site of an ancient 'Hospital for leprous maids'. He connected the two by appropriating the meadows that lay between them, now St James's Park. But up to his reign Kings and Commons had lived beneath its shadow. Great victories won by English armies were celebrated by processions and Te Deums beneath its roof. For three centuries parliaments frequently met in its stately Chapter House, the cradle of the parliamentary government of England and of her colonies. The church, too, though dedicated to St Peter, was practically that of the Royal Saint, Edward, just as St Thomas became almost the patron saint of Canterbury Cathedral. Innumerable pilgrims visited his shrine, and the various relics exhibited there. 'Indulgences' of definite amounts were accorded to visitors; and at the great festivals of the Church, when these relics were carried in procession, the building was thronged as on days of State pageants. Its two-fold character is well exhibited in a letter of Edward III, who writes of it not only as 'the monastery church of Westminster', but also as the 'special Chapel of our Principal Palace'. The national feeling is expressed in a letter of Edward IV to the Pope (A.D. 1478), wherein he speaks of the monastery of Westminster, 'as placed before the eyes of the whole world of Englishmen', an institution any favour to which would be 'welcome to all of English blood'. The interest that is so widely felt in the Abbey is by no means the birth of the last few generations.

You will now be in a position to visit the Abbey with some general knowledge of its character and history. You will perhaps approach it by the North Transept through what was once called 'Solomon's Porch'. The lower part, where the work done under Wren's direction had become greatly dilapidated, was restored in the last decade of the nineteenth century, after the designs of Sir Gilbert Scott, who is buried in the Nave. You will notice before you go in, the seated figure of Our Lord bestowing a benediction on two converging lines of figures representing kings, clergy, statesmen, warriors, poets, men of science and letters, whose services to God and man are commemorated in the Abbey. You are advised to pass at once through the Transept, and, turning to the right, to make your way to the great doors at the west end of the Nave. There you will take your stand beneath the statue of the younger Pitt, with his arm outstretched in defiance of the enemies of England; and, facing eastwards, will try first of all to get some clear notion of the general form and separate portions of the building, whose soaring roof you see stretching out before you.

First for its shape. The ground plan of the church is,

with some modifications, the same as that of the older church of the Confessor. It is in the form of a cross laid on the ground; the foot of the cross is towards the west, the head towards the east. Churches of this shape (called cruciform) were already known in England. The Norman builders first brought over by Edward the Confessor gave a great impulse to their construction, which henceforth became much more elaborate.

In such churches, reared in an age when reading and writing were confined to the few, great use was made of teaching by symbols. The broad upright beam of the cross, to which Our Lord's body was attached, was represented in architecture by the Nave, in which you are now standing. Notice the triple division of the Nave, with its two aisles (north and south) formed by the pillars on your right and left which sustain the roof. Pass your eye onward. Those two Transepts, or 'crosses', at right angles to the Nave were designed to recall the outstretched arms of the crucified Saviour. The head of the cross was represented by the easternmost portion, or Presbytery, here often called the Sanctuary, approached on steps from the central portion, or Lantern. At or towards the eastern end of this, which was sometimes, as here, of apsidal form, would be placed the altar. Further on, at the extreme east, would generally be added a 'Lady Chapel', or Chapel of the Virgin, representing the idea of the Virgin Mother supporting the head of her Son when lowered from the Cross. The easternmost end was looked on as the most sacred part; it was here, therefore, that Henry III began his work. The west he left to be completed by his successors. But, though this is the original type of such churches as that in which you are standing, you will notice one or two important modifications.

First, instead of the beam, or 'body' of the cross, being appropriated to the Nave, the Choir, or part used for singing the ordinary services, encroaches on it. The number of monks, novices, boys and others was large. The 'Sanctuary', therefore, or Presbytery before the High Altar, was reserved for the celebration of masses. The seven nightly and daily services were performed in the Choir, which you see before you, running far into the Nave, and separated from it by a stone wall or screen. At the foot of this screen, on the western side, was an altar, called the Altar of the Holy Cross, the principal Nave altar. The exact position of the great crucifix or rood is uncertain, but it probably hung between two pillars with steps up and down for the use of the worshippers who went up to kiss the Saviour's feet. Below this was another altar dedicated to St Paul. Mass was said at the Holy Cross

Altar in the presence of the people, who were not admitted within the Choir without payment. The Nave was thus used both as a place of worship for the laity and also as the scene of processions on great occasions, but not as a place of burial till after the Reformation. All the gravestones and monuments that you see are comparatively modern. But the point which you should notice more especially is that what in many cathedrals is an open nave is here divided between the Nave, with its north and south aisles, and the Choir, with the north and south Choir aisles on each side of it. Again, if you look at the ground plan of the Abbey, you will see that the simple cruciform or cross shape, already spoken of, though preserved, is greatly modified. First, the church does not end at the screen behind the altar or Holy Table, in the Sanctuary, but it is continued for some distance, as a glance at the roof from here will show you, in a rounded or apsidal form. And in that curved eastern end was deposited by Henry III the body of the Saint. It is the Chapel of the Confessor, and the burial-place of kings. Secondly, on the right and left of the 'head of the cross', or east end, are added chapels dedicated to different saints, on the exterior side. On the south side, immediately beyond the South Transept, are three chapels, those of St Benedict, the Italian founder of Western monasticism, whose head, presented by Edward III, was one of the most prized of the relics kept in the Confessor's Chapel; St Edmund, the English royal saint, said to have been taken prisoner by the Danes in Suffolk, and tied to a tree as a mark for arrows – over his supposed remains stood the great Benedictine monastery of St Edmundsbury (now Bury St Edmunds); and St Nicholas, the patron saint of Russia, the special protector of children, especially of boys, and of sailors. On the north side, the eastern aisle of the threefold North Transept was once divided into three chapels, beyond which come first Abbot Islip's small chapel, and then those of St John the Baptist and St Paul; each of these, though now crowded with tombs, had at one time its own altar. If you notice also that the South Transept, or 'Poets' Corner', is narrower on the ground floor than the other, or Statesmen's Transept, its western aisle being encroached on by the East Cloister, and that the extreme east of the church terminates in Henry VII's Chapel – which took the place of the Lady Chapel built in Henry III's boyhood, nominally by that King, the building carried on by Abbot Humez, largely paid for from the indulgences offered to contributors – you will have no difficulty in understanding the general features of the church which you have come to visit.

THE ARCHITECTURE OF THE ABBEY

The following sketch of the architecture of the Abbey was written by the late Mr A. J. Grahame. It has been revised and in part re-written in order to incorporate the results of recent research into the history and architecture of the Abbey Church.

CHRONOLOGY OF THE BUILDING OF THE PRESENT CHURCH

Bases of pillars and walls on each side of the Sanctuary and the foundations discovered in the Nave (1932) are the only remains of the Confessor's Church.

Thirteenth century. Eastern portion, including the chapels round the apse, both Transepts, and five bays west of the Crossing, built by Henry III, 1245 to 1272, also the Chapter House.

Fourteenth, fifteenth and sixteenth centuries. New Nave commenced by Abbot Litlyngton, who laid foundation stone 3 March 1376, in the name of the late abbot, Cardinal Simon Langham, who gave money during his life and left large bequests to the building fund on his death. The Norman Nave took eleven years to demolish, during which time the outer wall was raised along its whole circuit. 1387–1403. – Outside walls completed up to Triforium level and marble pillars placed, under Abbot Colchester and Peter Combe, the sacrist, warden of the new works. Richard II gave considerable sums of money for the purpose. 1403–13. – Work discontinued for want of funds under Henry IV. 1413–22. – Henry V, shocked by the ruinous state of the Nave, undertook to pay 1,000 marks a year to continue the work, which was supervised by his surveyor, Richard Whityngton, and carried on under Abbot Harweden. 1422–67. – Progress very slow under Henry VI, no royal help. Work hindered by restoration of rose window in South Transept (1460–2). 1468–71. – Building recommenced under Abbot Millyng, who found the Nave again in a ruinous condition. Contributions towards the work given by Edward IV and his family, £519 9s. 8d. in all. 1471–98. – Nave roofed in, West Window, and gable end finished under Abbot Esteney. 1498–1500. – His successor, Abbot Fascet, made good the financial deficit, £599 9s. 2d. – i.e. about £6,000 in our coinage. 1500–2. – Abbot Islip completed the building by vaulting two bays and west towers, paving the Nave, and glazing the great West Window as well as those in the Clerestory. 1503. – Foundation stone of Henry VII's Chapel laid; the whole Chapel completed in 1519; the total cost was £14,000 – the greater part of this given and bequeathed by Henry VII.

Seventeenth century. Wren repaired the whole fabric, and built lower portion of Western Towers (1722); his design for upper portion altered and completed by Hawksmoor and others (1745) after Wren's death.

WESTMINSTER ABBEY is in truth only a part of the original Abbey of Westminster. When the church was built, more than six hundred years ago, it formed part of a Benedictine monastery. The monastery itself was much older; we can trace it back nine hundred, if not eleven hundred, years; and when it was first established it stood on an island called Thorneye or Thorn Island, between the River Thames and the marshes which now form the water of St James's Park. The number of monks at first was very small, only a dozen or so; but Edward the Confessor, who had his palace close by, where the Houses of Parliament now stand, before his death in 1066, greatly enlarged it, making provision for seventy monks, and erecting buildings for them, part of which still remain. As he intended to be buried there himself he took great pains with the church; and having Continental leanings he, naturally enough, made use of the new style of architecture then growing up on the Continent: and thus it is that the old Abbey Church of Westminster was one of the earliest examples in England of the Norman style of building. 'It was,' says an old historian, 'in the new mode of construction,' which many persons who afterwards built churches imitated in its sumptuous expense.' The 'many persons' were the Norman bishops who came over a few years later with William the Conqueror, and covered the land with splendid cathedrals.

England at that time was full of such monasteries; hence the numerous 'abbeys', 'priories', and 'minsters' still existing. Many of them survive as cathedral churches, but Westminster is unique in this respect; that although not a cathedral – that is, not the seat of a bishopric – it is built in the style peculiar to the great age of cathedral building – the thirteenth century. It is peculiar also in this respect: that though originally only an abbey, like Sherborne or Romsey, it did not share the fate of most English abbeys at the Reformation, when the monasteries were dissolved, but it was established with a dean and canons just as if it had been a cathedral. Westminster, being close to the royal palace, was always favoured by the King; and the Abbot of Westminster had, like his successor the Dean, a position of peculiar independence.

The church which was built in the reign of King Edward the Confessor was made in the shape of a cross with an apse, or round east end, a central tower, and two western ones, topped by short spires with a porch at the west end. Its architecture was heavy and solid, with flat buttresses and round-headed windows. It had aisles and numerous chapels above and below. Of the church there are practically no remains, but some of the Norman monastic buildings can still be seen.

The old cloister is quite gone, but in the east walk of the present one, beyond the entrance to the Chapter House, there are low doors leading into vaulted rooms of Norman work, which formed the basement of the monks' dormitory. The low arched passage into the yard of Westminster School is also of this date, and some arches of the Norman Refectory in a garden behind the Cloister. The present church was begun by Henry III, who in the fourth year of his reign laid the foundation of a Lady Chapel at the east end of the Norman apse; Lady Chapels, or Chapels of the Virgin, were then coming into fashion. This chapel was destroyed to make way for Henry VII's. Twenty-five years later Henry III pulled down the Norman choir, transepts, and central tower, and in place of the low Norman structure erected the present magnificent building. It is 103 feet from the floor to the top of the vaulting, and in the Nave 35 feet wide: a proportion of three to one, and much greater than in any English building, though common enough in France. Another French feature is the circular east end, for thirteenth-century churches in England were usually built square to the east instead of ending in apses like the Norman churches. This arrangement, which Henry's Continental taste led him to adopt, is certainly an extremely beautiful one, and in this case the effect is enhanced by the great size of the chapels opening out of the apse. The absence of a large east window is amply made up by the gracefulness of the converging lines, the vista of piers and arches, and the feeling of completeness gained by the gathering in, as it were, of the walls of the church. As soon as the Choir, Transepts, and Central Tower, with one bay of the Nave to keep it steady, were built, Henry with great solemnity brought in the body of Edward the Confessor, who had been buried in the former church, and placed it in the splendid shrine he had prepared for it. The lower part to the shrine remains in its place behind the Altar.

The appearance of the church at this period must have been very curious. First came the low Norman Nave, with its western towers; then east of it the tall Early English Choir and Transepts, with their huge flying buttresses; while all the surrounding buildings, except the Chapter House, were of the original style. The Chapter House, and that part of the Cloister which forms the entrance to it, were finished between 1253 and 1260; before Henry III died the church was carried on one bay beyond the present screen, including the part now occupied by the Choir Stalls. The Choir, properly so called, is the part beyond the Transepts, but the Choir Stalls or 'ritual Choir' often take up, as here, the east end of the Nave.

The rest of the church went on so slowly that two hundred years later, when the Gothic style came to an end, the western towers were still unfinished. Sir Christopher Wren designed the lower portion of the towers, but they were not finished until after his death, by Hawksmoor and others (1745).

The church, as completed, consists of a Nave, Transepts, and Choir, with aisles throughout. It is rare to find aisles on both sides of the Transepts, but Westminster has them: only the western aisle of the South Transept has been encroached upon by the Cloisters, and forms their eastern walk, the upper part of the aisle overhanging the Cloisters. The aisle, where it is continued round the apse, is called the Ambulatory; and out of it open the radiating chapels, forming, as it were, a second outside aisle. At the extreme east end was the Lady Chapel, rather larger than the rest, but not so large as the later Chapel of Henry VII.

The Nave is very long, consisting of twelve bays or divisions, with richly moulded arches, carried by clustered piers. Above the first row comes the Triforium arcade of two arches to each bay: above that again, the Clerestory windows, one to each bay, with their heads fitting into the angles of the vaulting. Though the Nave was about 150 years in building, 1376–1528, the same design was kept throughout the church, and there is very little variety in the different parts, the late additions having been imitated from the original style of the Choir and Transepts. A close survey will detect eight shafts round the later piers instead of four, and a greater number of ribs in the later vaulting of the main roof, an absence of carving in the Triforium arches, and a loss of foliage and richness

generally about the work; but as far as the general effect goes the whole church might have been built in one century.

The thrust of the vaulting is sustained by those immense flying buttresses which form such a feature on the outside. They are thrown over the aisles and run down to the ground in projecting stages. The aisles are also vaulted in stone, and their roofs are kept in position by the lower part of the same buttresses. The main vault is sheltered from the weather by a high wooden roof covered with lead: those of the aisles by a similar covering sloping against the main vault just under the Clerestory windows. The top of the aisle vaulting forms the floor of the Triforium, which is itself the space between the stone and wooden roof of the aisles. At Westminster the aisle wall is run up a little way beyond the vaulting, and pierced with triangular windows, which light the Triforium. Otherwise it would be lighted only from the interior of the church. This arrangement is continued round the whole building, except at the ends of the Transepts, where there are only narrow passages in front of the windows. The Triforium gallery, from its beautiful shape and great richness, is one of the best features of the church.

The main entrance is by the great door at the west end, but in the south aisles there are two smaller doors leading from the Cloisters which run along the side of the Nave. The five eastern bays of the Nave are occupied by the Choir, the entrance to which is under a heavy stone screen across the central portion. Above this screen is the organ, which completely fills two of the bays. The ritual Choir ends at the great arch, the full height of the roof opening into the centre of the church, where the Transepts cross the Nave. The four arches thus formed sustain the tower, which is open to its roof, one storey above that of the church, and has a very fine effect as you look up from the Choir.

The ends of the Transepts are slightly varied from the general design. There being no aisles, the corresponding space is filled with graceful arcades, while the end of the gable above the Triforium gives room for a splendid rose window in each Transept. All along the eastern walls of both arms, between the arches, were ranged the chapels of the various saints specially honoured in the Church of Westminster, and these chapels were, of course, continued all round the apse. The three in the North Transept are those of St Michael, St Andrew, and St John the Evangelist; in the south is only St Benedict's; the Chapel of St Faith, a curious vaulted chamber at the end–from which there is a way into the Chapter House–being really the old revestry. It has been already noticed that the west aisle of this Transept is wanting being occupied by the Cloister; but above the Cloister roof and inside the church is an open gallery known as the 'Muniment Room', where the archives are kept. The South Transept has a little door at its southeast angle from the Poets' Corner; the North Transept is entered by the porch known as Solomon's Porch, and this is the most usual entrance to the church.

Coming to the eastern arm of the cross, the first half of the Choir forms the 'Sanctuary', or space in front of the Altar which is paved with beautiful mosaics brought from Rome by Abbot Ware in the thirteenth century. On the north side of the Sanctuary are three splendid tombs belonging to the first half of the 14th century, and on the other side the remains of the old *sedilia* or seats of the officiating clergy. Behind the Altar is the Altar Screen:

its front has been restored, but the back retains the old work. Two doors, one on each side of the Altar, lead into the shrine or chapel of Edward the Confessor, which occupies the further half of the Choir, and is bounded to the east by the circular arcade of the apse. To reach this it is necessary to go round by the Ambulatory, which at Westminster is usually entered by the south side, that nearest the Poets' Corner. At this point the Choir chapels begin; first St Benedict's, which is square, and opens from the Transept as well as from the Ambulatory; then St Edmund's and St Nicholas's, both octagonal in shape, and full of interesting tombs. These are on the right-hand side; on the left are the backs of the tombs surrounding the Confessor's Chapel. Following the Ambulatory, so called because in old days the processions used to walk round here, you pass under the arch of Henry V's Chantry, which fills the end of the apse, and up a flight of steps into Henry VII's Chapel.

Here we come to an entirely different style of architecture, nearly 250 years later than that of the Choir. The Chapel is divided, like the church, by two rows of piers, into a central and two side aisles, which are cut off from the central portion by the stalls, and are entered by separate doors. The spaces between the piers are filled with the seats of the Knights of the Bath, whose banners hang above them. The apse at the end has five chapels off it, corresponding in width to the aisles. Above the arches a row of sculptured figures of great interest runs round the whole building, including the chapels. In the centre, under the apse, stands Henry VII's tomb, of black marble, with bronze effigies, the work of the Italian Torrigiani, surrounded by a screen of bronze most elaborately worked. The entrance doors of the Chapel are fine examples of the same work, and should be carefully noticed.

The great feature of the Chapel is, of course, the roof. This is of the kind known as fan vaulting, and is peculiar to the Perpendicular period. The whole roof depends on the huge ribs of stone which may be seen crossing the entire span, through the network of smaller ribs and pendants hanging from them. The exterior walls between the buttresses are curved or angular in plan, and filled with Perpendicular traceried windows. The wall space both inside and out is covered with stone panelling, a mode of ornamentation imitated by Sir Charles Barry in the Houses of Parliament.

The chapels opening off the North Ambulatory by which you return to the North Transept are no less interesting than those on the other side, for the screens separating them from the Ambulatory and for the tombs they contain. These will all be noticed in their proper place. They are named after St Paul, St John the Baptist, Abbot Islip, St John the Evangelist, St Michael and St Andrew.

The Confessor's Chapel, which, as we saw, occupies the main apse, is entered by two flights of steps, one from the east end under Henry V's Chantry, and the other from the North Ambulatory. It contains a series of tombs whose historical interest is only equalled by the beauty of their design. An account of them will be found under the Confessor's Chapel. A more strictly architectural feature is the Chantry, where the tomb of Henry V stands under an arch flanked by two turrets, octagonal, with niches and statues in their different faces. These rise to a considerable height, and contain staircases leading to the upper floor of the monument, which was the Chantry

Chapel, and has an altar in its eastern wall. The upper floor is of greater extent than the lower part, and is supported where it bridges the aisles by arches profusely decorated with sculpture and panelling.

The architecture of this part of the church and of the Transept ends is the richest in ornament. The spandrels of the arches are filled with diaper work; the Triforium Arcade is adorned with carved foliage, and at the ends of the Transepts with figures of angels in the spandrels; the bosses of the roof are carved; and every here and there in going round the chapels you may see an arch or two of the beautiful wall arcade which once ran round the whole church at the ground level.

The windows should be noticed. In the Clerestory they are of two lights, with a cusped circle in the head; the Triforium arches show the same design more richly carried out; and they mark the period when stone tracery ceased to be merely a number of openings cut in a slab – a style known as 'plate tracery' – and became an arrangement of curved ribs known as 'bar tracery'. The curves are all geometrical, complete circles or portions of them; and this has led to the thirteenth-century or Early English style being sometimes called 'the Geometrical'. The windows at Westminster are early examples of this mode, and their mouldings are very simple. They still suggest the two lancet windows with a circle above them which was the earliest form of window decoration. The curved triangular openings which light the Triforium are not visible from the inside; below them come the windows of the aisle, which are similar in design to the Clerestory range.

Leaving the church by the little door in the south aisle we reach the Cloisters, which lie on the south side of the aisle. This was the usual position, as the monks were thus sheltered from the cold winds. Henry III rebuilt the Eastern Walk (which, it will be remembered, is really the aisle of the South Transept) in connexion with his other work there. He also built the fine entrance to the Chapter House just beyond the Transept, with its vestibule and steps richly decorated with sculpture, and the Chapter House itself, which was restored in 1865 by Sir Gilbert Scott. Formerly it had been used as a record office, divided into storeys and filled with cupboards and papers. At the nineteenth-century restoration all this was swept away, and its beautiful proportions were disclosed. It was begun in 1250, and shows in its windows the rapid advance made in the style. They are of four lights, occupying the whole space in the wall in each of the eight sides, one of which, however, is not pierced; and their heads are filled with large cusped circles and quatrefoils. The vaulting ribs spring from a central column, and radiate to the piers between the windows, which are strengthened outside by the huge flying buttresses visible from Poets' Corner. A rich trefoil-headed arcade runs round the inside, forming stalls for the monks when they met in the House for business or instruction. Those in the side opposite the door, richer, more deeply recessed, and having higher seats than the rest, were for the dignitaries of the monastery. There are remains of painting on the walls.

The vestibule has a door through the revestry into the Abbey, and formerly there was above it a passage connecting the South Transept with the dormitory, used by the monks when they rose for the midnight service.

Towards the end of the fourteenth century, when the Perpendicular style was in full force, Simon Langham, afterwards Bishop of Ely and Archbishop of Canterbury, left a sum of money for the completion of the fabric. The destruction of the old Norman nave seems to have commenced before Langham's time, but he continued to pull down the eastern part, and left his successor, Litlyngton, to superintend the new building, after his removal to the bishopric. When he died Litlyngton used part of his generous bequest, not only for the Nave, but also for the monastic buildings, which, it will be remembered, remained all this time as the Norman builders had made them – out of repair probably, certainly out of date. A considerable part of the buildings round the Abbey belong, therefore, to Litlyngton's time. Next to the Chapter House, in the same East Walk of the Cloister on an upper floor, was the dormitory where the monks slept – not in separate cells, but in one great room. It has been since divided into the Chapter library and the great schoolroom of Westminster School. The northern part of the vaulted chambers below it, of the Norman time, and once the monastic treasury, is now in the charge of Government officials and belongs to the Crown. At right angles to it, in the South Walk, was the Refectory where the monks dined together. This is gone, but a few of its windows are visible from the garden of Ashburnham House, now the property of the School. The West Walk has behind it the buildings of the Abbot's house, now the Deanery. The Abbot of Westminster was a great man, and his house was not unworthy of him. Besides the present Deanery, it included all the buildings looking on the little courtyard just inside the Cloister entrance.

One of these, the Abbot's dining-hall, is lent by the Dean to Westminster School for a dining-hall; the other with its low square window, is 'the Jericho parlour' leading into the famous Jerusalem Chamber. The latter is entered by a flight of steps from the Abbot's courtyard. It is panelled on the inside with cedar, and has a splendid cedar mantelpiece, put up at the time of Charles I's marriage. It was here that Henry IV was brought to die because it was the Abbot's 'withdrawing' room and reception room. The Westminster Confession was drawn up here, and in later times the committee sat here for the revision of the Bible. The Abbot had a private way into the Abbey and a private pew overlooking the Nave, both of which still exist.

The old walls of the Abbey enclosed the present Dean's Yard, then known as The Elms, and through it ran the stream which turned the Abbey mill and emptied itself into the Thames. Some of Litlyngton's work remains in the houses looking into it on the east side, with the two tower gateways. They were the quarters of officers, such as the bailiff, who looked after the outlying possessions of the Abbey; the cellarer, who had charge of all the property; and the sacrist, who was responsible for the conduct of the services.

Returning through the Cloister, and under the low arch at its south-east angle, we reach another low passage at right angles leading into a small court with a Classical colonnade, known as the Little Cloister. Here we have the exact site of the infirmary – the resort of those monks who, from age or sickness, were excused the regular duties of the monastery. It had a spacious garden, now reached by a door from the Little Cloister, and called the 'College Garden'. The malthouse, granary, brewhouse, and bakehouse were all placed in the south part of Dean's Yard, and were thus within easy reach of the kitchen, which lay behind the Refectory.

The mere mention of so many different buildings shows how large and important the monastic community was, and how thoroughly it was able to supply its own wants. The sixty or seventy monks, in fact, with the dependants who dwelt within the precincts, formed quite a large village; and many English towns owe their origin to the clustering of a small population round a great religious house.

The monks, except at meal-times and at night, and during the frequent daily services, spent their lives in the Cloister. There they wrote manuscripts, read, practised singing, taught schools, and went through the many other little duties which made absolute idleness impossible among them. In other orders, and amongst the Benedictines in early times – though probably not so late as the Confessor's foundation – they would also take part in those occupations on which the daily living of the monastery depended – in bakehouse or brew-house; and some might even here lend a hand in the constant building operations, as we hear of the vaulting at Gloucester being completed, not by ordinary workmen, but 'by the spirited energy of the monks themselves'.

A. J. GRAHAME

Professor Lethaby, aided by the researches of the Revd. H. F. Westlake and of Mr L. E. Tanner into the Abbey records, identified the first architects of the church of Henry III. These were Master Henry (died about 1253) who also planned the Royal Chapel at Windsor, Master John of Gloucester, and Master Robert of Beverley. All were Englishmen, and although there are traces of French influence yet 'the result is triumphantly English'.
The later Nave was designed by the great medieval architect Henry Yevele.

THE NORTH TRANSEPT [*See plan, page 18*]

THE NORTH ENTRANCE, or 'Solomon's Porch'. The name of 'Solomon's Porch' was probably first applied to a large porch erected against the central portal in Richard II's reign, of which no trace remains. The whole was much decayed at the beginning of the eighteenth century, when Wren and Dickinson recased it in Oxfordshire stone, paring and altering the details till the ancient character of the entrance was quite lost. The eighteenth-century front was entirely remodelled under the superintendence of Pearson (1884), who designed the upper part himself, and carried out Scott's plans for the triple portico, with slight modifications.

After the interment of Lord Chatham, the North Transept became 'The Statesmen's Aisle', the burial-place of statesmen, as the South Transept is of poets. Among them are monuments commemorating some of England's naval and military heroes.

William Pitt, Earl of Chatham, b. 1708, d. 1778, Prime Minister and Secretary of State (1756), created a peer (1766). Chatham's last appearance in the House of Lords was when, already crippled and dying, he insisted on coming to oppose Lord North's Government with regard to the severance of the American colonies. After delivering an eloquent appeal against 'the dismemberment of this ancient and noble monarchy', he fell down in a fit, and died a few weeks afterwards. He was temporarily buried at Hayes, in Kent, while St Paul's and Westminster contended for his remains; Parliament decided for the Abbey on the ground that he ought to be buried 'near to the dust of kings'. His funeral was attended 'almost exclusively by opponents of the Government . . . Burke, Saville, and Dunning upheld the pall. . . . The chief mourner was young William Pitt',[1] who was laid in the same grave twenty-eight years later. The monument is 33 feet high, and cost £6,000. The sculptor, *John Bacon,* was also the author of the inscription, which called forth George III's admonition, 'Now, Bacon, mind you do not turn author, stick to your chisel.'

Henry Grattan, b. 1746, d. 1820, statesman, the defender of the rights of Ireland. He first wished to be buried in his native country, but ultimately consented to have his grave in the Abbey; a plain stone marks the spot at the head of the grave of Charles James Fox, 'whom in life he so dearly valued, and near whom in death it would have been his pride to lie'.[2]

Henry John Temple, 3rd Viscount Palmerston, K.G., b. 1784, d. 1865, twice Prime Minister, 1855 to 1858, and 1859 to 1865. Statue erected by Parliament as a testimony of public admiration. Lady Palmerston, d. 1869, was interred in her husband's grave, an honour until then accorded to no other statesman's wife since Lady Canning's burial (1861). *R. Jackson sculpt.*

'The Three Captains', **William Bayne, William Blair, and Lord Robert Manners,** fell, 1782, in Admiral Rodney's two victorious engagements with the French in the West Indies. Buried at sea; monument erected by the King and Parliament. *Nollekens sculpt.*

Robert Stewart, Viscount Castlereagh, afterwards **2nd Marquess of Londonderry, K.G.,** b. 1769, d. 1822, one of the leading statesmen of his time, Minister for War 1807. Foreign Secretary 1814 to 1822. Castlereagh's policy at the First Congress of Vienna (1814), followed by the Triple Alliance (1815) secured the peace of Europe and led to the downfall of Napoleon. Finally, his mind having become unhinged, he committed suicide 12 August 1822. A terrible riot took place at his funeral. The mourners had to fight their way through a raging mob, and it was not till the doors were shut that there was silence in the building. In the hand of his statue is a scroll inscribed: 'Peace of Paris', which commemorates his greatest achievement. His widow, d. 1829, lies in the north-east angle of the Cloister. *J. E. Thomas sculpt.*

Against the southernmost pillar is the stone tablet erected by Parliament in memory of: **Herbert Henry Asquith,** b. 1852, d. 1928, created **Earl of Oxford and Asquith, K.G.** Prime Minister 1908–16. Mr Stanley Baldwin, then Leader of the House of Commons, unveiled the tablet in 1934. Buried at Sutton Courtenay, Berks. *Puiker sculpt.*

Sir Robert Peel, Bt., b. 1788, d. 1850, Prime Minister 1834 and 1841–46; the repeal of the Corn Laws (1846) was the marked feature of Peel's last administration. His death was caused by a fall from his horse on Constitution Hill, and he was buried by his own wish at Drayton. *Gibson* refused to undertake the statue unless he were allowed to adopt Classical costume, and the great statesman is represented addressing the House in a Roman toga.

Admiral Sir Peter Warren, b. 1703, d. 1752. Created a Knight of the Bath for his valour in an action with two French squadrons in the Channel. This monument is a typical example of the realistic taste of the eighteenth century: the face of the bust is pitted with smallpox. *Roubiliac sculpt.*

Benjamin Disraeli, b. 1804, d. 1881, created **Earl of Beaconsfield, K.G.** 1876. Famous Conservative leader; twice Prime Minister, 1868 and 1874. Through his influence Queen Victoria assumed the title of Empress of India, 1876. Author of brilliant political novels. Buried at Hughenden. *Boehm sculpt.*

William Ewart Gladstone, b. 1809, d. 1898. Four times Prime Minister 1868, 1880, 1886, 1892. Leader of the Liberal Party. He retired from public life, 1894, and was buried in this Transept at the public charge, by order of Parliament. The first State funeral here since that of Pitt, similar honours having been offered and declined in the case of Lord Beaconsfield. Mrs Gladstone, d. 1900, was buried in her husband's grave. *Brock sculpt.*

Sir John Malcolm, b. 1769, d. 1833, 'the soldier, statesman, patriot', one of the founders of the Indian Empire. *Statue by Chantrey.*

William Cavendish, 1st Duke of Newcastle, K.G., b. 1592, d. 1676, and his Duchess, Margaret sister of John, 1st Baron Lucas, d. 1673. Called the 'Loyall Duke' for

---

[1] *Macaulay's Essays, 'The Earl of Chatham'.*
[2] *Preface to Grattan's speeches.*

Detail of thirteenth-century sculpture in North Transept

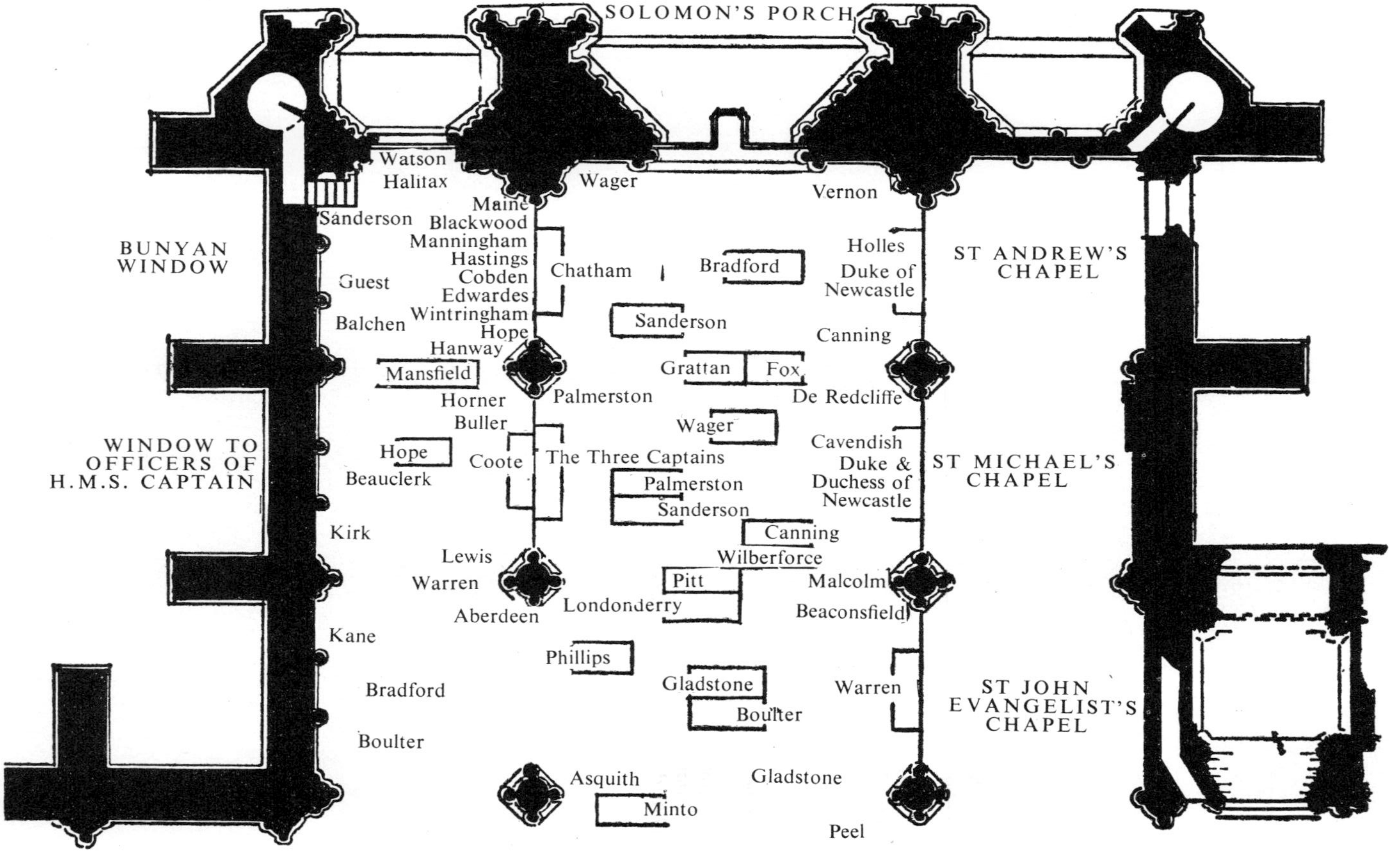

North Ambulatory

North Choir Aisle

ST ANDREW'S CHAPEL

ST MICHAEL'S CHAPEL

ST JOHN EVANGELIST'S CHAPEL

SOLOMON'S PORCH

BUNYAN WINDOW

WINDOW TO OFFICERS OF H.M.S. CAPTAIN

Vernon

Holles
Duke of
Newcastle

Canning

De Redcliffe

Cavendish
Duke &
Duchess of
Newcastle

Wilberforce

Malcolm

Beaconsfield

Warren

Peel

Gladstone

Bradford

Sanderson

Grattan

Fox

Wager

Canning

Palmerston

Sanderson

Pitt

Londonderry

Gladstone

Boulter

Gladstone

Minto

Wager

Chatham

Palmerston

The Three Captains

Asquith

Watson

Halitax

Sanderson

Blackwood

Manningham

Hastings

Cobden

Edwardes

Wintringham

Hope

Hanway

Maine

Mansfield

Horner

Buller

Coote

Lewis

Warren

Aberdeen

Phillips

Guest

Balchen

Hope

Beauclerk

Kirk

Kane

Bradford

Boulter

his devotion to Charles I, in whose cause he lost £941,308. 'The most distinguished patriot, general, and statesman of his age', says Cibber. He wrote works on horsemanship, besides being a liberal patron of learning, and the friend of Ben Jonson and Dryden. Exiled during the Commonwealth, he returned at the Restoration to build his own and his wife's tomb, and to write her inscription. The Duchess came of 'a noble familie, for all the brothers were valiant, and all the sisters virtuous'. She was a 'wise, wittie, and learned lady, which her many bookes do well testifie', and 'with her lord all the time of his banishment and miseries'. Indeed, as Pepys says, 'her whole story is a romance and all she does romantic'. She was a voluminous writer, and her attendants had to be ready any hour of the day or night 'to take down her Grace's conceptions'. Her effigy holds an open book, a pen case, and inkhorn, symbolic of her favourite pursuit.

In the same vault, but without any memorial, is buried the Duke's son-in-law **Edward Harley, 2nd Earl of Oxford**, b. 1689, d. 1741. Collector of the vast collection of manuscripts which were sold by his widow to the nation in 1753 and now form the Harleian Collection in the British Museum.

Statues of: **Stratford Canning, 1st Viscount Stratford de Redcliffe, K.G.**, b. 1786, d. 1880; for fifty years our Ambassador in the East. Buried at Frant, Sussex.

> Thou third great Canning, stand among our best
> And noblest, now thy long day's work hath ceased,
> Here silent in our Minster of the West,
> Who wert the voice of England in the East.

Epitaph by Tennyson
Statue by Boehm.

George Canning, b. 1770, d. 1827, statesman and orator, made Prime Minister and Chancellor of the Exchequer by George IV, 1827. When Foreign Secretary (1822–7) he defended the claims of Greece against Turkish aggression and by acknowledging the independence of the Spanish American Colonies he 'called the New World into existence, to redress the balance of the Old'. This statue is a replica of the original, which belonged to the 1st Duke of Sutherland and stood at Trentham Hall. In 1932 it was presented to the Greek Government, and has been re-erected in Canning Square, Athens. His son: **Charles, 1st Earl Canning, K.G.**, b. 1812, d. 1862, Viceroy of India (1856). *Foley sculpt.* **Charlotte**, d. 1861, wife of Earl Canning, daughter of Charles, Baron Stuart de Rothsay. All buried in the same vault, east of Pitt.

John Holles, b. 1662, d. 1711, **3rd Earl of Clare**, and, by his marriage with the 'Loyall Duke's' granddaughter, created **Duke of Newcastle, K.G.** He filled several offices of State in Queen Anne's reign. Buried in St John's Chapel, near his kinsmen Vere and Holles. The tomb was designed by *Gibbs*, and the work executed by *Bird.*

Admiral Edward Vernon, b. 1684, d. 1757, called 'Old Grog' from his grogram boat cloak, a nickname which gave rise to the word 'grog', as applied to the sailors' official drink, rum and water, a mixture introduced by Vernon. His chief victory was the capture of Portobello with only six ships in 1739; but his choleric temper, and his exposure of the naval abuses in print and in Parliament, led to his dismissal from the Navy six years later. *Rysbrack sculpt.*

Admiral Sir Charles Wager, b. 1666, d. 1743. Knighted in 1709 for his gallantry in the West Indies, Wager became Admiral of the White, Lord of the Admiralty, and finally Treasurer of the Navy. The bas-relief represents his most dashing exploit, the capture of some Spanish treasure-ships in the West Indies. *Scheemakers sculpt.*

Sir William Webb Follett, b. 1798, d. 1845, Attorney-General, considered the best advocate of his generation. *Statue by Behnes* (now in St Michael's Chapel).

In this Transept are also buried: **General Richard Philipps**, b. 1651, d. 1750, Governor of Nova Scotia for twenty-nine years (1720–49), who risked his life by distributing copies of the proclamation announcing William of Orange's approaching arrival in London round the Jacobite camp at Blackheath. He was arrested, and the halter was actually round his neck when the news of William's landing dispersed his captors. Philipps distinguished himself at the battle of the Boyne. He afterwards (1712) raised the Fighting 40th Foot at his own expense.

Gilbert Elliot, 1st Earl of Minto, b. 1751, d. 1814, Governor-General of India, 1806–13; and his brother **Hugh Elliot**, b. 1752, d. 1830, a distinguished diplomatist, Governor of the Leeward Islands and of Madras successively, lie in one vault.

Charles Abbott, 1st Baron Colchester, b. 1757, d. 1829. Speaker of the House of Commons 1802–16.

West Aisle

George Gordon, 4th Earl of Aberdeen, K.G., b. 1784, d. 1860, Prime Minister 1852–5. He was an accomplished scholar, especially learned in Athenian antiquities. Byron calls him 'the travelled Thane, Athenian Aberdeen'. Buried at Stanmore, Middlesex. *Bust by Noble.*

Elizabeth Warren, d. 1816, widow of **John Warren, Bishop of Bangor** (d. 1800), whose memorial, upon the opposite wall, is by the same sculptor, *Sir Richard Westmacott.* Mrs Warren was distinguished for her extensive charity, which is typified on the monument by a beggar girl holding a baby.

Sir George Cornewall Lewis, b. 1806, d. 1863, successively Chancellor of the Exchequer, Home Secretary, and Secretary for War. Editor of the *Edinburgh Review* and author of political pamphlets. *Bust by Weekes.*

General Sir Eyre Coote, b. 1726, d. 1783, who drove the French out of the Coromandel coasts, 1761, and defeated Hyder Ali's forces in the Carnatic, 1781. Monument erected by the East India Company. *Banks sculpt.*

Francis Horner, b. 1778, d. 1817, politician, called by Stanley 'the founder of our modern economical and financial policy'. Buried at Leghorn. The inscription is by Sir Henry Englefield. *Statue by Chantrey.*

A bust of **Charles Buller**, b. 1806, d. 1848, politician. 'The British Colonies will not forget a statesman who so well appreciated their desires and their destinies.' From inscription by Lord Houghton. *Weekes sculpt.*

Brigadier-General Henry Hope, d. 1789, Lieutenant Governor of Quebec. *Bacon sculpt.*

Warren Hastings, b. 1732, d. 1818, Governor-General of Bengal, 1774–85, was a King's Scholar (with Elijah Impey) at Westminster School. He entered the service of the East India Company, 1750. After a distinguished career in India, Hastings retired (1785); in 1788 he was impeached on charges of cruelty and corruption during his Indian administration. His trial lasted over seven years, and resulted in his triumphant acquittal, but the immense cost, £70,000, practically beggared him. The Company assisted him to pay this; he was made a Privy Councillor and honoured by royalty, a proof of the general belief in his innocence. Hastings died and was buried at Daylesford, 'the home of his race'. His second wife, formerly Baroness Imhoff, erected this monument. *Bacon, jun., sculpt.*

Jonas Hanway, b. 1712, d. 1786, City merchant, philanthropist and traveller, is said to have been the first person in England to carry an umbrella. Hanway was one of the founders of the Marine Society (1756), and his gift to them of the first training ship in the world is commemorated on his monument by the figure of Britannia presenting sailors' uniforms to small boys. He also devoted time and money to ameliorating the lot of outcast women and poor children, by financing sundry Acts of Parliament on their behalf, and by assisting in the foundation of the Magdalen and Foundling Hospitals. *J. F. and J. Moore sculpt.*

Major-General Sir Herbert Edwardes, b. 1819, d. 1868. He distinguished himself in the insurrection in the Punjab, in 1848, when, among other brilliant exploits, he kept an army of 12,000 Sikhs at bay for seven hours until the reinforcements sent to help him arrived. He also did good service at the outbreak of the Mutiny (1857), by persuading the native chiefs to rally round him and send levies of horse and foot, thus greatly contributing 'to the Security of the Frontier, and to the Salvation of the British Empire in India'. *Theed sculpt.*

Richard Cobden, b. 1804, d. 1865, statesman, buried at West Lavington; the hero of the repeal of the Corn Laws and the successful champion of free trade. *Bust by Woolner.*

Sir Henry James Sumner Maine, b. 1822, d. 1888. Legal Member of Council in India for seven years. Master of Trinity Hall, Cambridge, and Professor of International Law. Author of *Ancient Law. Boehm sculpt.*

Major-General Coote Manningham, d. 1809, Colonel of the 95th Foot. He began his military career at the siege of Gibraltar, when the fortress was held for three years and seven months (1779–82) against the French and Spaniards. He fought under Sir John Moore at Corunna, and died soon after the battle, worn out by the hardships of the retreat. His friend, Sir Thomas Hislop, Commander-in-Chief at Bombay, put up the tablet.[1]

George Montagu Dunk, 2nd Earl of Halifax, b, 1716, d. 1771. First Lord of the Admiralty, 1762; Lord-Lieutenant of Ireland, 1761–3; twice Secretary of State, 1762, 1771; styled the 'Father of the Colonies' for his success in extending American commerce. He also helped in the foundation of the Colony of Nova Scotia; the capital was called Halifax after him. *Bacon sculpt.*

Sir William Sanderson, d. 1676, historian of Mary, Queen of Scots, James I, and Charles I, Gentleman of the Bedchamber to Charles. 'After great hardships sustained under the late Tyranny of Rebels' and 'after a full length of 90 years of this troublesome Life', 'he went to a better'. His wife, **Dame Bridget**, daughter of Sir Edward Tyrell, d. 1681, 'Mother of the Maids of Honour to the Queen Mother and to her that now is', with whom he had lived 'very amicably' for fifty years, erected the monument, and is buried in his grave (in front of Chatham's monument). *Edward Marshall sculpt.*

Rear-Admiral Charles Watson, b. 1714, d. 1757. He and Clive together avenged the tragedy of the Black Hole of Calcutta. They reduced Chandernagore, the last fortified French stronghold in Bengal, 1757, and restored the settlement of the East India Company. Watson's name was forged by Clive's connivance, to a fictitious treaty to deceive Omichund. He died shortly after, and was buried in Calcutta. The monument was erected by the East India Company. Watson's statue stands in Classical costume; at his feet kneels an Oriental woman, representing Calcutta. *Scheemakers sculpt.*

Lieut.-General Joshua Guest, b. 1660, d. 1747, 'who closed a Service of Sixty Years by faithfully defending Edinburgh Castle against the Rebells, 1745'. Buried East Cloister. *Taylor sculpt.*

Admiral Sir John Balchen, b. 1670, d. 1744, Commander-in-Chief of the fleets of England and Holland, lost with his ship, the *Victory*, in the Channel in a violent storm. *Scheemakers sculpt.*

Lord Aubrey Beauclerk, b. 1710, d. 1740, youngest son of Charles, 1st Duke of St Albans (illegitimate son of Charles II by 'Nell' Gwynne), killed on Vernon's expedition to Carthagena; his legs were shot off during the bombardment of Boca-Chica. The epitaph to 'dauntless, loyal, virtuous Beauclerk' is said to be by the poet Thomson. *Scheemakers sculpt.*

Lieut.-General Percy Kirk(e), b. 1684, d. 1741, succeeded his father as commander of the Old Tangier regiment, derisively called 'Kirke's Lambs', after their cruelty to Monmouth's adherents at Sedgmoor, the regimental badge was a Paschal lamb. Percy was a distinguished soldier, he fought under Marlborough, and was wounded at Almanza, 1708. In later life he was made Keeper of Whitehall Palace—buried in this Transept. *Scheemakers sculpt.*

William Murray, b. 1705, d. 1793, created **Earl of Mansfield** 1776. Lord Chief Justice of England for thirty-two years, 1756–88. He was educated first at Perth grammar school. His father then entered him as a boarder at Westminster School and though only thirteen he rode all the way on a pony starting from Perth 15 March 1718, and arriving at Westminster on 20 May, having visited his parents on his way; the pony was sold to pay his expenses. Bishop Newton called him: 'the oracle of law, the standard of eloquence and the pattern of all virtue, both in public and private life'. Chatham was his only rival as a Parliamentary speaker, and Pope justly called him 'the silver-tongued Murray'. Owing to his approval of the Roman Catholic Relief Bill, Murray's Bloomsbury house was sacked and burnt with all his furniture and books by the Gordon rioters. He retired from the Bench in 1788, and spent the remainder of his long life in the house built for him by his friend, the famous architect, Robert Adam[2] at Caen (Ken) Wood, Highgate, which is now open to the public, and where his portrait by Sir Joshua Reynolds still hangs. *Flaxman* designed the statue on the tomb from this picture. He was buried in the Abbey by his own wish from the love which he bore to the place (Westminster School) of his early education.[3]

Brigadier-General Richard Kane, b. 1666, d. 1736, distinguished in the wars of William III and Anne. Held Gibraltar for eight months against the Spaniards for George I. George II made him Governor of Minorca, where he is buried. *Rysbrack sculpt.*

Samuel Bradford, b. 1652, d. 1731, Dean of Westminster and Bishop of Rochester (1723). Succeeded

---

[1] *Now removed to Triforium.*

---

[2] *See page 49.*

[3] *This monument which was formerly on the west side of the North Transept has been moved to the west aisle of the Transept.*

Atterbury in these posts while the latter was in the Tower. He was the first Dean of the revived Order of the Bath. Buried close by. *Cheere sculpt.*

Hugh Boulter, b. 1672, d. 1742, the 'munificent statesman prelate'. Bishop of Bristol and, later, Primate of Ireland (1723). At the time of his death he was for the thirteenth time one of the Lord Justices of Ireland, and showed such energy and philanthropy 'as practically brought the direction of the Government under his care', while his charities won him the respect of all classes of the people in Ireland, where, says Dr Johnson, 'his piety and charity will be long honoured'.[1]

---

[1] *Johnson's* Lives: *'Life of Ambrose Phillips'.*

THE NAVE [*See plan, page vii*]

The Unknown Warrior

At the west end of the Nave is the grave of the **Unknown Warrior,** whose body was brought from France to be buried here on 11 November 1920. The grave, which contains soil from France, is covered by a slab of black Belgian marble from a quarry near Namur. On it is an inscription, written by Dean Ryle, which embodies the text 'They buried him among the Kings because he had done good toward God and toward his House'.

The burial was attended by King George V, his two elder sons (the Prince of Wales and the Duke of York), four Queens (Queen Mary, Queen Alexandra, and the Queens of Spain and Norway) and other members of the Royal Family. There were also present the Prime Minister, Members of the Cabinet and the Service Chiefs, while a Guard of Honour of a hundred V.C.s lined the Nave.

The idea of such a burial first came to a chaplain at the Front in 1916, who had noticed a grave in a back garden at Armentières, at the head of which was a rough cross on which was pencilled the words: 'An unknown British Soldier'. It was, however, largely due to Dean Ryle that this idea, which captured the imagination of the world, was carried into effect, and from the day of the funeral the grave has become a place of pilgrimage for people from all over the world.

On the pillar near by is placed the **Congressional Medal** (the highest honour which can be conferred by the United States of America) which was delivered into the keeping of the Dean by General Pershing, the Commander-in-Chief of the United States Army on 17 October 1921. Above it hangs the Union Jack known as 'the Padre's Flag' which was presented by the Revd. David Railton, the chaplain mentioned above. It had covered the coffin of the Unknown Warrior at the burial, as it had covered the bodies of many of those killed on the Vimy Ridge, on the Ypres Salient, on the Somme and elsewhere, and had been used to drape the altar at many services at the Front. It was dedicated by the Dean on 11 November 1921, the third anniversary of the Armistice, 'to the memory of all those who gave their lives' in the 1914–18 war.

Grave of the Unknown Warrior

North-west or Belfry Tower

'This spot,' says Dean Stanley, 'by the monuments of Fox and Holland, of Tierney, the soul of every opposition, and of Mackintosh, the cherished leader of philosophical and liberal thought and the reformer of our criminal code, has been consecrated as the Whigs' Corner.'[1] The figure in the window traditionally represents Edward the Confessor, but is in reality made up of fragments of ancient glass.

In the centre is a large monument to **Captain James Montagu,** b. 1752, who was killed while commanding the *Montagu* in the engagement off Brest under Lord Howe on 'the glorious first of June', 1794. *Flaxman sculpt.*

Across the eastern bay of this tower, is *Westmacott's* monument[2] to the Whig statesman **Charles James Fox,** b. 1749, d. 1806. He first took office under a Tory Government, but on the question of the American War he went over to the Opposition, and from that time became the Whig leader of the House of Commons. He is represented dying in the arms of Liberty; a negro, kneeling at his feet, is thanking him for his share in the abolition of the slave trade. Fox and Pitt, rivals to the last, died in the same year, and are buried close together in the North Transept.

George, 3rd Viscount Howe, b. 1725, d. 1758, brother of the great admiral. He was killed on the first expedition to Ticonderoga in North America. Wolfe called him 'the noblest Englishman that has appeared in my time, and the best soldier in the British Army'. The monument was put up by the Province of Massachusetts, before its separation from the mother country. *Scheemakers sculpt.*

Sir James Mackintosh, b. 1765, d. 1832, philosopher and jurist. He devoted himself during his Parliamentary career to the improvement of the Penal Code. Buried at Hampstead. *Theed sculpt.*

George Tierney, b. 1761, d. 1830, a Whig statesman, notable for his strenuous opposition to Pitt, with whom he fought a bloodless duel in 1798. A tablet put up by his friends.

Henry Vassal Fox, 3rd Lord Holland, b. 1773, d. 1840, nephew of Charles James Fox. Statesman and writer, the centre of a notable literary circle at Holland House, Kensington. The monument represents the 'Prison House of Death': there is no inscription. *E. H. Baily sculpt.*

Lieut.-Colonel the Hon. George Augustus Lake, who fell 17 August 1808, at the head of his grenadiers storming the heights of Rolica, in Portugal, Lord Wellington's first victory in the Peninsular War. He had fought in India under his father General Viscount Lake, and was wounded at Laswari, one of the decisive battles which helped to break the power of the Mahratta family. *J. Smith sculpt.*

Henry Petty-Fitzmaurice, 3rd Marquess of Lansdowne, b. 1780, d. 1863, Home Secretary 1828, and Leader of the Opposition on Peel's death. He was actively associated with the Whig Party, and took part in all its leading measures, such as the abolition of slavery, and the repeal of the penal laws.

John, Earl Russell, K.G., 3rd son of the 6th Duke of Bedford, b. 1792, d. 1878, Prime Minister 1846–52, created Earl Russell in 1861, and, on Palmerston's death in 1865, again Prime Minister. In 1866, when his party was defeated on the Reform Bill, Russell resigned, and

never again held office. Buried at Chenies. *Two busts by Boehm.*

Lieut.-Colonel Sir Richard Fletcher, R.E., b. 1768, d. 1813. Wellington's chief engineer officer, who constructed from his general's plans the lines at Torres Vedras, which baffled the French Army; he afterwards directed the siege works at Badajos. Killed at San Sebastian. *E. H. Baily sculpt.*

Rear-Admiral Sir George Hope, b. 1767, d. 1818, erected at the expense of several Captains of the Royal Navy, who served under him as Midshipmen. *P. Turnerelli sculpt.*

William Horneck, d. 1746, one of 'the earliest of our great English engineers, who learned his military science under the Duke of Marlborough'. His father, Anthony Horneck, d. 1697, a German by birth, became Prebendary of Westminster, and is buried with his son in the South Transept. *Scheemakers sculpt.*

Major Charles Banks Stanhope, b. 1785, great-grandson of the first Earl Stanhope (page 32), and nephew of William Pitt; he fell at the battle of Corunna, 1809.

Major James Rennell, b. 1742, d. 1830, Surveyor-General of Bengal, distinguished for his military service in India. He won European fame as a geographer and antiquary; author of many scientific and literary works. Buried in the Nave. *Bust by Hagbolt.*

Dr Thomas Arnold, b. 1795, d. 1842. Head Master of Rugby School from 1828–42. The bust was subscribed for by his old pupils. *Pinker sculpt.*

Zachary Macaulay, b. 1768, d. 1838, an African merchant, father of the historian. The inscription, by Sir James Stephen, records his labours on behalf of the abolition of the slave trade. *Bust by Weekes.*

Joseph Chamberlain, b. 1836, d. 1914, statesman. Thrice he was Mayor of Birmingham. Chancellor of the University of Birmingham (1901), Secretary of State for the Colonies under Lord Salisbury and Mr Balfour. Chamberlain's name will always be associated with the cause of Tariff Reform, also with the Imperialist movement, which began in the late nineteenth century under his auspices. *John Tweed sculpt.*

Major-General Charles George Gordon, R.E., b. 1833, d. 1885, known as 'Chinese Gordon' after his services in China, where he assisted the Imperial Government to suppress the Taiping rebellion (1863–4), and received the Yellow Jacket and Peacock's Feather, denoting a mandarin of the first rank. He devoted the rest of his life to Africa, and finally became Governor of Khartoum, where he was slain by the Mahdi's forces before the relief expedition arrived. A bronze bust given in 1892 by the Royal Engineers. *Onslow Ford sculpt.*

Robert Cecil, b. 1830, d. 1903, **3rd Marquess of Salisbury, K.G.,** thrice Prime Minister, and leader of the Conservative Party in the last decade of the nineteenth century. A black marble altar tomb, erected by Parliament, 1909, with recumbent effigy in bronze. Lord Salisbury was Master of Trinity House, Warden of the Cinque Ports, Chancellor of Oxford, and High Steward of Westminster, and these coats of arms will be found on shields at his head and feet. On the sides of the tomb are bronze statuettes of his father, the second Marquess, and his mother; also of his great ancestors, Lord and Lady Burghley, with their son, Sir Robert Cecil, first Earl of Salisbury, and his wife, Elizabeth. The earl holds a model of Hatfield House in his hand. Buried at Hatfield. *W. Goscombe John sculpt.*

---

[1] *Memorials of Westminster Abbey (1882 ed.), page 245.*
[2] *Originally in the north aisle of the Choir.*

West End of Nave

William Pitt, b. 1759, d. 1806, Lord Chatham's second son. He became Prime Minister at the age of twenty-four (1783), and remained in office, with a break of only three years, until his death. He died insolvent, and was buried at the public expense; Parliament, in recognition of his services to the country, voted £40,000 to pay his debts. On his monument, over the west door, the great orator is represented speaking, while history records his words, and anarchy – the French Revolution – crouches in chains at his feet. *Westmacott sculpt.*

(*North of Door*) – **John Conduitt,** b. 1688, d. 1737, married Sir Isaac Newton's niece, and succeeded him as Master of the Mint. Buried near Newton. After the last transit of Venus (1874) a memorial tablet with inscription by Dean Stanley, was inserted to **Jeremiah Horrocks,** d. 1641, a young clergyman, Curate of St Michael's Church, Hoole, who first observed this phenomenon, 4 December 1639. *Cheere sculpt.*

A statue of the philanthropist, **Anthony Ashley Cooper, 7th Earl of Shaftesbury, K.G.,** b. 1801, d. 1885, was erected here in 1888. *Boehm sculpt.*

Beneath Lord Shaftesbury's statue lies **Angela Georgina, Baroness Burdett-Coutts,** b. 1814, d. 1906, well known for her philanthropic work.

(*South*) – **Admiral Sir Thomas Hardy,** b. 1666, d. 1732; served under Rooke at Cadiz. He was descended from Clement le Hardy, of Jersey, the protector of Henry VII, who, when Earl of Richmond, landed in Jersey on his way to exile in France, and was safely conveyed to Normandy by Clement, 'at the hazard of his own life'. Buried near the west end of the Choir. *Cheere sculpt.*

To the south of the west door is a case with a Roll of Honour containing the names of civilians who were killed by enemy action 1939–45.

Above this case is a memorial plaque to **Franklin Delano Roosevelt,** b. 1882, d. 1945. 'A faithful friend of freedom and of Britain, four times President of the United States. Erected by the Government of the United Kingdom.' Unveiled by the Prime Minister (Mr Attlee) and by Mr Winston Churchill on 12 November 1948. *H. W. Palliser sculpt.*

The Warriors' Chapel

Was formerly used as the Baptistery, but the Font has been removed to Henry VII's Chapel. The Consistory Courts were also held here; the judge's seat still remains on the south wall. The glass in the window is a composite figure traditionally known as the Black Prince. This Chapel has been remodelled and richly decorated. On 24 June 1932, Edward, Prince of Wales,[1] dedicated it to the memory of the men and women who had lost their lives in the First World War. The cost £4,000, was defrayed mostly by an anonymous gift,[2] in part by pennies collected from the women of the empire by the Mothers' Union, and from the gifts of private persons. The alterations to the Chapel and the decorations are from the designs of *Sir J. N. Comper,* architect, the work was carried out by his assistants, *B. Pegram* and *W. F.*

[1] *King Edward VIII.*
[2] *The donor, Mr John Denham of Johannesburg, died before the completion of the Chapel.*

Knight. The altar, which is dedicated to St George, is enriched with many ornaments and tapestries; above it on the east side are remains of the original stone screen. Against the western wall is a decorated tablet, which was unveiled by Edward, Prince of Wales, President of the Imperial War Commission, 19 October 1926. It commemorates the million citizens of the British Empire to whom this Chapel was afterwards dedicated. The tablet is from the design of Lieut.-Colonel Lafontaine. On the wooden panelling at the back of the seats are the names of the nine Abbey servants who were killed in the war.

Beneath the tablet to the million citizens of the British Empire is a small tablet, unveiled in 1950, to **Major-General Sir Fabian Ware, K.C.V.O.,** b. 1869, d. 1949. Vice-Chairman Imperial War Graves Commission.

Above on the South Wall is the monument to **James Craggs,** b. 1686, d. 1721, son of the Postmaster-General. Craggs became a Privy Councillor and Secretary of State before he was thirty-two, but his brilliant career was cut short by smallpox at the early age of thirty-five. He was a mourner at Addison's funeral, and, before two years had passed, his own coffin was laid upon his friend's. Pope, who had a great admiration for Craggs, superintended the erection of his monument, and wrote the epitaph, which was cut on it by the sculptor *Bird*.

> Statesman, yet friend to truth of Soul sincere,
> In Action faithful and in Honour clear,
> Who broke no Promise, serv'd no private end,
> Who gain'd no Title, and who lost no Friend;
> Ennobled by Himself, by All approv'd,
> Prais'd, wept, and honoured, by the Muse he lov'd.

Had Craggs lived until the inquiry into the South Sea Bubble was concluded this panegyric could hardly have been written, for the Secretary of State and his father were down in the company's subscription lists for the fictitious sum of £330,000. *Guelfi,* an Italian sculptor.

Henry Fawcett, b. 1833, d. 1884. The monument was erected (1887) to commemorate the blind statesman. He was Postmaster-General 1880–4, and established parcel post 1882. Underneath is a memorial to his wife: **Dame Millicent Garratt Fawcett,** b. 1847, d. 1929, who helped to fight the battle for women's suffrage. Below are small portrait heads of Mr and Mrs Fawcett. *Alfred Gilbert sculpt.*

Two busts commemorate **Fredk. Denison Maurice,** b. 1805, d. 1872, preacher and writer. Buried at Highgate. And his 'Disciple', **Charles Kingsley,** b. 1819, d. 1875, writer and poet, Canon of Westminster and rector of Eversley. Buried at Eversley. *Woolner sculpt.*

The bust of the poet and essayist **Matthew Arnold,** b. 1822, d. 1888, presented by his relatives and friends, was unveiled by Lord Coleridge, 31 October 1891. *Bruce Joy sculpt.*

The first interment in this Chapel took place shortly after the dedication when, 18 July 1932, **Field-Marshal Herbert, 1st Viscount Plumer, G.C.B.,** b. 1857, d. 1932, was buried here, with full military honours. He was a distinguished Commander of the Second Army in the First World War. Governor of Malta 1919–24; Commander-in-Chief in Palestine 1925–8.

Field-Marshal Edmund, 1st Viscount Allenby, G.C.B., etc., b. 1866, d. 1936. One of the great Commanders in the First World War. To him was due the recapture of Jerusalem.

Portrait of Richard II

On the pillar just outside St George's Chapel is now placed the contemporary **portrait of Richard II,** which used to hang over the Lord Chancellor's stall on the south side of the Choir, but the wigs of the occupants injured it greatly, and it was removed to the Jerusalem Chamber in 1775, whence Dean Stanley transferred it to the Sanctuary. The picture was restored by Sir George Richmond in the nineteenth century, at which time the pattern of raised and gilt gesso work had already disappeared. The vivid colours of the costume still remain unimpaired, as described by Dart in the eighteenth century–the green vest powdered with the golden letter R, the crimson robe lined with ermine, the ermine cape, the vermilion socks, and gilt shoes. The artist is conjectured to have been a Frenchman, André Beauneve of Valenciennes, portrait-painter to Charles V, who is known to have visited the English Court about 1398.

South Aisle

Above the Deanery entrance is a small oak gallery, called the 'Abbot's Pew', built, with the rooms behind it, by Abbot Islip, early in the sixteenth century.

A stone in the floor near the Deanery entrance and by the Screen of St George's Chapel commemorates **Robert, 1st Baron Baden-Powell,** b. 1857, d. 1941, the founder of the Scout Movement. He died and was buried at Nyeri, Kenya. Above it are placed the flags of the Boy Scouts and Girl Guides. It was unveiled on St George's Day, 1947.

Henry Wharton, b. 1664, d. 1695, divine and author. 'This wonderful and surprising gentleman, to whose example and labours the worlds of piety and learning are so much indebted', was Archbishop Sancroft's favourite chaplain. Though he died young, Wharton was already famous, and had written ecclesiastical works, of which the best known is the *Anglia Sacra.* He was buried with much pomp in the South Nave. Archbishop Tillotson attended his funeral. Purcell composed the anthems.

Below the Abbot's Pew are the graves of two deans: **Francis Atterbury,** b. 1663, d. 1732; King's Scholar, Westminster School, under Dr Busby, and Scholar and Fellow of Christ Church, Oxford; the famous Jacobite Dean of Westminster and Bishop of Rochester, noted as a brilliant orator and controversial writer. His High Church principles brought him preferment with the Tory Government, but he lost their favour under the Hanoverians. He was sent to the Tower charged with conspiracy to place the Pretender on the throne, deprived of his offices and condemned to perpetual exile in 1723. Nine years later he died in Paris, and was buried here by his own desire, expressed in a letter to Pope, 'as far from Kings and Caesars as the space will admit of'. Under Atterbury the school dormitory was rebuilt, and he also left his mark on the structure of the Abbey. He chose the subjects for the rose window in the North Transept, and himself superintended the repairing of the North Front by Wren, then the Surveyor of the Abbey, and, it is said, complacently 'watched the workmen hewing smooth the fine old sculptures'.

George Granville Bradley, D.D., b. 1821, d. 1903, Dean of Westminster for twenty-one years, 1881–1902, is buried near Atterbury, close to the Deanery door. Dr Bradley began his career as Assistant-Master (1846) at Rugby School, where he had been educated under Dr Arnold, passing thence in 1858 to the Head Mastership of Marlborough College, and in 1870 returned to University, his old college at Oxford, as Master. In 1881 he was made a Canon of Worcester and succeeded his friend Arthur Stanley the same year as Dean of Westminster. Dr Bradley devoted himself to the ordering of the services, to the finances of the Collegiate Body, and, like his predecessors Atterbury and Wilcocks, made the preservation and restoration of the fabric one of his chief duties. He officiated at many great functions, notably at the first Jubilee of Queen Victoria (1887), and took his official part at the coronation of King Edward VII and Queen Alexandra (9 August 1902). He resigned the Deanery in October[1] 1902, and died 13 March 1903. Brass presented by the Dean and Chapter. *Clayton and Bell.*

---

[1] *Succeeded as Dean by Dr Armitage Robinson, who was transferred to the Deanery of Wells, 1911, retired in 1933, and died the same year. Buried in Wells Cathedral.*

View westwards through the Crossing to the Na

A wall monument to **William Congreve**, b. 1670, d. 1729, considered the first dramatist of the age by his contemporaries. Dryden compared him with Shakespeare, Pope flattered him, and Swift both satirized and eulogized him. His most successful plays were *Love for Love* (1695), *The Mourning Bride* (1695) and *The Way of the World*, which was revived on the London stage in 1922. His funeral was a very pompous ceremony. The body lay in state in the Jerusalem Chamber, and the Prime Minister was one of the pall-bearers. Henrietta, Duchess of Marlborough[1] (daughter and heiress of the great Duke), to whom Congreve left the bulk of his fortune, erected the monument and wrote the epitaph. She spent the legacy on a diamond necklace, and an ivory statue of the poet, moved by clockwork, was set daily at her table, with which she talked as if it were the 'living Mr Congreve'. She also had a wax doll made in imitation of him, whose feet were regularly blistered and anointed by the doctors in memory of Congreve's sufferings from gout. He left a legacy of £200 to Mrs Bracegirdle (see page 109) who had always acted his heroines and spoken the prologues and epilogues of his plays. *Bird sculpt.*

Dr John Freind, b, 1675, d. 1728, eminent physicist and scholar, favourite of George II and Queen Caroline. Imprisoned in the Tower for his intimacy with the Jacobite Dean Atterbury, and released through Dr Mead's influence (see page 28). Buried at Hitchin. His brother Robert, Head Master of Westminster School, wrote this, and other inscriptions here, of which Pope says:

Freind, for your epitaphs I'm grieved
   Where still so much is said,
One half will never be believed,
   The other never read.

Designed by Gibbs: bust by *Rysbrack*.

Ann Oldfield, b. 1683, d. 1730 (a stone in the floor). She was the chief actress of her day, and had a magnificent funeral, her body lying in state in the Jerusalem Chamber. She was buried in 'a very fine Brussels lace head, a Holland shift with a tucker and double ruffles of the same lace, a pair of new kid gloves, and her body wrapped up in a winding sheet'. Hence Pope's lines:

'Odious! in woollen! 'twould a saint provoke'
(Were the last words that poor Narcissa spoke);
'No; let a charming chintz and Brussels lace
Wrap my cold limbs and shade my lifeless face;
One would not, sure, be frightful when one's dead –
And, Betty, give this cheek a little red.'

Thomas Sprat, b. 1635, d. 1713, Dean of Westminster and Bishop of Rochester, a fervent Royalist, the friend of Cowley, whose epitaph he wrote. Buried in St Nicholas's Chapel. Dr Freind erected this monument, which was moved from St Nicholas's Chapel to make room for the Northumberland tomb (page 59). *Bird sculpt.*

Joseph Wilcocks, b. 1673, d. 1756, Dean of Westminster and Bishop of Rochester for twenty-five years, during which extensive repairs of the Abbey fabric were carried out, and the western towers built. The Dean was so proud of the towers that he caused a representation of them to be placed upon his monument, and chose his grave beneath the south-west tower. *Cheere sculpt.*

Rear-Admiral Richard Tyrrell, d. 1766. Tyrrell distin-guished himself while in command of the *Buckingham* by defeating single-handed three French men-of-war. The monument by *Read*, Roubiliac's pupil, had a great reputation in the eighteenth century. Nollekens ventured to disparage it: 'That figure of his (Read's) of Admiral Tyrrell going to heaven out of the sea looks for all the world as if he were hanging from a gallows with a rope round his neck.' Later on it received the name of the 'Pancake' monument from the shape of the clouds. But it has been cut down since, and the figure of the Admiral removed. Buried at sea by his own request.

Zachary Pearce, b. 1690, d. 1774, Dean of Westminster (1756) and Bishop of Rochester. He retired from the Deanery 1768, aged seventy-four, the first instance of the retirement of a Dean in the history of the Abbey. He left his books to the Chapter Library. Buried at Bromley. Inscription by Dean Thomas. *Tyler sculpt.*

A wall monument to **Mrs Katherine Bovey** (b. 1669, d. 1726), erected by Mrs Mary Pope, to mark their friendship of forty years. The ladies were caricatured by Addison as the 'Perverse Widow' and her 'Malicious Confidante' in *The Spectator*. Mrs Bovey was buried at Flaxley, where Mrs Pope put up another monument. *Gibbs des.*

John Thomas, b. 1712, d. 1793, succeeded Pearce as Dean of Westminster, 1768, and became also Bishop of Rochester. In this time the Festival of the Centenary of Handel's birth was held in the Nave of the Abbey, 1784. Thomas was an advocate for the removal of the disabilities of Roman Catholics. He was waylaid one day in the Cloisters, as he returned from service, 'by a band of tumultuous and misguided enthusiasts, who seized him by the robes and demanded "how he meant to vote in the House of Lords", to which with great presence and firmness the Bishop replied, "For your interests and my own." "What, then, you don't mean to vote for Popery?" "No," said he, "thank God, that is no part of our interests in this Protestant country". Upon hearing this one of the party clapped the Bishop on the back, and cleared the passage for him, calling out: "Make way for the Protestant Bishop!"'[2] The bust was copied from a picture by Sir Joshua Reynolds. *Bacon, jun., sculpt.*

John Ireland, b. 1761, d. 1842, Dean of Westminster, founder of the Theological Professorship and the 'Ireland' Scholarships at Oxford. Free admission to the Nave and Transepts of the Abbey was first given by Dean Ireland. *Bust by Ternouth.* Buried in the South Transept, with his old school fellow **William Gifford**, b. 1756, d. 1826, first editor of the *Quarterly Review*.

William Buckland, b. 1784, d. 1856, Dean of Westminster, twice President of the Geological Society, and author of works on geology. *Bust by Weekes.* Buried at Islip, Oxfordshire.

Ann Whytell, d. 1788, of Gilmonby Co. York. *John Bacon.*

John Laird Mair, 1st Baron Lawrence, b. 1811, d. 1879, Governor-General of India 1864. 'The great Viceroy, whose name was feared and loved throughout Upper India.' For his share in suppressing the Mutiny he was created a baronet and G.C.B., and after his resignation of the Governor-Generalship in 1868 raised to the peerage. *Bust by Woolner.*

Robert Cannon, b. 1663, d. 1722. Prebendary of Westminster (1715–22) and Dean of Lincoln (1721–2).

---

[1] *Buried in the south aisle.*

[2] *Stanley's* Memorials, *page 478.*

Field-Marshal George Wade, b. 1673, d. 1748, who assisted Kane (page 20) and Stanhope (page 32) in the conquest of Minorca and the Spanish wars, and was afterwards sent to Scotland as Commander-in-Chief to attempt to quell the Young Pretender's rebellion, 1745. The good roads he laid down through the Highlands are commemorated in the lines, which were inscribed on an obelisk once standing on the road between Inverness and Inveraray:

If you'd seen these roads before they were made,
You would hold up your hands and bless Marshal Wade.

Buried centre of Nave. *Roubiliac sculpt.*
Lieut.-General William Hargrave, b. 1672, d. 1751, Governor of Gibraltar, and his friend **Major-General James Fleming,** b. 1682, d. 1751, who died a few weeks later, are buried not far from the Choir Gates. Fleming had been wounded under Marlborough at Blenheim, and distinguished himself later at Falkirk and Culloden. He left his fortune to his nephew, a lieutenant in Hargrave's regiment, the Royal English Fusiliers, then stationed at Gibraltar. The monuments on the two window ledges are good examples of *Roubiliac's* style.
Lieut.-General Sir James Outram, b. 1803, d. 1863. 'The Bayard of India', who served his country in India 'forty years in war and council'. His name is inseparably connected with the defence of Lucknow, and he ranks as one of the saviours of India during the Indian Mutiny. The bas-relief represents the scene at the Residency when Lord Clyde relieved Lucknow. General Havelock stands between Outram and Clyde. *Noble sculpt.*
Charles Herries, b. 1745, d. 1819, a well-known merchant, buried here with military honours as Colonel of the London and Westminster Light Horse Volunteers. *Chantrey sculpt.*
Carola, d. 1674, and **Ann,** d. 1680, the two wives of **Sir Samuel Morland,** Oliver Cromwell's secretary, writer of the *History of the Evangelical Churches of Piedmont*; inventor of the speaking-trumpet, and improver of the fire-engine. He has displayed his learning in the Hebrew, Greek, Ethiopic, and English inscriptions which commemorate his wives. *Stanton sculpt.*
A tablet records the burials in the Nave of: **Sir William Temple,** b. 1628, d. 1699, Master of the Rolls in Ireland. A distinguished statesman, diplomatist, and man of letters and of **Dorothy Temple,** b. 1629, d. 1695,[1] daughter of Sir Peter Osborne, his accomplished wife, many of whose charming love-letters to her husband have been republished. The monument was restored in 1929, the tercentenary of Dorothy's birth, as a tribute to her memory, also their daughter **Diana,** d. 1679, and Temple's sister, **Martha Lady Giffard,** b. 1688, d. 1722, 'maid, wife, and widow in one day, her husband dying on their wedding day'. Swift was Temple's secretary and 'Stella' was waiting maid to Lady Giffard. Temple left legacies to them both, and entrusted the publication of his collected works to Swift.
Sir Charles Harbord and **Clement Cottrell,** who lost their lives in Southwold (Sole) Bay, 1672, a bloody action in which the Dutch fleet was held at bay for six hours and ultimately defeated. The friends might have saved themselves, but preferred to perish with their Admiral, the Earl of Sandwich, and his ship.[2] Harbord's father, who

was Surveyor-General, and a well-known resident in Westminster, put up this monument, leaving forty shillings annually to the poor of Westminster, as long as the memorial remained, 'whole or undefaced in the Abbey church'
Andrew Bonar Law, M.P., b. 1858, d. 1923, statesman and Prime Minister, a Canadian by birth and Scottish by descent, in the female line. Law entered Parliament as Conservative Member for the Blackfriars Division of Glasgow in 1900; was elected Lord Rector of Glasgow University in 1919, and represented the Central Division of Glasgow from early 1922 till his resignation on 23 October. His parliamentary career was a notable one. From 1911 to 1915 he led the opposition when the Liberals under Asquith were in office, joined the first Coalition Government as Colonial Secretary in 1915 and was a member of Lloyd George's war cabinet as Chancellor of the Exchequer, 1916. He held the office of Lord Privy Seal 1919–21, and led his party as Prime Minister during the last year of his life, 23 October 1922 to 20 May 1923. He resigned his post owing to failing health, and died a few months later, 20 October 1923.
Neville Chamberlain, b. 1869, d. 1940, statesman and Prime Minister 1937–40. Only son of Rt. Hon. Joseph Chamberlain by his second wife. A stone in the floor marks his burial-place.
Sidney, 1st Earl of Godolphin, b. 1645, d. 1712, who held office under Charles II, James II, and William III and was Chief Minister 'during the first nine glorious years' of Anne's reign. Burnet calls him 'the silentest and modestest man that was perhaps ever bred in a Court', but though he spoke little his judgment was 'always to the purpose'; and he maintained to his life's end the short character Charles II gave him when he was a page, 'He was never in the way and never out of the way.' Buried in the aisle. *Bust by Bird.*
Lieut.-Colonel the Hon. Roger Townshend (1759) killed, aged twenty-eight, when reconnoitring the French lines on the second expedition to Ticondernga. A bas-relief represents the fort, showing a skirmish between the French and British, who are dressed like Roman soldiers. It was designed by Robert Adam and Luc-François Breton and carved by John Eckstein and T. Carter. Flaxman considered this one of the best pieces of sculpture in the Abbey.[3]
Sir Palmes Fairborne, b. 1644, d. 1680, Governor of Tangier, killed defending that town against the Moors. Tangier came to the British Crown as part of the dowry of Charles II's Queen, Catherine of Braganza, but was finally lost soon after Fairborne's heroic defence. Dryden wrote the epitaph:

Yee sacred reliques which your marble keepe,
Heere undisturb'd by warrs, in quiet sleepe:
Discharge the trust which when it was below
Fairborne's disdaunted soul did undergoe:
And be the towns Balladium from the foe.
Alive and dead these walls he will defend.
Great actions great examples must attend.
The Candian siege his early valour knew;
Where Turkish blood did his Young hands imbrew:
From thence returning with deserv'd applause,
Against ye Moores his well-flesh'd sword he draws
The same the courage, and the same ye cause.

---

[1] *See Macaulay's Essays 'Temple'.*   [2] *See page 74.*   [3] *J. T. Smith*, Nollekins and his Times (*1920*), *vol. ii, page 238.*

More bravely british Generall never fell:
Nor Generall's death was 'ere reveng'd so well.
Which his pleas'd eyes beheld before their close,
Follow'd by thousand Victims of his foes.

Buried at Tangier; his widow erected the monument. *Bushnell sculpt.*

Major John André, b. 1751, d. 1780, Adjutant-General of the British Forces in America. André was sent on a secret mission to General Arnold, but was captured within the American lines, in a civilian's dress, with suspicious papers about him, and taken before General Washington. In spite of every effort made to obtain his pardon, he was hanged as a spy, 2 October 1780, aged twenty-nine. Forty years later his remains were, at the Duke of York's request, brought from America, and buried with the funeral service, near this monument, which was erected at the expense of George III. The chest in which they were enclosed is in the Triforium. On the bas-relief, Washington is portrayed receiving the petition, in which André vainly implored for a soldier's death, and André is seen on the way to execution. The heads of both have been often carried off, and Charles Lamb's allusion, in the *Essays of Elia*, to the dismemberment of this monument, caused a temporary rupture between himself and Southey who was very sensitive about his early political principles. Lamb calls it 'the wanton mischief of some schoolboy, fired perhaps with raw notions of transatlantic freedom. The mischief was done,' he adds, addressing Southey, 'about the time that you were a scholar there. Do you know anything about the unfortunate relic?' *Adam des., Van Gelder sculpt.*

Sir John Chardin, b. 1643, d. 1713, a French merchant, who became Court Jeweller to Charles II, and was sent by that King as Minister Plenipotentiary to Holland. He published some volumes of travels describing his early adventures in the East. Buried in Chiswick Church. *Henry Cheere sculpt.*

A small tablet to **Mrs Bridget Radley,** d. 1679, wife of Charles Radley, Gentleman Usher to Charles II.

North Aisle

Sir John Frederick Herschel, b. 1792, d. 1871, the celebrated astronomer, who, 'having explored the heavens, rests here near Newton' (from Latin inscription), a stone near by commemorates his father, **Sir William Herschel,** b. 1738, d. 1822, astronomer, who is buried at Upton, near Slough. **Charles Robert Darwin,** b. 1809, d. 1882, naturalist and biologist. Author of *The Origin of Species*.

Two small stones mark the graves of **George Stone,** b. 1708, d. 1764, Archbishop of Armagh, and of his brother **Andrew Stone,** b. 1703, d. 1773, Under-Secretary of State and Treasurer to Queen Charlotte.

Lieut.-General Thomas Livingston, 1st Viscount Teviot, b. 1652 (?), d. 1711, son of a colonel in the Dutch service, who was created a baronet by Charles II; he himself acquired his military reputation as Colonel of the Scots Brigade in the Dutch pay. He came to England with William of Orange, became Commander-in-Chief in Scotland (1690), and was made a viscount for his military services.

A tablet to a child of seven, son of **Sir Edward Carteret,** d. 1677, Gentleman Usher of the Black Rod to Charles II. **Hon. Philip Carteret,** b. 1692, d. 1711, son of George

1st Baron Carteret, a Queen's Scholar at Westminster School. Time holds a tablet inscribed with Latin verses by Dr Robert Freind, then Under, afterwards Head Master of the school. *Claudius David sculpt.*

Two monuments by *Bird*, covered with nautical emblems, pieces of artillery, and the grinning faces of sea monsters: **Henry Priestman,** d, 1712, a naval commander who fought all through the Dutch wars in the reign of Charles II, and received a post at the Admiralty under William III; and **Vice-Admiral John Baker,** b. 1661, d. 1716, who was second in command to Sir Cloudesley Shovel, and brought the fleet back from the Scilly Isles after his chief's shipwreck (page 35). He afterwards became Governor of Minorca – a possession now lost to England – and is buried there.

Dr Richard Mead, b. 1673, d. 1754, physician to George II, one of the first advocates of inoculation for smallpox. He stood at the head of his profession, and the following anecdote illustrates the weight attached to his medical opinion. Sir Robert Walpole fell ill during Dr John Freind's imprisonment in the Tower, and sent as usual for Mead to cure him, but the latter refused to prescribe unless his fellow-doctor were released, and the Premier, whether from fear or favour, yielded, and Freind was set free and never molested again. Mead was a collector of books and pictures, and Dibdin speaks of him as 'the ever-renowned Richard Mead, whose pharmacopoeial reputation is lost in the blaze of his bibliomaniacal glory'. Buried in the Temple Church. *Scheemakers sculpt.*

Spencer Perceval, b. 1762, d. 1812, Prime Minister and Chancellor of the Exchequer. Shot in the lobby of the House of Commons by Bellingham, a bankrupt, who had a grievance against the Government. The monument erected by the Prince Regent and Parliament, is an allegorical one by *Sir Richard Westmacott.*

A brass records the burial of **James Oswald,** b. 1715, d. 1769, successively Commissioner of the Navy, a Lord of the Treasury, and Vice-Treasurer of Ireland under George II and George III; the friend of David Hume and Adam Smith.

Gilbert Thornburgh, d. 1677, Gentleman of the Cellar to Charles II. A tablet with a quaint Latin inscription of which the following is a translation: 'Here lies Gilbert Thornburgh, who was always Faithful to his God, his Prince, and his Friends, formerly an earthly now a heavenly courtier. It shall no more be said in the age to come, *Who would become good must leave the Court*, when such shining piety as his shall appear there.'[1]

A tablet surmounted by flags and naval emblems, commemorates **Captain John Stewart, R.N.** d. 1811, who fought under Nelson and later in his ship, the *Seahorse*, defeated single-handed a Turkish squadron in 1808. (Buried in centre of Nave.)

Mrs Jane Hill, d. 1631, a curious monument of black touchstone. The lady's effigy kneels on a cushion; at the back are a skeleton in a winding-sheet and two mottoes: 'Mors mihi lucrum', and 'Solus Christus mihi sola salus'.

Next is a monument by the celebrated carver in wood *Grinling Gibbons* to **Miss Mary Beaufoy,** d. 1705, daughter of Sir Henry Beaufoy of Guys Cliff, Warwick.

Robert Killigrew, d. 1707, page to Charles II, and Brigadier-General of the forces under Anne. Killed at the Battle of Almanza, in Spain, where the British were defeated by the Spanish and French forces. *Bird sculpt.*

---

[1] *Dart's translation.*

Thomas Banks, R.A., b. 1735, d. 1805, a sculptor much patronized in his own day. Studied under Scheemakers and in Italy. His masterpiece, the tomb of a little girl, is in Ashbourne Church. His huge monument here to Sir Eyre Coote (page 19) is redeemed by the delicate moulding of the figures. Flaxman, in a funeral oration on Banks, attacked the popular sculptors Roubiliac and Rysbrack.

A modern paving-stone now marks the place of **Ben Jonson's** grave;[1] the ancient stone was placed against the wall in 1821 to preserve the inscription. The poet was buried standing on his feet. One story says that, dying in great poverty, he begged '18 inches of square ground in Westminster Abbey' from Charles I. Another, that 'one day being rallied by the Dean of Westminster about being buried in Poets' Corner, the poet is said to have replied, – we tell the story as current in the Abbey: "I am too poor for that, and no one will lay out funeral charges upon me. No, sir, 6 feet long by 2 feet wide is too much for me: 2 feet by 2 feet will do for all I want." "You shall have it," said the Dean, and thus the conversation ended.'[2] When, in 1849, the place was disturbed by Sir Robert Wilson's burial, the clerk of the works 'saw the two leg bones of Jonson fixed bolt upright in the sand . . . and the skull came rolling down among the same from a position above the leg-bones to the bottom of the newly-made grave. There was still hair upon it, and of a red colour.' The skull, 'with traces of red hair upon it', was again seen when Hunter's grave was dug. The inscription, 'O Rare Ben Jonson' has been ascribed to Davenant, on whose own gravestone in the Abbey is, 'O Rare Sir William Davenant'; but another tradition says: 'It was donne at the chardge of Jack Young, afterwards knighted, who, walking here when the grave was covering, gave the fellow eighteen-pence to cut it.'

General Sir Robert Romas Wilson, b. 1777, d. 1849, Governor of Gibraltar. Represented on his brass as a medieval knight.

John Hunter, b, 1728, d. 1793, the celebrated surgeon and anatomist, lies under a brass near Ben Jonson's grave. His remains were removed here from St Martin's-in-the-Fields, in 1859, by the Royal College of Surgeons, through the exertions of Frank Buckland.[3]

Colonel James Bringfield, d. 1706, Equerry to Prince George of Denmark, and aide-de-camp to the Duke of Marlborough '(the Victorious General of her Majestys Forces beyond ye Sea) who, while he was Remounting, his Lord, upon a fresh Horse, his former Fayling under him, had his Head fatally shott by a Cannon Ball, in ye Battell of Ramelies . . . and so haveing gloriously ended his days, in ye Bed of Honour, lyes interred at Bavechem in the Province of Brabant' (from inscription).

On the window ledge above is the bust by *Theed* of the great geologist **Sir Charles Lyell,** b. 1797, d. 1875, President of the Geological Society, and author of many works on geology. Buried in the Nave.

The Twysdens (three gallant young brothers) are commemorated on tablets here: **Josiah,** d. 1708, and **Heneage,** d. 1709, were soldiers, killed in Flanders and Hainault; **John,** a naval lieutenant, was shipwrecked (1707) with Admiral Shovel. They were the sons of Sir William Twysden, 3rd Bart.

---

[1] *His monument is in Poets' Corner, page 40.*

[2] *Cunningham's* Handbook, *page 36.*

[3] *b. 1826, d. 1880, son of Dean Buckland.*

Captains John Harvey (b. 1740, d. 1794) and **John Hutt** (b. 1746, d. 1794) fell in an action off Brest, under Lord Howe, fighting against the French, 1794. This cumbrous monument, by *Bacon Junior*, formerly stood on the floor of the Nave, beside another to **Captain Montagu,** who fell in the same action; but both have been removed, Harvey and Hutt to the window-ledge above Bringfield, and Montagu to the north-west tower (see page 22).

Dr John Woodward, b. 1665, d. 1728, Professor of Physic at Gresham College. Founder of the Geological Professorship called after him at Cambridge, and writer of many works on geology and natural history. He had incessant controversies with his fellow-doctors Mead and Freind (page 26), and is said to have fought a duel with Mead beneath the walls of the College of Physicians in Warwick Lane. Buried centre of Nave. *Scheemakers sculpt.*

Major-General Stringer Lawrence, b. 1697, d. 1775, was a marine under Wager, and afterwards served under General Wade in Flanders and Scotland. Appointed Major-General of the East India Company's forces in 1747, he helped by a brilliant series of campaigns to lay the foundations of the Indian Empire. Upon the monument, put up by the Company, is a bas-relief of Trichinopoly, which place Lawrence defended against the French from May 1753 to October 1754. *W. Tyler sculpt.*

A wall monument to **Mrs Martha Price,** b. 1640, d. 1678, wife of the Sergeant Trumpeter to Charles II, both buried in the Nave.

A white marble tablet to the **6,873 Officers, Non-Commissioned Officers, and Men of the Royal Army Medical Corps,** who fell in the First World War. H.R.H. Field-Marshal the Duke of Connaught unveiled the memorial, 13 July 1923, and presented a cheque for £10,100 to the Dean for the Abbey Preservation Fund, the balance of the sum raised in memory of the fallen, after part had been set aside for their dependants, and part used to defray the cost of the monument, and to inscribe the names in a golden book, which is in the Chapter House.

Sir Henry Campbell-Bannerman, b. 1836, d. 1908, Prime Minister, 1905 to 1908, during which time self-government was granted to South Africa; his policy with regard to the reform of the House of Lords was embodied in the Parliament Act. Bronze bust erected by Parliament. *Paul Montford sculpt.*

Gravestones mark the burial place of **Sidney Webb, 1st Baron Passfield,** b. 1859, d. 1947, and of **Lady Passfield** (Beatrice Webb), b. 1858, d. 1943, and **Ernest Bevin** (b. 1881, d. 1951), statesman and Foreign Secretary.

In a case near by is an illuminated Roll of Honour in memory of the officers and men of H.M.S. *Barham,* sunk off the coast of Libya on 25 November 1941.

(For **Charles James Fox,** see page 22.)

Centre of Nave and Choir Screen

A gravestone, east of that of the Unknown Warrior, marks the burial-place of **Herbert Edward Ryle, K.C.V.O., D.D.,** b. 1856, d. 1925, Dean of Westminster, 1911–25; President of Queens' College, Cambridge, 1888–1900; Bishop of Exeter, 1901–3; Bishop of Winchester, 1903–11. Dean Ryle officiated at the Coronation of King George V and Queen Mary (1911); at the marriages of Princess Patricia, only daughter of the Duke of Connaught (1919); of Princess Mary, King George V's only daughter, to Viscount Lascelles (1922); and of Albert, Duke of

York (King George VI), his second son, to Elizabeth, daughter of the Earl of Strathmore (1923).The years of the First World War were marked in the Abbey by many memorial services in which the Dean took a leading part. These culminated on 11 November 1920, in the burial of the Unknown Warrior, for the idea of which he was mainly responsible. Dean Ryle, in his official capacity as Dean of the Order, took part twice in the ceremony of the installation of the Knights of the Bath (in Henry VII's Chapel), which was revived by King George V on 12 July 1913, after the lapse of a century (see page 63). An appeal for money to repair the Abbey fabric was initiated by Dean Ryle with the help of *The Times*. A tablet, designed by *Oscar Cheadle*, was placed in 1928 above the vestry door in South Aisle of Nave.

Near Dean Ryle are buried:

William Foxley Norris, K.C.V.O., b. 1859, d. 1937, Dean of Westminster 1925–37. Officiated at the coronation of King George VI and Queen Elizabeth (1937).

William Hartley Carnegie, b. 1859, d. 1936, Canon and Sub-Dean of Westminster, and Rector of St Margaret's 1913–36. Also his wife, **Mary** (d. 1957), whose first husband was the statesman, Joseph Chamberlain (see page 22).

George Peabody, b. 1795, d. 1869, the American philanthropist. His remains rested beneath this stone for a few days, and were then afterwards reinterred in his native state, Massachusetts. His name is preserved in the houses built by his generosity for the London working classes.

Richard Chenevix Trench, b. 1808, d. 1886, divine and poet, Dean of Westminster for seven years (1856–63), Archbishop of Dublin twenty-three years (1863–86).

In the same grave lie two watchmakers and mechanicians, **Thomas Tompion,** b. 1638, d. 1713, the Father of English Watchmakers, and his friend and apprentice, **George Graham,** b. 1673, d. 1751. Tompion was elected a member of the Clockmakers' Company on its foundation in 1676, and Warden in 1704. A brass plaque to his memory and to commemorate the tercentenary of the Clockmakers' Company was placed (1935) in the Parish Church at Northill, Beds., his birthplace. **George Graham,** who succeeded to his business, was the greatest mechanician at that time. He invented many valuable astronomical instruments, working for the famous astronomers Halley and Bradley, also for the French Academy of Science. He constructed the first complete planetarium ever made, for the Earl of Ossory.

David Livingstone, b. 1813, d. 1873, the African explorer and missionary. After twice crossing the entire continent he died in the centre of Africa. His faithful servants carried his body through months of toil and danger to Zanzibar, whence it was shipped to England and interred in the Abbey, April 1874, eleven months after his death.

Robert Stephenson, b. 1803, d. 1859, engineer of the Birmingham Railway, and the Britannia Bridge, Menai Straits. Buried by his own wish next to Telford. In the Stephenson window above is also commemorated his father George Stephenson, b. 1781, d. 1848, inventor and founder of railways.

Sir Charles Barry, b. 1795, d. 1860, the eminent architect. His chief work, 'The Palace of Westminster' (the Houses of Parliament) is pictured on the brass. Belonging to the older classical school, he used with great effect the revived Gothic style which, as represented by him and Pugin, followed the architecture of the Tudor period.

Sir George Gilbert Scott, b. 1811, d. 1878, one of the foremost architects to lead in the revival of Gothic architecture. His pupil, **George Edmund Street,** b. 1824, d. 1881, and **John Loughborough Pearson, R.A.,** b. 1817, d. 1897, both masters of the Gothic style. Street died shortly before the completion of his chief work, the present Law Courts. Scott not only restored cathedrals and churches throughout Great Britain, but designed many new buildings, both ecclesiastical and secular. Amongst his chief works are the Treasury, Colonial and India Offices, St Mary's Cathedral, Edinburgh, the Albert Memorial, London, and the Martyrs' Memorial, Oxford. As Surveyor of the Abbey Fabric (1849), an office in which he was succeeded by Pearson, he restored the Chapter House, besides leaving plans for the triple portico, in the North Front. Pearson's greatest original work is Truro Cathedral (1879), the first cathedral consecrated in England since the Reformation. He designed many churches, and restored seven cathedrals–Lincoln, Peterborough, Canterbury, Bristol, Rochester, Exeter, and Chichester. When Surveyor of the Abbey he practically rebuilt the North Front, and refaced much of the exterior of the whole building, a work continued by his successors, Micklethwaite and Lethaby. He was also employed on secular work, notably the restoration of Westminster Hall, and designed various domestic buildings.

Sir Herbert Baker, R.A., b. 1862, d. 1946, architect. He designed the Government House at Pretoria, the Rhodes Memorial on Table Mountain, some of the Government buildings at New Delhi, the Winchester College War Memorial and many other buildings.

The early sixteenth-century hexagonal **Pulpit** (formerly in Henry VII's Chapel) with linen-fold panelling replaces a marble pulpit presented in 1862 and now in Belfast Cathedral. There is a tradition that Archbishop Cranmer preached from it at the coronation of King Edward VI.

Close together lie three heroes of the Indian Mutiny, **Lord Lawrence** (page 26), **Sir James Outram** (page 27), and **Sir Colin Campbell, 1st Baron Clyde,** b. 1792, d. 1863. Campbell entered the army at an early age, and distinguished himself in the Peninsular War; in the Sikh War of 1848–9; and won more honours in the Crimean War, especially at the battles of the Alma and Balaclava. In 1857 he was ordered to India to assume command against the mutineers, and there 'crowned his long and distinguished career by the recapture of Lucknow'. On the suppression of the Mutiny he received the thanks of both Houses of Parliament, and was rewarded by a peerage and the rank of Field-Marshal.

Another Indian veteran rests here, **Field Marshal Sir George Pollock,** b. 1786, d. 1872, who won military honours in the first Afghan War (1839–42) after the Cabul disaster, and received the thanks of Parliament and an eloquent tribute from Sir Robert Peel on his return.

Freeman Freeman-Thomas, 1st Marquess of Willingdon, b. 1866, d. 1941, Viceroy of India and Governor-General of Canada.

Beneath a small stone lies: **Lieut.-General Sir James Leith,** b. 1763, d. 1817, Governor of the Leeward Isles. Leith distinguished himself in Moore's Corunna retreat, and won a K.B. by his gallant conduct at Busaco, Badajos, and Salamanca, where he was severely wounded. He recovered in time for the assault on San Sebastian, when

he was again injured, and was personally congratulated by the Duke of Wellington.

Thomas Cochrane, 10th Earl of Dundonald, b. 1775, d. 1860, Admiral, had a brilliant and adventurous career; his exploits and inventive genius have justly won him a high place among our British admirals. He fell into disgrace in 1814, was fined, imprisoned, and his name struck off the rolls of the Knights of the Bath, his banner and brass plate removed from Henry VII's Chapel; but his reputation was afterwards cleared.

Against the Choir Screen are two large monuments, designed by *Kent* and executed by *Rysbrack*:

(*Right*)–**James, 1st Earl Stanhope,** b. 1673, d. 1721; greatly distinguished in the war of the Spanish succession; he was second in command under Peterborough at the siege of Barcelona, and in 1708 was made Commander-in-Chief of the forces in Catalonia. He took Port Mahon, defeated the Spanish at Almenara and Saragossa, and driving them before him to the gates of Madrid, killed their general with his own hand (1710). This brilliant campaign ended Stanhope's military career; he was defeated and taken prisoner by Vendôme, but ransomed in 1712, and on his return became the leader of the Whig Opposition. He was raised to the peerage by George I, made Chancellor of the Exchequer (1717), and Secretary of State (1718). The 2nd, 3rd, and 5th Earls are commemorated on the same monument. All buried at Chevening.

(*Left*)–**Sir Isaac Newton,** b. 1642 (the same year that Galileo died), d. 1727, philosopher and mathematician, author of the *Principia*, and the formulator of the law of gravitation. The body lay in state in the Jerusalem Chamber, and was followed to its grave before the Choir screen by all the Royal Society; the Lord Chancellor, two dukes and three earls were the pall-bearers. On the gravestone are the words 'Hic depositum est quod mortale fuit Isaaci Newtoni'.[1] The inscription on the monument called forth Dr Johnson's protest: 'Had only the name of Sir Isaac Newton been subjoined to the design upon his monument, instead of a long detail of his discoveries, which no philosopher can want, and which none but a philosopher can understand, those by whose direction it was raised had done more honour both to him and themselves.' Pope wrote a Latin inscription (ending with the two English lines given below) which was intended for the monument, but never placed there:

Nature and Nature's Laws lay hid in Night:
God said, *Let Newton be!* and all was Light.

William Thomson, b. 1824, d. 1907; created **Baron Kelvin of Largs,** 1902, scientist and inventor, is buried close to Newton, the foremost of the pioneers in the science to which Kelvin devoted his long life. He was knighted in 1866 for the part which he took in laying the Atlantic cable. Not far from his own grave lie Herschel and Darwin, close by are the memorials of Adams, Stokes, and Joule. With the latter Kelvin was associated in various ways, notably as one of the founders of the science of thermodynamics.

Near by are the graves of **Sir Joseph John Thomson, O.M.,** b. 1856, d. 1940, physicist and Master of Trinity College, Cambridge, and of **Ernest, 1st Baron Rutherford,** b. 1871, d. 1937, physicist; while inscriptions on the floor commemorate two earlier scientists, **Michael Faraday,**

(1791–1867), scientist, and **James Clerk-Maxwell** (1831–1879), physicist, who are buried elsewhere.

The outer **Choir Screen** was designed by Edward Blore and put up in 1834, but the inner stonework dates from the thirteenth century.

In front of the Choir Screen are placed the two **Bronze Candelabra** designed by *Benno Elkan* and presented to the Abbey by the late Lord Lee of Fareham in 1939 and 1942.

The present **Organ** has grown from one built in 1730 by Christopher Shrider, and rebuilt and enlarged by William Hill and Sons at various times since, notably in 1849, 1884 and 1909. It was completely rebuilt in 1937 by Harrison and Harrison Ltd, of Durham; it was first used at the coronation service of King George VI in that year, and is known as the Coronation Organ.

The hanging cases contain the Great and Choir organs, and part of the Pedal organ; the remainder of the Pedal and the Swell and Solo organs are above, out of sight, in the South Triforium.

Some of the pipework from earlier organs has been preserved and incorporated, after restoration and revoicing, including two stops made for the organ in use in 1694 by the celebrated builder Bernhard Schmidt ('Father Smith') –the 8 feet Stopped Diapason and 4 feet Nason on the Choir organ.

In 1895 a separate Echo or Celestial organ was given by Arthur D. Clarke; it stands in the West triforium of the South Transept. This was not included in the 1937 rebuild, and will need rebuilding before it can be made playable.

The organ has four manuals and pedals; there are 84 speaking stops, 26 couplers and 60 pistons. The Echo section, when rebuilt, will add 18 speaking stops, 8 couplers and 6 pistons to the above figures.

In July 1950 a roll of honour to the members of the **Metropolitan Police Force** who lost their lives in the First and Second World Wars was unveiled by H.M. King George VI and placed in a case at the Choir entrance to the North Choir Aisle.

The thirteenth-century sculptured shields of arms in the Choir Aisles and Nave should be noticed. Originally there were sixteen, eight on each side, and they reached as far as Henry III's work extended. Those which remain have been ascribed to (on the north side): the Holy Roman Emperor; the King of France; Richard de Clare, Earl of Gloucester; Roger Bigod, Earl of Norfolk; Simon de Montfort, Earl of Leicester; John de Warenne, Earl of Surrey; William de Forz, Count of Albemarle; (on the south side): Edward the Confessor, the King of England; Raymond Berenger, Count of Provence; Roger de Quincy, Earl of Winchester; Henry de Lacy, Earl of Lincoln; Richard, Earl of Cornwall; Richard, Earl of Ross. According to tradition these shields commemorate benefactors towards the building of the Abbey church.

A stone to the north of the Nave Altar marks the burial-place of **Paul Fulcrand Delacour de Labilliere,** b. 1879, d. 1946, Dean of Westminster 1938–46. Suffragan Bishop of Knaresborough 1934–8. From the earliest days of his appointment as Dean of Westminster Dr Labilliere took a deep interest in the history of the fabric and in the traditions of the great church over which he presided. It was always his aim to enhance the beauty of the fabric –the Nave Altar and the polished floor around it were due to him–and to increase the dignity of the services. With the war came increased anxieties and throughout

---

[1] '*Here lies what was mortal of Isaac Newton.*'

Shield of Simon de Montfort

the war years and during the worst of the bombing he was never absent from his post. In May 1941 the Deanery, in which he took great pride, and all his personal possessions were destroyed during a raid. He bore his loss and the damage to the Abbey with great courage and in a message he issued shortly afterwards he wrote: 'When all is said and done the Abbey, which is England, must suffer with England, but what has been knocked down will arise in the great pile of buildings, more glorious than ever. Our duty is to carry on, and, God helping us, carry on we will.'

He was spared to see that the Abbey itself had emerged safely from the war, but his death was undoubtedly hastened by the strain which these years had imposed upon him.

South Aisle of Choir[1]

(*South Wall*) – **Admiral George Churchill**, b. 1654, d. 1710, a brother of the great Duke of Marlborough, 'a Tory of the old school, virulent, domineering and foolish'.[2] Buried in this aisle. *Grinling Gibbons sculpt.*

John Methuen, b. 1650, d. 1708, Lord Chancellor of Ireland, 1697; twice Ambassador to Portugal, and author of the treaty between the Allied Powers and Portugal which bears his name. His son, **Sir Paul Methuen**, b. 1672, d. 1759, Ambassador to Portugal, Spain, and Savoy successively. Both buried in this aisle.

Major Richard Creed, who fell, shot through the head, at the Battle of Blenheim, 1704. His monument was originally placed in the vicinity of the one to Harbord and Cottrell (page 27) on which the death of the Earl of Sandwich (page 74), Creed's relative, is mentioned, 'whose heroic virtues he was anxious to imitate'. (Epitaph.)

Colonel Joseph Lemuel Chester, b. 1821, d. 1882, American genealogist. Edited, with very valuable genealogical notes the *Registers of Westminster Abbey*.[3]

Henry Francis Lyte (1793–1847), the writer of many hymns, including 'Abide with me'.

George Stepney, b. in Westminster, 1663, d. 1707, called by 'the courtesy of criticism' a poet, and as such included in Dr Johnson's *Lives*. His monument was placed here because he had been educated at Westminster School; he was also a distinguished diplomat, and his diplomatic honours are enumerated in the Latin inscription. Dart says the monument is 'as rich for marble but mean in design as Sir Cloudesley Shovel's, but erected to the memory of *a much greater man* – namely, Mr Stepney, a gentleman equally conversant with the world of fine letters and of business'. Buried in this aisle.

---

[1] *See plan on page 34.*   [2] *Wyon's* Reign of Queen Anne.

[3] *Harleian Society Publications (vol. x, 1875).*

Plan of Choir and Aisles

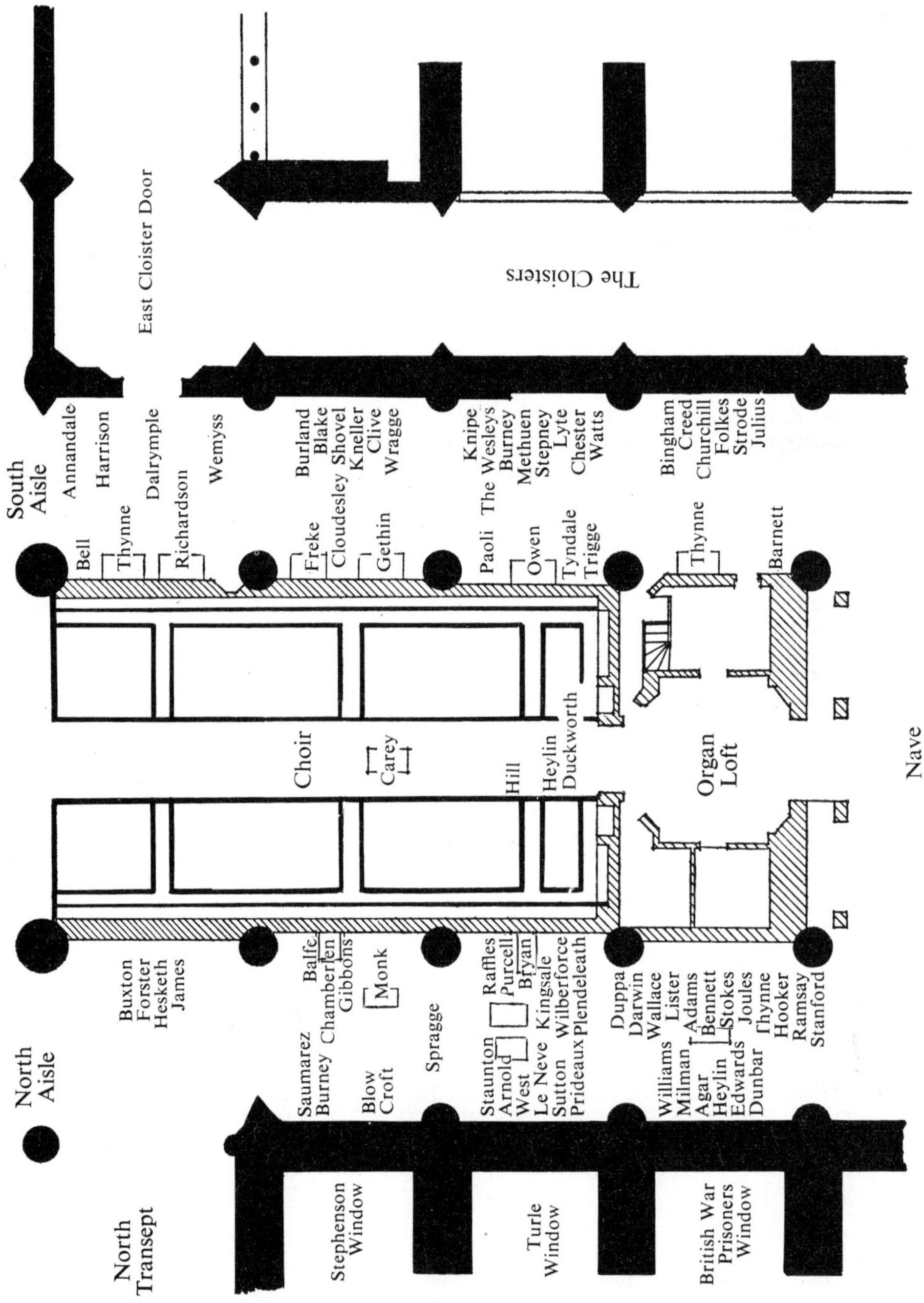

The Cloisters

East Cloister Door

South Aisle

Annandale
Harrison
Dalrymple
Richardson
Wemyss
Burland
Blake
Cloudesley Shovel
Kneller
Clive
Wragge
Knipe
The Wesleys
Burney
Methuen
Stepney
Lyte
Chester
Watts
Bingham
Creed
Churchill
Folkes
Strode
Julius

Bell
Thynne
Freke
Gethin
Paoli
Owen
Tyndale
Trigge
Thynne
Barnett

Choir

Carey

Hill

Heylin
Duckworth

Organ Loft

Nave

North Aisle

Buxton
Forster
Hesketh
James
Saumarez
Burney
West
Blow
Croft
Spragge
Balfe
Chamberlen
Gibbons
Monk
Staunton
Arnold
Le Neve
Sutton
Prideaux
Raffles
Purcell
Bryan
Wilberforce
Plendeleath
Kingsale
Duppa
Darwin
Wallace
Lister
Milman
Agar
Heylin
Edwards
Dunbar
Adams
Bennett
Stokes
Joules
Thynne
Hooker
Ramsay
Stanford
Williams

North Transept

Stephenson Window

Turle Window

British War Prisoners Window

Sir Richard Bingham, b. 1528, d. 1599, naval officer, distinguished in the wars of Mary I and Elizabeth I. Elizabeth employed him in Ireland, and made him Governor of Connaught, where 'he overthrew the Irish Scots, expelled the Traytor Orourke, suppressed dyvers Rebellions, and that with smale charge to her Matie.' A black tablet, with Bingham's arms above, put up by Sir John Bingley, 'sometime his servant'.

Dr Isaac Watts, b. 1674, d. 1748, hymn-writer and Nonconformist. Dr Johnson calls him 'one of the first authors that taught the Dissenters to court attention by the grace of language'. Buried in Bunhill Fields, *Banks sculpt.*

John Wesley, b. 1703, d. 1791, buried in the City Road Chapel-yard. **Charles Wesley,** b. 1707, d. 1788, buried in the old Marylebone churchyard. John, the most famous member of a distinguished family, was the leader and founder of the Wesleyan Methodists. Charles, 'the sweet Psalmist of the Church of those days', was associated with his brother in the establishment of Methodism; his hymns are familiar to all congregations in church and chapel alike. The monument was put up by private subscription in 1876. *J. Adams-Acton sculpt.*

Martin Folkes, b. 1690, d. 1754, numismatist, Newton's deputy at the Royal Society, and afterwards its President. Buried at Hillington, Norfolk. *Tyler des.; Ashton sculpt.*

Admiral Sir Cloudesley Shovel, b. 1650, d. 1707, the son of poor parents. Began his career as a common sailor, and rose to be Commander of the Fleet by repeated deeds of daring. As a boy distinguished himself in the Dutch war of 1666-7 by swimming from one ship to another under fire, carrying despatches in his mouth. On his return to England with the fleet in 1707, after the practical annihilation of the French Mediterranean squadron, a violent gale sprang up, the flagship was wrecked off the Scilly Isles, and the Admiral's dead body was found and buried on one of the islands by some fishermen. The remains were discovered, brought to London and reinterred in the Abbey two months after the shipwreck. Thirty years later a fisherman's wife confessed on her deathbed that she had found the Admiral lying unconscious on the rocks, and had put an end to his life for the sake of a valuable emerald ring upon his finger. This ring she had secreted ever since; it was sent by the clergyman who received her confession to Shovel's old friend, the Earl of Berkeley. 'Bird bestowed busts and bas-reliefs on those he decorated, but Sir Cloudesley Shovel's and other monuments by him made men of taste dread such honours.' This criticism of Bird by Horace Walpole was quite undeserved; recent research has proved that the celebrated *Grinling Gibbons* was the sculptor of this monument.

Robert Blake, b. 1598, d. 1657, Admiral and General of the Fleet-'who trusting in God and in the valour of his countrymen wrought great victories for England at sea and worthily maintained the honour of the Nation'. (See page 72.) *Gilbert Ledward sculpt.*

Robert Clive, 1st Baron Clive of Plassey, b. 1725, d. 1774, twice Governor of Bengal, one of the most famous of the East India Company's galaxy of distinguished men. During his three visits to India, which in all amounted to only twelve years, Clive helped to lay the foundations of the British Empire in India. Although a civilian and a clerk by training he got a commission in the army on his first visit and served under his friend Stringer Lawrence (page 29) in the south of India, establishing his own reputation as a military commander on the expedition

against Arcot, the first decisive step towards the foundation of the British Empire in India. Six years later (1757) in conjunction with Admiral Watson (page 20) Clive defeated and dethroned the Nawab of Bengal at Plassey, and thus established the British ascendancy in Bengal, of which province he was made the first governor. He returned to England in 1760, where he was received by the King and Ministers with much ceremony. He was afterwards raised to the peerage and made a K.B. A statue of him had meantime been placed in the East India House, and a medal struck in his honour. In 1764 he was made Governor of Bengal for the second time, but after a brief tenure of the office ill-health obliged his return to England. His conduct was severely criticized and although he triumphantly cleared himself, his reason gave way, and he committed suicide in 1774. The memorial was erected in 1919 by public subscription. *John Tweed sculpt.*

Sir Godfrey Kneller, b. at Lübeck about 1648, d. 1723, a famous portrait painter from the time of Charles II to George I. The only painter commemorated in the Abbey and, in accordance with his dying words to Pope— 'By God, I will not be buried in Westminster. . . . They do bury fools there'—not buried within its walls. Kneller himself designed the monument, for which he left £300, and chose a place for it in Twickenham Church; but the spot selected was already occupied by Pope's tablet to his father, and, as the poet refused to give place to the painter, it was, after a long dispute between Pope and Kneller's widow, placed in the Abbey.[1] Pope, by Kneller's own wish, composed the extravagant epitaph, which he confessed himself was 'the worst thing he ever wrote in his life':

> Kneller, by Heav'n, and not a master taught
> Whose Art was Nature, & whose Pictures Thought,
> When now two Ages, he had snatch'd from Fate
> Whate'er was Beauteous, or whate'er was Great,
> Rests crown'd with Princes Honours, Poets Lays,
> Due to his Merit and brave Thirst of Praise:
> Living, great Nature fear'd He might outvye
> Her Works; and dying, fears herself may dye.

Bust by Rysbrack.

Admiral John Harrison, d. 1791, who served against the French in the West Indies under Admiral Pocock, and afterwards went on Pocock's secret expedition to Havana (page 84), undergoing such terrible hardships on this latter voyage that he was crippled for the rest of his life. *Buried below.* Close by is a memorial recording the prowess of a midshipman, **William Dalrymple,** d. 1782, killed in a desperate naval engagement with the French off the coast of Virginia, and named in his captain's despatches home.

(*North Wall*)—**William Thynne,** d. 1584, 'by his long life covering the whole Tudor dynasty'. Receiver of the Marches under Henry VIII, 'went to sleep in the Lord' in Elizabeth's reign. A monument of marble and alabaster with a figure in armour, recumbent upon a quilt.

In 1938 a tablet was erected to **William Tyndale,** b. 1490, d. 1536, translator of the Bible. 'A martyr and exile in the cause of liberty and pure religion.'

Dr Andrew Bell, b. 1753, d. 1832, Prebendary of Westminster, inventor of the monitorial system in elementary education called the Madras scheme. *Behnes sculpt.*

Sir Thomas Richardson, b. 1569, d. 1635, Speaker of the

---

[1] *Its original place was at the west end of the Nave, where Fox's monument is now.*

House of Commons under James I; Lord Chief Justice of England under Charles I. 'This is that Judge Richardson who, to please the faction of his times, issued out an order against the ancient custom of wakes, and ordered every minister to read it in his church.' This order was protested against by the Bishop of Bath and Wells and seventy of his clergy, and a bishop presented the petition 'at the Council Table, where Richardson was so severely reprimanded (by Laud) that he came out complaining that he had been almost chok'd with a pair of lawn sleeves'. This same judge once had a flint stone flung at his head by a malefactor, but 'leaning low on his elbow in a lazy, reckless manner, the flint flew too high, and only took off his hat'. When his friends congratulated him on his escape, all he said was, 'by way of jest (as his fashion was to make a jest of everything), "You see now if I had been an *upright judge* (intimating his reclining position) I had been slain."'[1] Richardson went by the name of 'the jeering' judge; when he condemned Prynne he is said to have remarked that 'he might have the "Book of Martyrs" to amuse him in prison'. The monument of black marble, with a fine bronze bust of the judge in his hat and robes, is by *Hubert le Sueur*.[2]

Dame Grace Gethin, d. 1697, aged twenty-one, wife of Sir Richard Gethin, 2nd Bart. and daughter of Sir George Norton. After her death a book of devotions by this lady was published, purporting to be reflections noted down 'with a pencil at spare hours, or as she was dressing', which was prefaced by a poem, written in her honour by Congreve. This work, however, turned out to be merely a compilation of extracts from Bacon and other writers. She left a bequest for an anniversary sermon to be preached in her memory in the Abbey every Ash Wednesday. Buried at Hollingbourn.

Pasquale de Paoli, b. 1725, d. 1807, the champion of Corsican independence. Took refuge in England, where he died; buried in Corsica. *Bust by Flaxman.*

Thomas Owen, d. 1598, Judge of the Common Pleas in Elizabeth's reign. A fine recumbent alabaster figure, painted and gilt.

Thomas Thynne of Longleat, b. 1648, d. 1682, a favourite of Charles II, the 'Issachar' of Dryden's *Absalom and Achitophel,* called because of his wealth 'Tom of Ten Thousand'. He was assassinated in his coach in the Haymarket by three ruffians, who were in the pay of Count Königsmarck. The Count hoped by Thynne's murder to obtain the hand of his bride,[3] the heiress of the Percy family and child-widow of Lord Ogle, who had been forced to marry Thynne, and had fled to Holland directly after the ceremony. But she refused his suit, and married the 'proud' Duke of Somerset, thus becoming thrice a wife before she was sixteen. 'A Welchman, bragging of his family, said his father's effigy was set up in Westminster Abbey; being asked whereabouts, he said, "in the same monument with Squire Thynn, for he was his coachman."' The bas-relief represents the murder; the original eulogistic inscription was erased by order of Dean Sprat. The Count escaped abroad, but the assassins were hanged. *Quellin sculpt.*

Above the door to the Organ Loft is a monument put up by his widow to the memory of **Samuel Barnett,** b. 1844, d. 1913, social reformer, Vicar of St Jude's, Whitechapel, 1872–94. Founder and first warden of the Toynbee Hall University Settlement, 1884; Canon of Bristol, 1894–1906, and Canon of Westminster, 1906–13; buried at Brampton. Also **Dame Henrietta Barnett, D.B.E.,** his wife, b. 1851, d. 1936. *Sir George Frampton sculpt.*

---

[1] *Joe Miller's* Jests.   [2] *See the bust of Lady Cottington, page 78.*

[3] *Lady Elizabeth Percy.*

Murder of Thomas Thynne

North Aisle of Choir

(*South Wall*)–**Sir Thomas Fowell Buxton,** b. 1786, d. 1845, philanthropist, who worked for the abolition of the slave trade. He also worked for the improvement of prison discipline and the suppression of *suttee* in India. Buried at Overstrand. *Statue by Thrupp.*

William Edward Forster, b. 1818, d. 1886, statesman and Chief Secretary for Ireland, son of William Forster, philanthropist, nephew of Sir Fowell Buxton, and son-in-law of Dr Arnold (page 22). Buried at Burley-in-Wharfedale. The memorial was unveiled by Lord Knutsford in 1888; Dean Bradley wrote the inscription. *Pinker sculpt.*

Sir Thomas Hesketh, d. 1605, an eminent lawyer 'of deep acquaintance with the Law'. Attorney of the Court of Wards and Liveries in the reign of Elizabeth. A fine monument with reclining figure under a canopy, painted and gilt, was erected by **Juliana, Lady Hesketh** (d. 1629), a small figure of whom, kneeling at a desk, was formerly in the centre niche at the base of the monument.

Hugh Chamberlen, b. 1664, d. 1728, Court physician. Edmund Sheffield, last Duke of Buckinghamshire, erected the monument, which is by *Scheemakers* and *Delvaux,* the artists of his father's tomb in Henry VII's Chapel. The inscription was written by Dean Atterbury, whom Chamberlen had visited during his imprisonment in the Tower.

Sir Stamford Raffles, b. 1781, d. 1826, Lieut.-Governor during the period that Java was under British rule (1811–16), and the founder of the colony and city of Singapore, 29 January 1819. He was the first President of the Zoological Society of London, which was due to his initiative. *Statue by Chantrey.*

Almericus de Courcy, 1st Baron Kingsale, b. 1665, d. 1720, a favourite of Charles II and James II, and commander of a troop of horse under the latter. It was this peer who seems first to have asserted the alleged 'de Courcy Privilege' of remaining covered in the presence of royalty. By wearing his hat in the presence of William III he attracted the King's attention to whom he explained that he was asserting the privilege of his family 'granted to John de Courcy, Earl of Ulster, and his heirs, by John, King of England'. There does not, however, appear to be any basis for this claim.[1] His widow, Ann, erected the monument; both buried in this aisle.

A tablet above to a young guardsman, **Captain George Bryan,** who fell fighting under Wellington at Talavera, 28 July 1809, and is buried in Spain.

William Wilberforce, b. 1759, d. 1833, the philanthropist. He 'removed from England the guilt of the African slave trade and prepared the way for the abolition of slavery in every colony in the Empire'. Carried to his grave in the North Transept by the Peers and Commons of England with the Lord Chancellor, and Speaker at their head. *A sitting statue, by S. Joseph.*

Sir Thomas Duppa, d. 1694, who served Charles II, when Prince of Wales, and was rewarded, after the Restoration, by the post of Usher of the Black Rod. He was probably a relation of Charles's tutor, Bishop Duppa; the inscription says that the Bishop first introduced him at Court.

Lord John Thynne, b. 1798, d. 1880, 3rd son of the 2nd Marquess of Bath. Canon of Westminster for fifty, and Sub-Dean for forty-six years. *Armstead sculpt.*

---

[1] *See Note (vol. vii, page 287) in the* Complete Peerage *(1929), where the matter is discussed.*

Since the erection of Darwin's medallion portrait head above Thynne's monument this wall has been covered with memorials to other great scientists, who were his contemporaries. **Sir Joseph D. Hooker,** b. 1817, d. 1911, President of the Royal Society, 1873–8, Director of Kew Gardens, 1865–85. Darwin and Hooker were intimate friends and both were inspired by Lyell (page 29). Darwin claimed the discovery of the origin of species. Hooker investigated their distribution over the earth. *Frank Bowcher sculpt.* A medallion portrait head by *Charles Hartwell* to **Sir William Ramsay,** b. 1852, d. 1916, the distinguished chemist, the discoverer of helium, and argon (in conjunction with Lord Rayleigh), was placed beneath Hooker's medallion in 1922. A Laboratory of Chemical Engineering, University College, London, was opened 24 November 1924, as a memorial to Ramsay. **Dr Alfred Russel Wallace,** b. 1823, d. 1913, the publication of whose theory on the origin of species in 1858 coincided with Darwin's on the same subject, but Darwin had already (1844) communicated his thesis to Hooker. Wallace's *Flora of Tasmania,* a work embodying his discoveries, appeared four months before Darwin's famous book, *The Origin of Species* (1895). *Bruce Joy sculpt.* A tablet to **James Prescott Joule,** b. 1818, d. 1889, physicist, whose discoveries strongly influenced Kelvin; medallion heads of: **Sir George Stokes,** b. 1819, d. 1903, Lucasian Professor of Mathematics at Cambridge, 1849–99, author of over 100 scientific works. *Hamo Thorneycroft sculpt.* **John Couch Adams,** b. 1819, d. 1892, discoverer of the planet Neptune by mathematical calculations. *Bruce Joy sculpt.* The great surgeon, **Joseph Lister, 1st Baron Lister,** b. 1827, d. 1912, the pioneer of antiseptic treatment in hospitals. *Brock sculpt.*

James Henry Monk, b. 1784, d. 1856 (*a brass*), Bishop of Gloucester and Bristol, and Canon of Westminster (1830–56).

(*North Wall*) **Sir George Leonard Staunton,** b. 1737, d. 1801, diplomatist. One of the Commissioners who concluded the treaty with Tippoo Sahib in 1784, and was rewarded for his services by a pension of £500 from the East India Company and a baronetcy. He went as Secretary on our first Embassy to China, and wrote an account of it. Dr Johnson had a great liking for him, and sent him a letter of advice when he first went to the West Indies. Buried in this aisle. *Chantrey sculpt.*

Vice-Admiral Temple West, b. 1713, d. 1757, son-in-law of Admiral Balchen (page 20), distinguished himself in two victorious actions against the French. *Roubiliac sculpt.*

Richard le Neve, d. 1673, a dauntless young naval officer, who was 'Kill'd in the flower of his age, being but 27 yeares old, after hee had signaliz'd his valour to admiration in that sharp engagement with the Hollanders which happen'd on the 11th of August, 1673'. (Epitaph.) Buried in this aisle.

Admiral Sir Edward Spragge, killed in the same action, 11 August 1673. As Vice-Admiral he had taken a brilliant part in the victory of Southwold Bay[2] (1672), and in his last fight so hotly engaged Tromp that when his own flagship was disabled he shifted his flag to Sir George Rooke's, and after this had also been put out of action, was on his way to a third vessel in a small boat when it was sunk by a round shot, and the Admiral drowned. His body was recovered six weeks later, and buried here.

---

[2] *See page 74.*

Dr Peter Heylin, b. 1600, d. 1662, the historian, author of a *Life of Laud*, whose chaplain he was, besides other works. Was Sub-Dean of Westminster in Charles I's reign, and defied Dean Williams from the Abbey pulpit. After Williams's imprisonment he became the supreme authority in the Abbey, at which time he superintended the repairs of the fabric, and 'new-vaulted the curious arch over the preaching-place'. During the Civil War he was stripped of his property and obliged to hide himself, but returned to his post at the Restoration, and died two years afterwards. He was buried, in accordance with a dream he had before his last sickness, beneath the Sub-Dean's seat. He dreamed that his 'late Majesty', Charles I, stood before him, and said: 'Peter, I will have you buried under your own seat in church, for you are rarely seen but there or at your study.' A black marble tablet, the inscription written by Dr Earle, then Dean of Westminster.

In this, called the **Musicians' Aisle,** since the burials of Purcell and Blow, organists, beneath the organ, which once stood above it, are collected the graves and monuments of many British composers:

(*South Wall*)–**Michael William Balfe**, b. at Dublin, 1808, d. 1870, a well-known composer, chiefly of English operas. Some of the most popular ballads of his day were written by Balfe. Buried at Kensal Green. *Malempré sculpt.*

Dr Orlando Gibbons, b. 1583, d. 1625, organist of the Chapel Royal (1604), and Court composer. Commanded by Charles I to compose the music for the reception of Henrietta Maria (1625), and to be present at Canterbury on this occasion; he died there, and was buried in the cathedral. Gibbons is celebrated as a composer both of madrigals and motets. In 1907 a service was held in the Abbey, in commemoration of himself and his son **Christopher Gibbons,** d. 1676, who was the first organist here after the Restoration; he lies in the North Cloister. The black marble bust, presented in 1907 by C. D. L. Crews, Master of the Worshipful Company of Musicians, is a copy of the one on his monument in Canterbury Cathedral. *A. G. Walker sculpt.* **Dr Samuel Arnold,** b. 1740, d. 1802. He was educated at the Chapel Royal (where he was afterwards organist), under Bernard Gates,[1] and Dr Nares, and became composer to Covent Garden Theatre in his twenty-third year. He was sub-director of the Handel Commemoration in Westminster Abbey in 1784, and in 1793 succeeded Dr Cooke[2] as organist of the Abbey. Buried in this aisle.

Henry Purcell, b. about 1658, d. 1695, one of the greatest English composers. His short life was connected with Westminster from beginning to end. He was born close by, in St Ann's Lane, and probably, like his sister (an entry of whose baptism occurs in the register), baptized in the Abbey, where his own children were also baptized and buried. At the age of twenty-two he took Blow's place both at the Abbey (1680) and at the Chapel Royal (1682). During his fourteen years as organist here he arranged and composed the music at many State ceremonials, which included the marriage and coronation of Queen Anne, and the coronation of William and Mary. His only opera *Dido and Aeneas* was composed in 1682. He died of consumption 21 November 1695, and was interred here 'in a very magnificent manner'; the anthem which he had composed for Queen Mary's burial was sung at his own funeral. His wife was laid in the same grave ten years later. His pupil and patroness, Lady Elizabeth Howard, Dryden's wife, probably wrote the epitaph, which used to be ascribed to Dryden: 'Here lyes Henry Purcell, Esqr, who left this Life, And is gone to that Blessed Place Where only his Harmony can be exceeded.' Purcell's tablet was put up by his former pupil Annabella, wife of Dryden's brother-in-law the dramatist, **Sir Robert Howard,** b. 1626, d. 1698, who is buried in St John the Baptist's Chapel.

Beneath gravestones in this aisle lie: **Sir William Sterndale Bennett,** b. 1816, d. 1875, Professor of Music at the University of Cambridge, Principal of the Royal Academy of Music, London, 1866, and the foremost English musician in his own day.

Sir Charles Villiers Stanford, b. 1852, d. 1924, musician. Like Bennett he was Professor of Music at Cambridge, and was also Professor of Composition and Orchestration, at the Royal College of Music, London, from its foundation in 1883 until his death. He was also conductor of the orchestra at the Royal College under three successive directors, Sir George Grove, editor of the *Dictionary of Music and Musicians,* Sir Hubert Parry, and Sir Hugh Allen.

Ralph Vaughan Williams, O.M., b. 1872, d. 1958, musician and composer.

(*North Wall*)–**Dr John Blow,** b. 1648, d. 1708, 'his own Musical Compositions (Especially his Church Musick) are a far nobler monument to his memory than any other can be raised for him'. In 1680 he resigned his post as organist of the Abbey in favour of his pupil Henry Purcell, but resumed it again on Purcell's death in 1695. Blow was organist of the Chapel Royal, and Composer in Ordinary to James II. The King once challenged him to write an anthem as good as that of one of his Italian composers, and on the following Sunday Blow produced, 'I beheld, and lo! a great multitude'. James sent his confessor to compliment the composer, but unfortunately Father Petre added the remark: 'I myself think it too long.' 'That,' replied Blow, 'is the opinion of but one fool, and I heed it not.' Fortunately for the irascible musician's Court favour, the dispute was cut short by the revolution of 1688, and he remained undisturbed in his posts till his death in the reign of Queen Anne. Beneath the tablet is a canon composed by Blow.

Dr Charles Burney, b. 1726, d. 1814, author of the celebrated *History of Music*. He was an intimate friend of Dr Johnson, and contributed many anecdotes of him to Boswell's *Life*. In 1789 he was appointed organist of Chelsea College, and lies in the burial-ground there. His daughter Fanny–Mme D'Arblay, the author of *Evelina*, wrote the florid inscription.

Dr William Croft, b. 1677, d. 1727, composer, organist of the Chapel Royal (1707), Blow's pupil and successor as organist of Westminster Abbey (1708). 'It was in the discharge of the duties of the latter office that Croft produced for the frequent public thanksgivings for victories, etc., many of those noble anthems which have gained him so distinguished a place among English church composers.'[3] The end of the Latin inscription may be translated as follows: 'He emigrated to the Heavenly Choir with that concert of angels for which he was better fitted, adding his Hallelujah.'

---

[1] *Buried in North Cloister, page 108.*
[2] *Buried in West Cloister, page 106.*

---

[3] *Grove's* Dictionary of Music and Musicians.

Captain Philip de Saumarez, b. 1710, d. 1747, a distinguished naval officer, who fought under Anson and Hawke, and was killed in Anson's victory over the French fleet off Cape Finisterre 3 May 1747. Below the portrait medallion head of Saumarez, is a bas-relief of this battle. *Cheere sculpt.*

THE SOUTH TRANSEPT [*See plan, page 42*]

Poets' Corner[1]

'In the poetical quarter I found there were poets who had no monuments, and monuments which had no poets.' – ADDISON, *Spectator*.

The name 'Poets' Corner' was originally applied only to the eastern portion of the Transept; it was not until after the burial of Spenser near the tomb of Chaucer that this part of the Abbey was appropriated to the poets. In time their monuments overflowed into the rest of the southern end, but the western wall was early called the 'learned', or 'historical' side.

In the Aisle of the S. Transept by St Benedict's Chapel is the bust of **John Dryden**, b. 1631, d. 1700, Poet Laureate to Charles II and James II. He was educated at Westminster School under Dr Busby. In early life Dryden was an ardent admirer of Cromwell, but after the Restoration he became an enthusiastic Royalist, and held several offices under the Crown. Soon after the accession of James II he turned Roman Catholic. In consequence of his principles he suffered much from the revolution of 1688. His finest works, *All for Love* (1678), *Aurengzebe* (1675), a rhymed tragedy, and *Absalom and Achitophel* (1681), the greatest English political satire, were published before he changed his religion, but his poem *The Hind and the Panther* (1687) was written after his conversion. Dryden's ode on *Alexander's Feast*, set to music by Purcell, and his poem in honour of *St Cecilia's Day*, are perhaps the best known of his poems. He was deprived of his Laureateship and died in poverty in Gerrard Street, Soho. He was buried 13 May 1700, with much ceremony, near Chaucer's empty grave, and Dart states that the tombstone was sawn asunder to make room for his monument. This monument (which has since been altered) was erected in 1720 by Dryden's friend John Sheffield, Duke of Buckinghamshire, whose widow replaced the first bust in 1731 with the present fine one by *Scheemakers*. Pope's proposed epitaph was rejected for the plain inscription.

Henry Wadsworth Longfellow, b. 1807, d. 1882, the American poet. Bust erected in 1884 by his English admirers. *Brock sculpt.*

Abraham Cowley, b. 1618, d. 1667, a poet whose great contemporary reputation quickly waned. The epitaph by his friend and biographer, Dean Sprat, calling him the 'Pindar, Horace, and Virgil of England', bears witness to his extraordinary though short-lived fame. He was educated at Westminster School and Trinity College, Cambridge, from whence he was driven in 1643 by his Royalist principles. He followed Queen Henrietta Maria to Paris, where he lived for several years, acting as her confidential secretary. He returned to England after the Restoration expecting recognition of his services, but 'found his reward very tediously delayed'.[2] He died in retirement at Chertsey. Cowley published several volumes of poems, but is chiefly remembered today as the inventor of the 'Pindaric Ode'. *Bushnell sculpt.*

We now come to the tomb from which Poets' Corner 'derives the origin of its peculiar glory'. **Geoffrey Chaucer**, b. about 1343, d. 1400, poet and civil servant. As the author of the *Canterbury Tales* he is, next to Shakespeare, perhaps the most famous English poet. He began his career in the service of Lionel, third son of Edward III, and subsequently held various offices in the King's household. He was sent abroad on several diplomatic missions, and on one of these spent twelve months in Italy, which exercised a marked influence on his writings. His patron and constant friend was John of Gaunt, whose first wife's death was the occasion of Chaucer's poem on *The Death of Blaunche the Duchess*. Gaunt's third wife is said to have been the sister of the poet's wife. For a short time Chaucer held the office of Clerk of the King's Works at Westminster. During the last years of his life he took a long lease of (and seems to have lived in) a house near the old Lady Chapel which was later pulled down to make room for Henry VII's Chapel. It was probably owing to these circumstances that he was buried in the Abbey, at the entrance of St Benedict's Chapel. For 150 years his only memorial was a leaden plate 'whereon,' Caxton tells us, 'was wreton his epitaphye, maad by a Poet-laureate' (Surigonius of Milan), which hung on the adjacent pillar. In 1555 Nicholas Brigham, himself a poet, presented the grey marble tomb. Behind it was a portrait of Chaucer, and there were in the eighteenth century traces of another figure, conjectured to be that of Brigham, who is said to have been buried near Chaucer.

Alfred Tennyson and **Robert Browning**, the two greatest poets of the Victorian era, lie side by side before Chaucer's monument.

Alfred, Lord Tennyson, b. 1809, d. 1892, succeeded Wordsworth in 1850 as Poet Laureate. *In Memoriam*, published the same year commemorates his grief on the death of his friend, Arthur Hallam. The *Ode on the Death of the Duke of Wellington* (1854), the *Idylls of the King*, and many volumes of poems were published in quick succession afterwards. In later life Tennyson published several historical plays, some of which were produced on the stage by Sir Henry Irving. His poem *Crossing the Bar*, set to music by Sir Frederick Bridge, was first sung at his own funeral in the Abbey. A bust – one of three by *Woolner* – was placed on the pillar near his grave in 1895.

Robert Browning, b. 1812, d. 1889, poet. His longest work, *The Ring and the Book*, published in 1862, was succeeded by many other volumes of poetry. He married the poetess Elizabeth Barrett, in 1846, and lived in Italy until her death in 1861. Browning died at Venice, whence

---

[1] *The memorial window to the Duke of Westminster at the south end is described on page 118.*

[2] *Johnson's* Lives of the Poets.

his body was brought to the Abbey. His last work, *Asolando*, was published on the day (16 December) of his death. The gravestone is composed of Italian marbles and porphyry.

Above Chaucer's tomb is a tablet (by *R. Hayward*) to **John Roberts** (d. 1772), politician.

John Phillips, b. 1676, d. 1708, poet, buried in Hereford Cathedral; author of the *Splendid Shilling* and a poem called *Cyder*. His epitaph is memorable not only for its 'elegant Latinity', but for the mention of Milton. Dean Sprat had the epitaph erased on account of this allusion, but it was restored by Atterbury four years later, and in time Milton's monument was erected close by.

Barton Booth, b. 1681, d. 1733, actor, succeeded Betterton in public estimation. Buried with his wife at Cowley, Middlesex. Barton and Cowley Streets, Westminster, recall his connexion with Westminster. *Hayward sculpt.*

Michael Drayton, b. 1563, d. 1631, poet. The monument was presented by Anne Clifford, Countess of Dorset, Pembroke and Montgomery; the bust is by *Edward Marshall*. The epitaph (attributed both to Quarles and

Ben Jonson) testifies to the poet's contemporary fame, but he was quickly forgotten, and his chief work, *Polyolbion*, is now little read. 'As we walked along to a particular part of the temple, "There," says the gentleman, pointing with his finger, "that is Poets' Corner; there you see the monuments of Shakespeare and Milton, and Prior and Drayton." "Drayton!" I replied: "I never heard of him before." '[1]

Ben Jonson, b. 1574, d. 1637, dramatist and poet, the friend of Shakespeare and Bacon. He was educated at Westminster School, under Camden the antiquary, and afterwards passed through many vicissitudes, being for a short time a bricklayer, a soldier, a student at Cambridge, travelling tutor to Sir Walter Raleigh's son, an actor as well as dramatist, and finally, in 1619, he succeeded Daniel as Poet Laureate. Jonson was always improvident and, in spite of gifts from the King, died in great poverty, in a house which stood between the Abbey and St Margaret's Church. Of his many tragedies and comedies, *Catiline*, *Every Man in his Humour*, and

---

[1] *Goldsmith's* Citizen of the World.

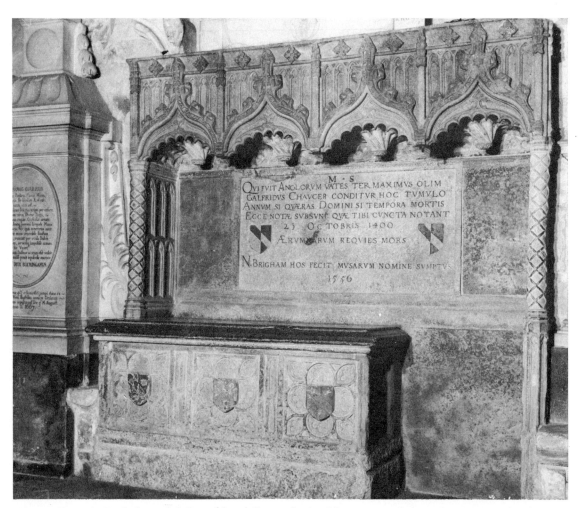

(Above) *Chaucer's Tomb;* (opposite) *Part of Poets' Corner showing Monuments to Spenser, Ben Jonson and Milton*

The Silent Woman are the most celebrated. He was also well known as a writer of masques. He was buried in the Nave (page 29), under a stone bearing the same inscription as his monument, which was erected before 1728 by the Earl of Oxford. *Gibbs des., Rysbrack sculpt.*

Edmund Spenser, b. 1553, d. 1599, poet, author of the *Faerie Queene*, which he dedicated to Queen Elizabeth. He spent his latter years on an estate granted him in Ireland, but this was finally devastated by the natives, his house set on fire, and he and his wife obliged to fly with their four young children. Shortly afterwards, according to his friend and brother poet, Drummond of Hawthornden, 'he died for lack of bread in King Street (Westminster), but refused twenty pieces sent to him by my Lord of Essex, adding "he was sorry he had no time to spend them".' There is, however, no authentic foundation for this story. A memorable gathering of his contemporaries assembled at the funeral, and all, probably including Shakespeare, threw their elegies, with the pens which wrote them, into the grave. Ann Clifford, Countess of Dorset, erected his monument in 1620; but this falling into decay, was replaced in 1778 by an exact copy, for which the poet Mason set on foot a subscription. Notice the epitaph:

> Heare lyes (expecting the Second comminge of our Saviour Christ Jesus) the body of Edmond Spencer the Prince of Poets in his tyme whose Divine Spirrit needs noe othir witnesse then the works which He left behinde him.

Samuel Butler, b. 1612, d. 1680, satirist, buried at St Paul's, Covent Garden, because there was no money to pay the Abbey fees for a grave here. The author of *Hudibras* did not reap much profit from its popularity, and, after passing from the service of one great person to another, died in great poverty. The monument was erected in 1721 by John Barber, a printer, when Lord Mayor, in order 'that he who had been denied almost everything in life might not in death be denied a tomb'. This inspired Pope's spiteful lines:

> But whence this Barber? that a name so mean
> Should joined with Butler's on a tomb be seen.

John Milton, b. 1608, d. 1674, poet, buried in St Giles's, Cripplegate, born in London. He was educated at St Paul's School and at Christ's College, Cambridge. The earlier part of his life was spent in laborious study, but in

1639 the gathering of the great political storm and his own strong Puritan bias called him home from a journey in Italy. For ten years he was Latin secretary to the Council of the Commonwealth, during which time he published many controversial writings on political, social, and religious subjects. After the Restoration Milton was forced to conceal himself for a short time. He lived later on in London unmolested, neglected, and totally blind, devoting himself to the great works of his life, *Paradise Lost*, which was published in 1667, *Paradise Regained* and

Samson Agonistes in 1671. Until 1737, when this monument was erected by Auditor Benson, the Abbey contained no memorial of Milton, the strength of Royalist feeling against him having delayed public recognition of his genius. Addison in his *Spectator* criticism led the way for the inevitable reaction. Speaking of it, Dr Gregory remarked to Dr Johnson: 'I have seen erected in the church a bust of that man whose name I once considered as a pollution of its walls.' Dr Johnson said to Boswell on another occasion, in allusion to the egotistical

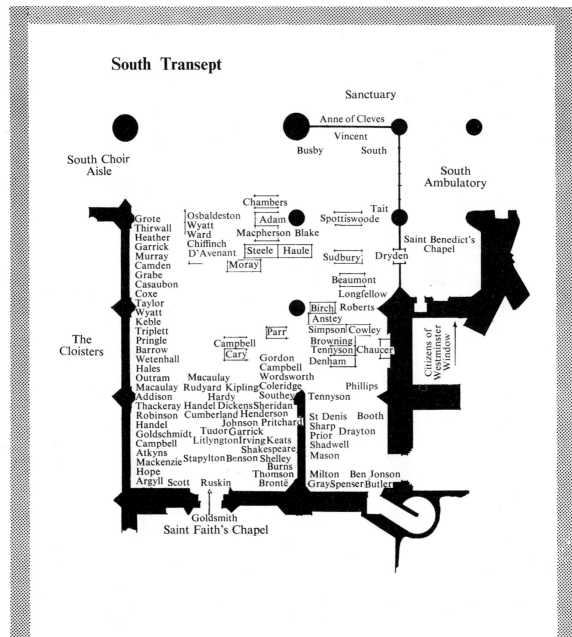

South Transept

inscription: 'Mr Benson has bestowed more words upon himself than upon Milton.' Pope also had his say:

On poets' tombs see Benson's titles writ.

Rysbrack sculpt.

Thomas Gray, b. 1716, d. 1771, poet, buried at Stoke Poges, the scene of his *Elegy written in a Country Church-yard.* The lyric muse holds a medallion with his portrait, and points to the bust of Milton. The epitaph is by **William Mason,** b. 1724, d. 1797, poet, the friend and biographer of Gray, buried at Aston, Yorks. Dr Hurd, Bishop of Worcester, wrote his inscription. Both monuments are by *J. Bacon, sen.*

Thomas Shadwell, b. 1642 (?), d. 1692, poet. He was the rival of Dryden, and succeeded him as Poet Laureate. Dryden satirized him in *MacFlecknoe.* He died of opium-eating at Chelsea, where he is buried. *Bird sculpt.*

Matthew Prior, b. 1664, d. 1721, a poet of great contemporary reputation. He held several offices under William III, and was for a time Plenipotentiary at the Court of Louis XIV, who presented him with this bust by *Coysevox.* He was buried, as he desired, at the feet of Spenser. Dr Freind, Head Master of Westminster School, wrote the epitaph on his old pupil. Prior had composed the following lines, but Dean Atterbury forbade their insertion:

To me 'tis given to dye, to you 'tis given
To live; Alas! one moment sets us even.
Mark how impartial is the will of Heaven!

Gibbs des.; Rysbrack sculpt.

Granville Sharp, b. 1735, d. 1813, philanthropist, one of the earliest and most devoted opponents of the slave trade. The monument was erected by the African Institution in gratitude for his efforts. *Chantrey sculpt.*

Charles de St Denis, Seigneur de St Evremond, b. 1613, d. 1703, a famous wit at Charles II's Court.

Christopher Anstey, b. 1724, d. 1805. Buried at Bath. Widely known in his day as the author of the *New Bath Guide. Horwell sculpt.*

On the column near Tennyson is the bust of **Adam Lindsay Gordon,** b. 1833, d. 1870, the poet of Australia, born and educated in England. He emigrated to the Colony in 1853 and henceforth made Australia his home; supporting himself by horse-breaking and riding in steeplechases, he became the most famous amateur steeplechaser in Australia. His bush ballads and galloping rhymes are the best of his many verses, and on the last day of his life the volume containing these, amongst them *The Sick Stockrider* and *How we beat the Favourite* was published. The marble bust was given to commemorate the centenary of the poet's birth and was unveiled by the Duke of York, on 11 May 1934. *Lady Kennet sculpt.*

Thomas Campbell, b. 1777, d. 1844, poet, the author of *The Pleasures of Hope, Hohenlinden, Ye Mariners of England,* and *The Battle of the Baltic,* etc. The lines engraved are from his own *Last Man.* He died at Boulogne, whence his remains were brought here for interment. *Wm. Calder Marshall sculpt.*

Mrs Hannah Pritchard, b. 1711, d. 1768, the celebrated actress. Whitehead, then Poet Laureate, wrote the epitaph. *Hayward sculpt.*[1]

Robert Southey, b. 1774, d. 1843, Poet Laureate, the author of *Thalaba* and the *Curse of Kehama.* Buried at

---

[1] *Now removed to Triforium.*

Crosthwaite. Wordsworth 'wrote the epitaph. *Weekes sculpt.*

Samuel Taylor Coleridge, b. 1772, d. 1834, poet, philosopher, and critic. *The Ancient Mariner, Christabel,* and *Kubla Khan* are his best-known poems. *Thorneycroft sculpt.* The bust was given by Dr Mercer, an American, and unveiled 7 May 1885, by Mr Lowell, the United States Minister.

Wordsworth, Southey, and Coleridge formed the famous triumvirate of Lake poets; beneath their busts is the seated statue of the greatest of the three friends, **William Wordsworth,** b. 1770, d. 1850, who succeeded Southey as Poet Laureate (1843), and whose first published poems were written in collaboration with Coleridge. All his poetry was inspired by an absorbing love of Nature, and written amidst the lakes and mountains where he spent most of his life. His gifted sister Dorothy (1804–47), whose letters are models of English prose, lies by her brother and his wife in Grasmere Churchyard. *Thrupp sculpt.*

John Keats and **Percy Bysshe Shelley,** poets. Two oval tablets erected by the Keats-Shelley Memorial Association and unveiled in 1954. *Frank Dobson sculpt.*

William Shakespeare, b. 1564, d. 1616. Shortly after his death there was much talk of removing his remains from Stratford-on-Avon to the Abbey; the idea was soon abandoned, but it gave rise to Ben Jonson's famous lines:

My Shakespeare, rise! I will not lodge thee by
Chaucer or Spenser, or bid Beaumont lie
A little further on to make thee room:
Thou art a monument without a tomb,
And art alive still while thy book doth live,
And we have wits to read and praise to give.

And to Milton's protest:

What needs my Shakespeare for his honour'd bones
The labour of an age in piled stones?

The monument, which Horace Walpole called 'preposterous' was erected by subscription in 1740. On the scroll are inscribed some lines from *The Tempest*; the heads at the corners of the pedestal represent Queen Elizabeth, Henry V, and Richard III. *Kent des.; Scheemakers sculpt.*

Robert Burns, b. 1759, d. 1796, Scotland's most famous poet, author of *The Cotter's Saturday Night, Auld Lang Syne, The Banks o' Doon,* etc. This memorial, erected eighty-nine years after his death, the work of a Scottish artist, and paid for in shilling subscriptions contributed by all classes from highest to lowest, attests the Ayrshire poet's hold over the hearts of his countrymen. The bust was unveiled by Lord Rosebery, 7 March 1885. *Sir John Steel sculpt.*

James Thomson, b. 1700, d. 1748, poet, author of *The Seasons,* which are represented in bas-relief on the pedestal. Buried in Richmond Parish Church. The monument was erected in 1762, the expenses covered by a subscription edition of his works. *Adam des.; Spang sculpt.*

The Brontës. A tablet to the three Brontë sisters (**Charlotte,** 1816–55, novelist, author of *Jane Eyre* and other novels. **Emily Jane,** 1818–48, author of *Wuthering Heights.* **Anne,** 1820–49, authoress) was presented by the Brontë Society and unveiled in July 1947.

Nicholas Rowe, b. 1674, d. 1718, Poet Laureate. He translated Lucan's *Pharsalia,* and wrote several plays, 'which pleased the town', Evelyn said, but are now forgotten, though one – *Jane Shore* – furnished Mrs Siddons with an effective part. His widow erected the monument, with an epitaph (attributed to Pope) commemorating her inconsolable grief. She, however, afterwards disconcerted the author of it by marrying again. *Rysbrack sculpt.*[1]

John Gay, b. 1685, d. 1732, poet and dramatist, made his original reputation as a prose writer by the *Fables*, a series of tales written for Prince William, afterwards the Duke of Cumberland, son of George II (page 68). Swift and Pope were his literary sponsors, dukes, duchesses and Court ladies his patrons. After nearly two centuries of comparative oblivion his name was restored to fame by the revival in 1920 of his chief dramatic work, the *Beggars' Opera* and of its sequel *Polly*. The former, refused by the manager of Drury Lane, was first produced on the stage at Lincoln's Inn Fields (29 January 1728) and at once made its author's name a household word. Hogarth painted pictures of the various scenes, in which portraits of Rich, the manager of the theatre, and Gay himself appear in the distinguished audience. When *Polly* was ready for rehearsal the Lord Chamberlain, instigated by Gay's enemy Sir Robert Walpole, forbade the performance by royal command. The affair gave rise to a violent squabble, Congreve's friend the Duchess of Marlborough (see page 26) gave £100 for a single copy of the play, and Gay's chief patroness, the Duchess of Queensberry, was banished from the Court with her husband. Henceforth, the author, who was always in pecuniary difficulties, spent the few remaining years of his life with the Queensberrys, who husbanded his money, gave him a magnificent funeral in the Abbey and erected this monument, by *Rysbrack*. Pope wrote the epitaph in which the lines: 'In wit a man, simplicity a child', exactly describe the poet's character, but Gay's flippant verse was inscribed on the pedestal by his own desire:

> Life is a jest and all things show it,
> I thought so once and now I know it.

In 1936 **two wall-paintings** representing St Christopher and the Incredulity of St Thomas were discovered on the wall to the east of the door leading into St Faith's Chapel and immediately behind and hidden by the monuments to Gay and Rowe. They date from about 1280–1300 and the late Professor Tristram described them as 'amongst the most important survivals of wall painting . . . in the whole of England'.

Oliver Goldsmith, b. 1728, d. 1774, buried in the Temple Churchyard, author of *The Vicar of Wakefield*, *She Stoops to Conquer* and *The Deserted Village*. His life was a perpetual struggle with poverty, for he was incapable of managing money affairs, and died burdened with debt. Sir Joshua Reynolds chose the site for his monument, and Dr Johnson wrote the epitaph. *Nollekens sculpt.*

Beside this monument a memorial to the author of the Waverley Novels, **Sir Walter Scott** (b. 1771, d. 1832), was placed in 1897. It is a replica by *John Hutchinson, R.S.A.*, of the *Chantrey* bust at Abbotsford.

Above Scott is a bronze medallion portrait head of **John Ruskin**, b. 1819, d. 1900, author of the *Stones of Venice*, *Modern Painters*, and other works, one of the greatest artistic and social influences in his generation. *Onslow Ford sculpt.*

John Campbell, 2nd Duke of Argyll and 1st Duke of Greenwich, b. 1680, d. 1743, buried in Henry VII's Chapel.

This orator and soldier, familiar to us in the pages of Scott's *Heart of Midlothian*, was one of the main instruments of the Union of England and Scotland. His allegorical monument blocks up the place where once a staircase led up to the monks' dormitory. Minerva and Eloquence stand below the recumbent figure; History inscribing his titles, stops short at Gr— to show that the dukedom of Greenwich expired with him. *Roubiliac sculpt.*

General Sir Archibald Campbell, b. 1739, d. 1791. As Governor of Madras, at the end of his career, Campbell arranged the important Arcot Treaty (1787). The monument also commemorates his nephew, **Lieut.-General Sir James Campbell, Bt.**, d. 1819. *J. Wilton sculpt.*

A monument to the **Atkyns** family, three of whom were Barons of the Exchequer in the seventeenth century. Their descendant, **Sir Robert Atkyns**, b. 1647, d. 1711, also commemorated on the monument, was the author of a topographical work on Gloucestershire.

A tablet commemorates **Mrs Mary Hope** (d. 1767) and near by is a tablet and medallion by *Nollekens* to **Rt. Hon. James S. Mackenzie**, d. 1800, Lord Privy Seal of Scotland.

George Frederick Handel, b. 1685, d. 1759. The composer of the *Messiah* and *Israel in Egypt*. The statue, with its unwieldy figure, is said to be an exact likeness; the face was modelled from a cast taken after death. A tablet above recalls the first Handel Festival held in the Abbey in 1784. *Roubiliac sculpt.*

Below the composer was placed in 1894 a portrait head of **Jenny Lind-Goldschmidt**, b. 1820, d. 1887, the well-known singer ('The Swedish Nightingale').

William Makepeace Thackeray, b. at Calcutta 1811, d. 1863, novelist and essayist, editor of the *Cornhill*, 1860–2. Thackeray contributed with pen and pencil to *Punch* (1842–52), where the celebrated *Snob Papers* first appeared. *Vanity Fair* (1848) established his reputation; *Pendennis*, *Esmond*, and other novels followed in quick succession. Buried at Kensal Green. *Marochetti sculpt.*

Joseph Addison, b. 1672, d. 1719, buried in the north aisle, Henry VII's Chapel. The first of English essayists, 'the noblest purifier of English literature', had no monument in the Abbey until this statue was erected in 1809. 'His body lay in state in the Jerusalem Chamber, and was borne thence to the Abbey at dead of night. The choir sang a funeral hymn. Bishop Atterbury,[2] one of those Tories who had loved and honoured the most accomplished of the Whigs, met the corpse, and led the procession by torchlight round the shrine of St Edward and the graves of the Plantagenets to the Chapel of Henry VII.'[3] Tickell has described the scene in some well known lines. Addison's paper in the *Spectator* on the Abbey should be read by all who visit this Church. *Westmacott sculpt.*

Thomas Babington Macaulay, 1st Baron Macaulay, b. 1800, d. 1859, the historian and poet was buried at the foot of Addison's statue. *Bust by Burnard.*

Dr Stephen Hales, b. 1677, d. 1761, physiologist and botanist; the first inventor of ventilators. Augusta, Princess of Wales, mother of George II, erected this memorial. The figures of Religion and Botany support the medallion portrait. Buried at Teddington. *Wilton sculpt.*

Dr Isaac Barrow, b. 1614, d. 1677, mathematician, and Classical scholar. He was Master of Trinity College, Cambridge, and tutor to Sir Isaac Newton, in whose favour he resigned his Mathematical Professorship.

---

[1] *The monuments to Gay and Rowe have now been moved to the Triforium.*

[2] *See page 24.*   [3] Spectator, *No. 26, 30 March 1711.*

Dr Thomas Triplett, d. 1670, Canon and Sub-Dean of Westminster and a distinguished scholar. His tablet fills the place previously occupied by a monument destroyed at the Restoration, to Thomas May, d. 1650, the Parliamentary historian.

John Keble, b. 1792, d. 1866, author of *The Christian Year.* Keble College, Oxford, was founded in his memory. Keble, Newman, and Pusey formed the triumvirate of the Oxford Movement in 1832. *Woolner sculpt.*[1]

---

[1] *The bust was formerly in the Warriors' Chapel.*

Handel's Monument in Poets' Corner

Sir Richard Coxe, d. 1623, 'Taster' to Queen Elizabeth, and Steward of the Household to James I.

On a pillar near by a bronze bust of **William Blake,** b. 1757, d. 1827, poet and painter, was placed here in 1957 on the bi-centenary of his birth. *Epstein sculpt.*

Isaac Casaubon, b. at Geneva, 1560, d. 1614, Classical scholar and editor of *Persius* and *Polybius.* On the death of his patron, Henri IV, in 1610, 'the learned critik was fetcht out of France by King James (I) and preferred Prebendary of Canterbury. But, alas! death here stopped him in his full speed, and he lieth entombed in the south

GEORGE FREDERICK HANDEL, Efq'
born February XXIII. MDCLXXXIV.
died April XIV. MDCCLIX. *L.F.Roubiliac inv'd et*

ile of Westminster Abbey . . . next the monument of Mr Camden.'[1] The monument was erected at the cost of Morton, Bishop of Durham (1632–59), 'that great lover of learned men, dead or alive'.[2] Notice the initials I.W. and date, 1658, traditionally said to have been scratched by Izaak Walton author of *The Compleat Angler*, on the tablet.

John Ernest Grabe, b. 1666, d. 1711, the Prussian Orientalist, whose veneration for the English Church led him to settle in this country. Buried at St Pancras. *Bird sculpt.*

William Camden, b. 1551, d. 1623, the famous antiquary, surnamed the 'Pausanias of England'; author of the *Britannia* and *Annals of the Reign of Queen Elizabeth*. Camden's father was a painter who belonged to the Guild of Master Painters, and William received a good education at Christ's Hospital and Oxford. His abilities attracted the attention of Dean Goodman, who made him second master at Westminster School, where he pursued his antiquarian researches. In 1593 he was appointed Head Master of the School, although a layman, by Queen Elizabeth, that 'he might be near to her call and commandment, and eased of the charge of living'. He was subsequently given the post of Clarenceux King of Arms that he might have greater leisure for his work. He loved to meditate among the tombs, and to him we owe the first Abbey guide-book, a Latin list of the chief monuments, published in 1600. He was buried in the South Transept, 19 November 1623; his friend Heather was his sole executor. Ben Jonson, who was one of his pupils at Westminster, has commemorated him with grateful affection:

Camden, most reverend head, to whom I owe
All that, I am in acts, all that I know
(How nothing's that), to whom my country owes
The great renown and name wherewith she goes.
Than thee the age sees not that thing more grave,
More high, more holy, that she would more crave.
What name, what skill, what faith hast thou in things
What sight in searching the most antique springs!
What weight and what authority in thy speech!
Men scarce can make that doubt, but thou canst teach.

After the funeral of the Earl of Essex (1646)[3] some rioters destroyed the nose of Camden's effigy, which damage was repaired by the University of Oxford about 1780.

William Heather, b. 1563, d. 1627, musical composer, was a chorister and lay vicar in the Abbey choir, and a gentleman of the Chapel Royal. He had a house in the Almonry precincts, where he nursed Camden (see above) through two serious illnesses; in 1609 Camden went to live with Heather at Chislehurst. Heather and Orlando Gibbons (page 38) both received the degrees of Bachelor and Doctor of Music on 17 May 1622. By Camden's will Heather was appointed sole heir to his property and he followed him to his grave in the South Transept (close to the place where he now lies himself) 19 November 1623. In 1626 Heather founded the Music Professorship at Oxford called after his name, and himself appointed Nicholson, the organist of Magdalen, as the first lecturer. In May 1926, a musical festival was held at Oxford, in commemoration of the Tercentenary of the foundation of the Heather Chair, and on 18 June 1926, a special service was held here, at which the Chancellor of the University of Oxford, Viscount Cave, unveiled an in-

scribed stone close to Camden's monument, to mark Heather's grave.

Gilbert Murray, O.M., Classical scholar, b. 1866. His ashes were buried here in 1957.

David Garrick, b. at Hereford, 1716, d. 1779, the famous actor. He was Dr Johnson's solitary scholar when he set up a school near Lichfield, from whence master and pupil came up to London to seek their fortunes together. Garrick retired at the height of his fame, and died three years afterwards at his house in the Adelphi. His funeral train stretched from there to the Abbey, and included all the most celebrated members of the Literary Club. Dr Johnson was seen standing by his grave at the foot of Shakespeare's monument 'bathed in tears'. Charles Lamb says in the *Essays of Elia*: 'Taking a tour the other day in the Abbey I was struck with the affected attitude of a figure which I do not remember to have seen before, and which upon examination proved to be a whole length of the celebrated Mr Garrick. . . . I own I was not a little scandalized at the introduction of theatrical airs and gestures into a place set apart to remind us of the saddest realities. Going nearer I found inscribed under this burlesque figure a farrago of false thought and nonsense.' Mrs Garrick (d. 1822) was buried in her husband's grave. The statue of Garrick was erected by his old friend, Albany Wallis, an eminent solicitor, whose grave is in the East Cloister, near the tablet which Garrick put up to commemorate Wallis's[4] only son, a Westminster scholar. *Webber sculpt.*

The two historians of Greece, **Connop Thirlwall, Bishop of St David's**, b. 1797, d. 1875 (*bust by Davis*), and **George Grote**, b. 1794, d. 1871, are buried in the same grave. A bust of Grote, by *C. Bacon*, is close by.

Starting from Dryden's monument we find the following gravestones in the floor over persons who have no monuments. To the right is a stone with the indent of a brass of a man in armour, the brass having been torn off. This represents **Robert Haule**, murdered in 1378 by the followers of John of Gaunt in the Choir, where he had taken sanctuary. After this desecration the Abbey was closed for four months until the rights of sanctuary were freshly decreed to it. His friend **John Shakel**, who escaped from the murderers, was buried in the same grave in 1396.

Near Dryden, lie **Sir John Beaumont**, b. 1583, d. 1627, a writer of graceful verse; and his brother, **Francis Beaumont**, b. 1584, d. 1616, the dramatist, who entered the Inner Temple in 1600. He wrote chiefly in conjunction with Fletcher; the two friends '"lived together on the Bank side," in Southwark, "not far from the play-house" (the Globe), and wrote for the theatre' (1606–16). Among their joint productions are *The Maid's Tragedy*, *The Knight of the Burning Pestle*, *Philaster*, etc. The well known lines on the tombs in Westminster Abbey are usually ascribed to Francis Beaumont:

Mortality, behold and fear
What a change of flesh is here!
Think how many Royal bones
Sleep within these heaps of stones.
Here they lie, had realms and lands,
Who now want strength to stir their hands
. . . Here are sands, ignoble things,
Dropt from the ruin'd sides of kings
Here's a world of pomp and state,
Buried in dust, once dead by fate.

---

[1] *Fuller's* Church History.   [2] *Ibid.*   [3] *See page 82.*

[4] *See page 110.*

South Transept and Rose Window seen from the No

Near his friend Cowley, on whose death he wrote a fine elegy, lies **Sir John Denham,** b. 1615, d. 1669, made surveyor of the works and a K.B. by Charles II. His poem *Cooper's Hill*, the earliest example of English descriptive poetry, was praised by Dryden, Pope, and Dr Johnson.

Abbot Nicholas de Litlyngton, d. 1386, succeeded Langham as Abbot here (1362–86). Partly out of his predecessor's bequest and partly from his own money he rebuilt the West and South Cloister, part of the Abbot's Lodgings including the Jerusalem Chamber and College Hall, the conventual buildings on the east side of Dean's Yard and the boundary wall of the monastery, part of which can be seen in Great College Street. He also enlarged the Monastic Frater or Refectory and went on with the re-building of the Nave during Langham's lifetime, and continued it with the Cardinal's legacy after his death.

Edward Tudor, son of Owen Tudor by Queen Catherine, widow of Henry V and uncle of Henry VII. He is probably to be identified with Edward Bridgewater who was a monk of Westminster from 1468–9 to 1471–2.[1]

Sir Robert Stapylton, d. 1669, a French Benedictine monk. Later he became a Protestant and a dramatist at the English Court, 'too gay and poetical for a monkish cell'.

Dr Samuel Johnson, b. 1709, d. 1784, lexicographer and critic, is, thanks to Boswell, the most living and familiar figure in the eighteenth century. He was born at Lichfield and educated at the grammar school there and at Pembroke College, Oxford. After an unsuccessful attempt at schoolmastering, in 1737 he went up to London accompanied by his pupil Garrick, in search of a career. The master's success, however, was much slower than that of the pupil, and continual struggles with poverty and ill-health lay before him. The great *Dictionary of the English Language*, the *Lives of the Poets*, and the *Rambler* are his chief works. The inscription was re-cut at the cost of his old college, Pembroke, Oxford. His monument is at St Paul's. In 1939 a bust of Dr Johnson by *Nollekens* was placed on the wall above his grave.

Richard Brinsley Sheridan, b. 1751, d. 1816, the eloquent Parliamentary orator and dramatist, author of *The Rivals* and *The School for Scandal*. Notwithstanding his great reputation he died in extreme poverty, and the help which came too late served only to furnish him with a magnificent funeral.

Richard Cumberland, b. 1732, d. 1811 dramatist, and friend of Dr Johnson.

Charles Dickens, b. 1812, d. 1870, novelist, whose books have had perhaps the largest circulation of any English works of fiction. *The Pickwick Papers* and *David Copperfield* are the best known. Dickens also edited two journals, *Household Words* and *All the Year Round*, and took part in advocating the abolition of the Slave Trade, and in other philanthropic works.

Rudyard Kipling, b. at Bombay 1865, d. 1936, author and poet. The British Empire was ever in Kipling's thoughts, and expressed in his written words. Kipling succeeded Sir James Barrie as Rector of St Andrew's University in 1922, and was made an associate of the French Academy in 1933; he also received honorary degrees from English and foreign universities. A member of the War Graves Commission he chose the words: 'Their name liveth for evermore', carved on stone pillars

[1] *See E. H. Pearce,* Monks of Westminster, *page 161.*

in the French War Cemeteries. The *Recessional* written after Queen Victoria's Diamond Jubilee was sung at his own funeral. He lies beside Thomas Hardy and, as at the latter's burial, the Prime Minister, Stanley Baldwin, was one of the distinguished pall-bearers.

Thomas Hardy, b. 1840, d. 1928, the Wessex novelist and poet, whose ashes are buried near Dickens. His heart lies with his family in Stinsford Churchyard, the 'Mellstock' of *Under the Greenwood Tree*. Hardy's novels are all connected with Dorset. *Far from the Madding Crowd* (1874) and *Tess of the d'Urbervilles* (1896) are two of the best known. The *Dynasts*, a poetical chronicle of English history was his greatest achievement in verse (1903–6).

Sir Henry Irving, b. 1838, d. 1905, actor and actor-manager, who revolutionized the dramatic art of the nineteenth century by his revivals of Shakespeare, and other plays at the old Lyceum Theatre (1878–99). Whilst playing Becket in Tennyson's play of that name at Bradford, Irving was struck down by an illness which proved fatal in a few hours. His grave is near Garrick's.

John Henderson, b. 1747, d. 1785, called the 'Bath Roscius', an actor who was considered second only to Garrick.

The **Rev. Henry Francis Cary,** b. 1772, d. 1844, the translator of Dante.

Thomas Parr, d. 1635, said to be aged 152 years, and to have lived in the reigns of ten sovereigns. One of his portraits, by Van Dyck, is at Dresden, another is in the National Portrait Gallery, London.

Sir William D'Avenant, b. 1606, d. 1668, the 'Sweet Swan of Isis', succeeded Ben Jonson as Poet Laureate, and, himself a Cavalier, was buried in the grave from which his Roundhead rival Thomas May had been cast out at the Restoration. D'Avenant was manager of the Duke's Theatre, which was amalgamated after his death with the King's company at Drury Lane. **Thomas Killigrew,** b. 1612, d. 1683, dramatist, manager of the King's Theatre, is buried close by.

Sir Robert Moray, b. 1603, d. 1673, chemist and mathematician, the first President of the Royal Society, and one of its original founders. He fought for the King in the Civil Wars, and was knighted by Charles I at Oxford; he was in high favour at the Restoration Court, and Charles II paid the expenses of his funeral.

James Macpherson, b. 1736, d. 1796, translator of the alleged poems of Ossian, the authenticity of which was disputed by Dr Johnson. His body was brought here from Inverness.

Dame Mary Steele, d. 1718, the second wife of Sir Richard Steele, the 'dearest Prue' of his correspondence.

Thomas Chiffinch, b. 1600, d. 1666, and **John Osbaldeston,** d. 1667, Pages of the Bedchamber to Charles II. Chiffinch was also keeper of the King's Private Closet and Comptroller of the Excise. He is said to have been brought to Charles I's Court by Bishop Duppa (page 75).

Dr Joshua Ward, b. 1686, d. 1761, celebrated for his various chemical preparations, was the inventor of the remedy called 'Friar's Balsam'. He established works near London for the manufacture of sulphuric acid. In Westminster, where he founded a hospital near Buckingham Palace, Ward was known as the 'Father of the Poor'. Many allusions to him occur in contemporary literature and in caricature. Pope satirized him in his *Imitations of Horace*. George II, Hogarth, and Fielding were amongst his patients.

Five architects are buried or commemorated here:

Thirteenth-century sculpture: Eastern Censing Angel   *Thirteenth-century sculpture: Western Censing Angel*

Robert Adam, b, 1728, d. 1792, architect, the most talented of four celebrated brothers.

Sir William Chambers, b. 1723, d. 1796, the architect of Somerset House.

Sir Robert Taylor, b. 1714, d. 1788, an architect of the Classical revival, who built the Mansion House and part of the Bank of England.

James Wyatt, b. 1746, d. 1813, surveyor of the Abbey fabric (1776), whose misdirected zeal as a restorer of Gothic architecture earned him the title of the 'destroyer'.

Sir Thomas Robinson, b. 1700, d. 1777, an amateur architect, called 'long Sir Thomas', who ruined himself by his love of building. Governor of Barbados for a time. He was famed for his splendid entertainments. At the coronation of George III he acted as deputy for the Duke of Normandy, the last occasion that the Duke performed homage.

Richard Hakluyt, b. 1553, d. 1616, 'the father of modern geographers', educated at Westminster School, and later a Prebendary (1602–16), the compiler of the *Voyages and Travels*. He was one of the promoters of the South Virginia Colony. Buried probably in this part of the Abbey.

Dr Richard Busby, b. 1606, d. 1695, Head Master of Westminster School, the most celebrated schoolmaster of his time. He died in the reign of William III, having held his post for fifty-five years. 'He used to declare that the rod was his sieve, and that whoever could not pass through that was no boy for him.' Sir Roger de Coverley says, standing before his tomb: 'Dr Busby, a great man! Whipped my grandfather–a very great man! I should have gone to him myself if I had not been a blockhead. A very great man!'[1] He was buried beneath the black-and-white pavement which he presented to the Choir. A finely modelled reclining statue by *Bird*.

Dr Robert South, b. 1634, d. 1716, a pupil of Busby's.[2] He died Archdeacon of Westminster, having refused the

[1] *Addison's* Spectator, *No. 139*.
[2] *Buried by his own wish near Busby*.

Deanery. He was a famous preacher, and the violence of an attack on Cromwell in one of his sermons so amused Charles II that he fell into a violent fit of laughter, and vowed Dr South should have a bishopric if he was put 'in mind of him at the next death'. The next death was, however, the King's own. *Bird sculpt.*

Between Busby's and South's monuments may be seen a portion of the tomb, attributed to *Theodore Haveus* from Cleves, of **Anne of Cleves,** d. 1557, daughter of the Duke of Cleves and fourth wife of Henry VIII. She lived quietly in England for sixteen years after her divorce from the King, and, dying a Roman Catholic (at Chelsea), was buried here by the monks. The marble slab over the tomb dates only from 1606, and cost £7. The decoration, the skull and crossbones, is said to be the earliest example of the kind in England.

A slab on the floor, **William Spottiswoode,** b. 1825, d. 1883, President of the Royal Society and Printer to the Queen.

Against the pillar is the bust of **Archibald Campbell Tait,** b. 1811, d. 1882, Archbishop of Canterbury (1869–82). *Armstead sculpt.*

The Chapel of St Faith at the south end of this Transept is reserved for prayer and meditation, and is also used occasionally for confirmations, marriages, and funerals. It formed the eastern portion of the Monks Revestry, and has an altar dedicated to St Faith.

Some early wall paintings still exist here. A figure of the Saint herself, wearing a crown, holding a book and a gridiron, the emblem of her martyrdom, is above the altar; below is the Crucifixion. On the left is a small half figure of a praying Benedictine monk; from his lips issues a scroll with the words:

'Me quem culpa gravis premit, erige, Virgo suavis.
Fac mihi placatum Cristum, delasque reatum.'

('From the burden of my sore transgressions, sweet Virgin, deliver me; make my peace with Christ and blot out my iniquity.')

On the south wall is a tablet to **Jocelyn Henry Temple Perkins,** b. 1870, d. 1962; Minor Canon and Sacrist 1899–1958.

Just within the South Transept was an altar, the gift of the Prior, Richard de Merston (1362–76). It was dedicated to St Blaise, an Armenian bishop, martyred with iron combs about 316, and hence the patron saint of woolcombers. As late as 1825 his festival was still celebrated at Bradford, with trade processions, and a poem recited in his honour.

Outside the Poets' Corner door a tablet was placed in 1954 to commemorate the fact that near that spot **William Caxton** set up the first printing press in England in 1476.[1]

[1] *See L. E. Tanner, 'William Caxton's Houses in Westminster' in* The Library (*Fifth Series, vol. xii, No. 3, Sept. 1957*).

THE CHOIR AND SANCTUARY [*See plan, page 52*]

The Choir was formerly separated from the Transepts by wooden parcloses or partitions; these were replaced by iron gates, which were removed in the nineteenth century. The greater part of the present stalls and pews were set up in 1848, and designed by Blore, then architect to the Dean and Chapter. Above the Dean's stall at the west end of the Choir are emblazoned the coat of arms of the Collegiate Church, and further east on the north side a stall with the City arms over it has been allotted to the Mayors of Westminster; stalls, with arms above, have also been assigned to the High Commissioners of Australia, Canada, and New Zealand. The Head Master and Under Master of Westminster School have stalls further west, above the seats allotted to the Queen's Scholars.

Beneath the pavement in front of their own stall lie two sub-deans, **Dr Peter Heylin** (see page 38) and:

Dr Robinson Duckworth, C.V.O., b. 1834, d. 1911, Canon of Westminster for thirty-six years, Chaplain to Queen Victoria, King Edward VII, and King George V. Duckworth accompanied King Edward, when Prince of Wales, to India in 1875, and was governor to his brother, Prince Leopold, Duke of Albany.

In the centre of the pavement a Latin inscription marks the grave of **Dame Anne Carey,** d. 1660, daughter of Sir Nicholas Hyde (d. 1631), Chief Justice of England, widow of Sir Ross Carey, who was knighted for his services on the memorable expedition to the Isle of Rhé.

The present **Pulpit (seventeenth century)** was replaced in its original position in 1935. It had been removed in 1781, at the same time that Keene the Abbey surveyor destroyed the thirteenth-century choir stalls. Dean Ryle placed it in the Nave but it was again stored away after the coronation of Edward VII. The pulpit has now been repainted and gilded, and put upon a modern pedestal.

The carved English walnut **Lectern,** inscribed to the memory of **William Carey** (1761–1834), missionary in India and translator of the Bible, was presented to the Abbey in 1949 by the Baptist Missionary Society. (*Designed by A. E. Richardson, R.A.*)

The **Sanctuary** or Presbytery–i.e., the space within the altar rails, often inaccurately called the 'Sacrarium'– was formerly hung round with cloth of arras, adorned with legends of the Confessor. This was replaced in Queen Anne's reign by a wooden wainscoting, which entirely concealed all those portions of the fine tombs which could not be seen from the Ambulatories. The wainscoting was removed in 1820. The **Ceremony of Coronation** takes place before the Altar, and is now always performed by the Archbishop of Canterbury, who on that occasion only can claim a place in the Choir by right. The Sovereign afterwards ascends a raised throne erected under the Lantern and receives the homage of the Peers. The first coronation here was possibly that of Harold, the last of the Saxon kings, January 1066. Twelve months afterwards, on Christmas Day, 1066, William the Conqueror, the first Norman sovereign, was crowned by Aldred, Archbishop of York, before the High Altar. Since that time all the sovereigns (except Edward V and Edward VIII) have been crowned in the Abbey. The present **High Altar** and reredos were erected in 1867, after Sir Gilbert Scott's design. The sculptured figures of the reredos were executed by *Armstead*, the mosaic, representing the Last Supper, was designed by J. R. Clayton (of Clayton and Bell's) and carried out by *Salviati*.

The thirteenth-century Pavement is Cosmati work and is composed of various kinds of mosaic and porphyry set in squares and circles. The design represents the probable duration of the world according to the Ptolemaic system. The inscription, of which only a few brass letters remain, incorporated the date (1268), the name of the reigning king (Henry III), and the city (Rome) from whence the materials came. It has been suggested that the pavement might have been presented by the Pope.

Underneath the pavement on each side of the Altar are the bases of pillars which formed part of the Confessor's Church.

Three fine tombs occupy the north side of the Sanctuary. They are very similar in design, and two of them, Edmund's and Aveline's, may, perhaps, be attributed either to Master Alexander of Abingdon or to Master Michael of Canterbury. Aymer's tomb is later, and may be by Master Richard of Reading. The exact dates of their erection are unknown, but they were probably executed between 1300 and 1326. The design was suggested by the hearse and lights which stood in the church during the funeral ceremonies; the little figures round the basements represent the mourners. All three monuments show traces of having been richly painted and gilt; the two last were decorated with coloured glass enamel, of which a fragment can be seen in a corner of Edmund Crouchback's tomb.

Aveline, Countess of Lancaster, d. 1274, daughter of

High Altar from the Choir Sta

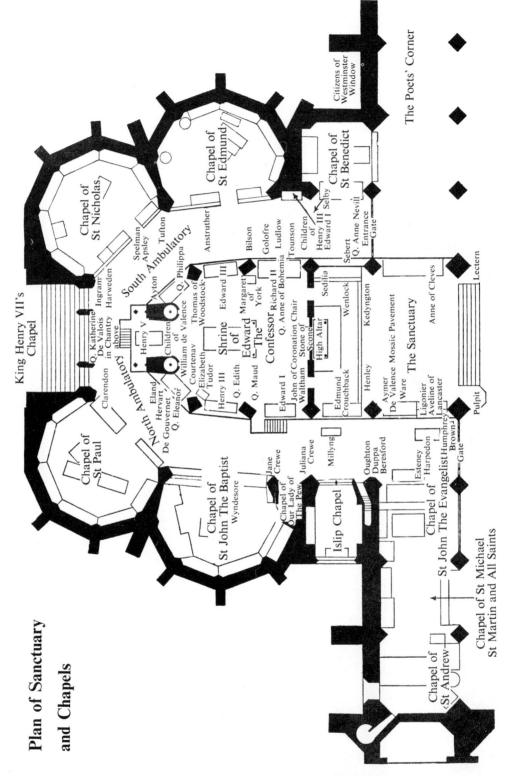

Plan of Sanctuary and Chapels

King Henry VII's Chapel

Chapel of St Nicholas

Chapel of St Edmund

Chapel of St Benedict

Chapel of St Paul

Chapel of St John The Baptist

Chapel of Our Lady of The Pew

Islip Chapel

Chapel of St John The Evangelist

Chapel of St Michael St Martin and All Saints

Chapel of St Andrew

North Ambulatory

South Ambulatory

The Poets' Corner

The Sanctuary

Shrine of Edward The Confessor

Citizens of Westminster Window

South Transept

North Transept

Clarendon

Q. Katherine De Valois in Chantry above

Ingram
Harweden
Spelman
Apsley
Tufton

Eland
Hervart
De Gouvernet
Q. Eleanor

Ayton
Q. Philippa
Thomas of Woodstock
Edward III
Margaret of York

Bilson
Golofre
Ludlow
Tounson
Anstruther

Children of Henry III
Edward I Selby
Sebert
Q. Anne Nevill
Entrance Gate

Henry V
Children of
William de Valence
Courtenay
Elizabeth Tudor
Henry III
Q. Edith
Q. Maud

Richard II
Q. Anne of Bohemia

Sediia
Wenlock
Kedyngton
Henley

Aymer De Valence Mosaic Pavement
Ware

Ligonier
Aveline of Lancaster
Humphrey Brown
Gate
Pulpit

Anne of Cleves
Lectern

Edward I
John of Waltham
Coronation Chair Stone of Scone
High Altar

Edmund Crouchback

Wyndesore
Jane Crewe
Juliana Crewe
Millyng

Oughton Duppa Beresford

Esteney
Harpedon

St John The Evangelist

William de Forz, Count of Albemarle, one of the greatest heiresses of England and a famous beauty; she was married by Henry III to his second son, Edmund Crouchback, who is buried close by, in April 1269, the first wedding in the new building. Aveline died childless, and her wealth endowed the future House of Lancaster, of which her husband became the founder by his second marriage. The recumbent figure of Aveline, her head supported by two angels, rests upon an altar tomb, and is probably by the same sculptor as her husband's effigy. She is dressed in a long mantle, and wears the stiff head-dress, the close coif and wimple of the time. In front of the basement are six figures (now headless or defaced), standing in the arched niches. The pointed canopy is supported by the buttresses, and has been greatly injured. The whole was once richly coloured, and traces of painted vine leaves can still be seen in the vaulting of the trefoiled arch and on the adjacent tomb of Aymer de Valence.

Aymer de Valence, Earl of Pembroke (b. *c.* 1270, d. 1324), son of William de Valence (page 56) and cousin to Edward I. He was a tall, pale man, nicknamed by Piers de Gaveston, from his appearance, 'Joseph the Jew'. Aymer was much employed in the wars with Scotland, where he captured and put to death Nigel, the brother of Robert Bruce, and he also took part in the execution of Gaveston. In 1321 he assisted Edward II to defeat the Barons at Pontefract, and to execute Thomas, Earl of Lancaster, son of Edmund Crouchback. He died suddenly in France when on an embassy to Charles IV. Aymer's first wife Beatrice, daughter and co-heir of Raoul de Clermont, Sire de Néelle and Constable of France, died in 1320. He married secondly Mary, daughter of Guy de Châtillon, Comte de St Pol; she, who was the foundress of Pembroke College, Cambridge, died in 1377. The little figures of weepers (mourners) on the lower part of the Earl's tomb, though now mutilated, and Aymer's effigy in armour are very fine. Two angels at the head support his soul, a small figure wrapped in a mantle. His feet rest on a lion; his shield has disappeared. Above on the richly carved canopy he is again represented in bas-relief, fully armed and on horseback. This magnificent tomb was in danger of being removed to make way for the memorial to General Wolfe. Horace Walpole protested against the idea, and intended, if his remonstrance proved ineffectual, to have Aymer's monument set up in his garden at Strawberry Hill. The Dean, Zachary Pearce, on hearing that Aymer was not, as he had supposed, one of the Knights Templars, 'a very wicked set of people',[1] allowed it to remain.

Edmund, Earl of Lancaster (b. 1245, d. 1296), surnamed Crouchback, youngest son of Henry III. He became Earl of Lancaster in 1267, and married Aveline de Forz in 1269. After her death he married Blanche, widow of Henry, King of Navarre, and daughter of Robert, Count of Artois. Crouchback was employed actively in England, Wales (where in 1282 he captured and beheaded Llewellyn ap Gruffydd), and France. He died at Bayonne in 1296 while besieging Bordeaux. Crouchback's monument is the largest and most elaborate of the three; a triple canopy richly decorated (probably by Master Alexander of Abingdon) rises over the fine sculptured effigy of the Earl, who is in armour; his hands are folded in prayer. There are ten trefoil arched niches on either side of the tomb, containing crowned figures and coats of arms.

---

[1] *Walpole's* Letters (*ed. Toynbee*), *vol. v, page 95 and Supplement, vol. ii, page 120.*

The canopy, like so many others in the Abbey, has suffered much from the preparations made for coronations in former days. The Earl appears again on the pediment in full armour on horseback.

The grave of **Richard de Ware**, Abbot of Westminster from 1258 till his death in 1283, author of the *Customary*, i.e., rules for the daily life of the monastery in his time, is on the north side of the Presbytery, beneath the pavement which was laid down under his superintendence. The place was formerly marked by this inscription:

Abbas Richardus de Wara qui requiescit
Hic, portet lapides, quos huc portavit ab urbe.

His successor **Walter de Wenlock**, d. 1307, lies on the south side of the Altar; the little head wearing a mitre on the sedilia above may be his portrait. He was at first high in the King's favour and Lord Treasurer of England, but fell under a cloud after the robbery of the royal treasure, which had been placed in the monastic treasury during Edward's absence in Scotland. In his time also occurred the great fire which consumed many of the monastic buildings.

Two oak chairs for the Dean and Sub-Dean were placed on the north side of the Presbytery in 1922. About thirty shields appear on the Dean's Chair, which was made by Messrs. Jack. The back of the chair is decorated with the royal arms, below are the arms of the Order of the Bath, and the Keys of St Peter, the arms of the Collegiate Church and of Dean Ryle. Below these is the word 'Decanus' in carved and gilded letters; the reading desk in front is carried on octagonal posts. Between the posts are eight panels upon which are painted in colours the arms of the Deans of Westminster, from William Bill, first Dean since the foundation of the present collegiate church, to Bishop Ryle's predecessor, Joseph Armitage Robinson (1902–11, afterwards Dean of Wells). There are also two reading desks for the Canons and Minor Canons.

The ancient **sedilia** rest on Sebert's tomb, and used to be mistaken for part of it. They were erected under Edward I in the time of Abbot Wenlock, and are richly decorated; the glass enamel has almost all disappeared, but the paintings and carvings have been recently cleaned. On the north of the Sanctuary side two of the panels are painted with full-length figures of kings and these are probably Henry III and Edward I, but the identity of the ecclesiastic between them is uncertain; the other figure has completely disappeared. On the Ambulatory side restoration has uncovered the figure of the Confessor holding the ring out to the Pilgrim, of whose figure no traces remain, and also part of a fourteenth-century painting of the Annunciation, of which only the lower portion is intact.

In front of the sedilia, in an unmarked grave, lies buried **Queen Anne Nevill** (d. 1485), wife of Richard III (for a tablet to her memory, see page 55).

On the south side of the Presbytery hangs a sixteenth-century piece of tapestry, which traditionally formed part of the scenery used in the annual performance of the Latin play at Westminster School.

On this tapestry hangs a fifteenth-century altar-piece painted on panel by Bicci Di Lorenzo (1375–1452) and bequeathed to the Abbey in 1948 by the late Viscount Lee of Fareham. It represents the Madonna and Child enthroned in the centre, with St Anthony of Padua and St Giovanni Gualberti on her right, and St John Baptist and St Catherine of Egypt on her left.

THE CHAPELS AND SOUTH AMBULATORY

Chapel of St Benedict

THIS LITTLE CHAPEL ADJOINS the South Transept. It is dedicated to the founder of the great Benedictine Order, to which the monks of Westminster belonged. The head of St Benedict, a much valued relic, was presented to the Abbey by Edward III in 1355; he is said to have brought it from the Abbey of Fleury, in France. There are heraldic tiles to be seen in the pavement. Against the south wall is a mural monument with the kneeling figure of **Gabriel Goodman**, b. 1529, d. 1601, Dean of Westminster for forty years under Queen Elizabeth. He addressed the House of Commons in defence of the rights of sanctuary at Westminster, and in consequence of his opposition to the Bill for their suppression, they were preserved, in cases of debt only, until the reign of James I. He was chaplain to Lord Burghley (which displeased the Puritans), and a friend of William Camden, the antiquary, whose expenses he defrayed 'in some of his journeys after anti- quity'. Lady Burghley founded two scholarships for Old Westminsters at St John's College, Cambridge, which bear the name of Dean Goodman. Goodman founded Christ's Hospital and the grammar school, Ruthin, and left money to several Cambridge colleges.

The place of the Altar is occupied by the tomb of **Frances, Countess of Hertford**, b. 1554, d. 1598, the daughter-in-law of Protector Somerset, wife of Edward (Seymour), Earl of Hertford and sister of Lord Howard of Effingham, the Lord High Admiral who repulsed the Spanish Armada. The monument (28 feet high) is a fine example of the period; the initials F.H. are introduced among the decorations.

William de Curtlington, Abbot of Westminster from 1315 till his death in 1333, was buried before the Altar. The brass figure and inscription which formerly marked the place have disappeared. **Simon de Langham**, d. 1376, Abbot of Westminster from 1349 to 1362, when he became Bishop of Ely; and from 1362 to 1366, Lord Chancellor of England. In 1366 he was made Archbishop of Canterbury by Edward III, the only Westminster Abbot to attain to that dignity. On receiving a cardinal's hat from Pope Urban V, Langham was obliged to give up the arch- bishopric (1368) and go abroad to the Papal Court, but he returned to England in 1369, where Edward III con- ferred fresh ecclesiastical benefices upon him. Recalled by Pope Gregory XI, in 1373, he was made Bishop of Palestrina, and died at Avignon three years later. He was buried by his own desire in the Abbey, to which he was a great benefactor. Besides many gifts in money, plate, and vestments during his lifetime, including £200 a year towards the rebuilding of the Nave, Langham bequeathed the whole of his vast fortune to the monastery, and his successor, Abbot Litlyngton,[1] ably administered the funds. The monument, erected c. 1395, is by *Henry Yevele* and *Stephen Lote*; the canopy was destroyed at the coronation of George I, and little remains of the brass inscription round the ledge. A statue of St Mary Magdalene (on whose feast, 22 July, Langham died), which was pre- sented by one William 'de Reliquiis' at the cost of ten shillings, originally stood near the Cardinal's feet, and his cardinal's hat formerly hung above his tomb.

In the centre is the large altar tomb of **Lionel Cranfield, Earl of Middlesex**, b. 1575, d. 1645, and Anne, his second wife, daughter of James Brett of Hoby, Co. Leics., who erected the monument. Cranfield rose from one post to another through his great business capacity, and was finally made Lord High Treasurer under James I. He was impeached at the instigation of the Duke of Buckingham, whose extravagance he had opposed, and to whom he was indebted both for his rise and for his fall. He was pardoned in 1625.

William Bill, d. 1561, the first Dean of Westminster after the establishment of the Abbey as a Collegiate Church by Elizabeth I in 1560. A brass figure of 'an antient man in a doctor's habit', with a laudatory Latin epitaph, rests on the low altar tomb. Another inscription in brass letters once surrounded the ledge.

Under a blue slab lies the learned **William Vincent**, b. 1739, d. 1815, Head Master of Westminster School, 1788–1802; Dean of Westminster, 1802–15. Vincent secured ten acres in Tothill Fields for the boys' play- ground, called Vincent Square after him. He was responsible for the restoration of the original stone work outside Henry VII's Chapel by the architect, Wyatt. (See page 63.)

John Spottiswoode, Archbishop of St Andrews, b. 1565, d. 1639, the historian of the Scottish Church, was buried in this Chapel.[2] In 1633 he crowned Charles I King of Scotland at Edinburgh. His younger brother **James Spottiswoode**, b. 1567, d. 1645, buried close by, was made Bishop of Clogher, Ireland, in 1621.

In 1878 an old doorway of the Chapel, which had long been concealed by a tablet, was again opened to view, and is now known to have led to the Abbey Anchorite's cell.

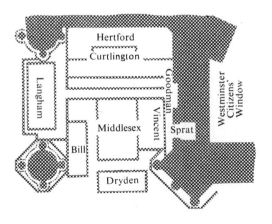

---

[1] *See page 48.*   [2] *An inscribed stone has been placed outside.*

The South Ambulatory [*See plan, page 52*]

(*Before passing through the iron gates each person must obtain a ticket – 2s.* (*Members of H.M.'s Forces in uniform free*) – *for admission to the Chapels, from the desk in Poets' Corner, except on Friday, which is a free day.*)

Immediately within the gates of the Ambulatory to the left, is the arched recess containing the supposed tomb of **King Sebert**, d. about 616, the traditional founder of the Abbey. Although the legend which connected this King of the East Saxons with Westminster has no historical foundation, the tomb has always been shown as his since the erection of the building, and was reputed to contain also the bones of Sebert's queen, Ethelgoda, and his sister Ricula. The segmental arch, with its mouldings, once painted and gilt, belongs to the earliest years of the fourteenth century. The decoration at the back of the recess is evidently of later date as it contains the *rose en soleil*, the

Dean Goodman's Monument

badge of Edward IV. During the rebuilding of the church by Henry III the stone coffin was removed and deposited on the southern side of the Chapter House entrance until after the completion of the Choir, when it was placed with great ceremony by the monks in its present position. Above it are remains of the painted figures of the Confessor and Pilgrim, contemporary with those on the north side of the sedilia (about 1308); recent restoration has uncovered traces of a painting of the Annunciation in the other recess.

In 1960 a bronze tablet (designed by *J. S. Comper*) was erected on the wall by Sebert's tomb to **Queen Anne Nevill** (1456–85), wife of Richard III and daughter of Richard, Earl of Warwick, 'The Kingmaker'. She lies buried in front of the sedilia (page 53) with nothing to mark her grave.

Under a segmental arch in the wall between the chapels of St Edmund and St Benedict is a small altar tomb over the remains of **Katherine**, d. 1257, aged five years, and of **four other children of Henry III**; with these were afterwards laid **four children of Edward I**. The loss of their dumb but beautiful little daughter Katherine was a great grief to Henry III and his Queen. He ordered a richly decorated monument for her, inlaid all over with precious marbles and mosaics, perhaps the remains of those brought over for St Edward's shrine, but these have disappeared from almost everywhere except the slab, where something of the design can still be traced. There were also two images, lost long since; one of brass, which Master Simon of Wells came to London to set up, and one of silver (probably representing St Katherine), for which William de Gloucester, the King's goldsmith, received 70 marks. The back of the recess was painted with four kneeling figures; these may have been either the Princess Katherine and her brothers, or have been added later by Edward I when his children were laid to rest in the same grave. The space between the arches over the tomb was elaborately painted and gilt; an image of a saint occupied the centre.

In the pavement are the graves of:

Thomas Bilson, b. 1547, d. 1616, Bishop of Winchester (1597–1616). 'As reverend and learned a prelate as England ever afforded' (Fuller). He 'put the completing hand' to the authorized translation of the Bible by command of James I.

Sir John Golofre, d. 1396, the second husband of Philippa, Duchess of York (page 59). He was Ambassador to the Court of France in the time of Richard II, with whom he was a great favourite, and by whose orders his remains were brought here from their burial-place at Wallingford. A few fragments of what must have been a very handsome brass are preserved in the Abbey Museum. The original large Purbeck marble slab, badly cracked, can be seen south of Richard II's tomb.

Robert Tounson, b. 1575, d. 1621, Dean of Westminster, 1617; Bishop of Salisbury, 1620. While he was Dean, Sir Walter Raleigh was imprisoned in the old Gatehouse, once the monastery prison, which formerly stood at the entrance of what is now Tothill Street. Dean Tounson went to pray with Raleigh both the night before and the morning of his execution, and was amazed if not shocked at the courageous gaiety with which he faced death.

Sir Robert Anstruther, d. 1645, Privy Councillor, a favourite at the Courts of James I and Charles I, and a successful ambassador abroad during both reigns.

Sir Henry Spelman, b. 1564 (?), d. 1641, antiquary, was

buried by order of Charles I with much state close to the entrance of St Nicholas's Chapel. He wrote several learned works on legal and ecclesiastical history, and was an intimate friend of Archbishop Laud.

Ralph Selby, d. 1420, a learned Westminster monk, the favourite of two kings, Henry IV and Henry V.

Richard Harweden, Abbot of Westminster from 1420 till his resignation in 1440 (d. *c.* 1441). He was one of the treasurers of the money given by Henry V for rebuilding the west part of the Nave. Nothing remarkable occurred in his time except the 'most solemn burial' of Henry V. His grave was at the foot of the steps to Henry VII's Chapel on the south side, and the large Purbeck marble slab there is known to have had a brass on it with a mitred effigy.

Richard de Berkyng, Abbot of Westminster from 1222 till his death in 1246, one of the witnesses to the Magna Charta. He held several high offices in the State, and was a great favourite with Henry III, from whom he obtained important charters and grants for the Abbey. He was first buried in the old Lady Chapel, but on its demolition for the building of Henry VII's Chapel, his remains are said to have been removed here, but the actual place is unknown.

A bust by *Fanelli* of **Sir Robert Ayton,** b. 1570, d. 1638, poet and philosopher, a friend of Ben Jonson and Thomas Hobbes. He was secretary to Anne of Denmark and Henrietta Maria.

Beneath is a much injured thirteenth-century **Retable,** probably by a French artist, representing the Ministry and Majesty of Christ, which is believed to have formed part of the thirteenth-century High Altar. It was discovered by Edward Blore, the Abbey architect, about 1827, on the top of one of the cases containing the wax effigies, after they were moved to the Islip Chantry. The central figure, Christ in Glory, holds a small globe upon which are painted in miniature the sea, with men in a boat; the land, with sheep feeding; a stork and other birds in the sky; the sun and moon; on either side are figures of the Virgin and St John the Evangelist. The background was decorated with gilding and coloured glass. In star-shaped panels are represented the Miracles of Christ.[1]

A tablet to **Sir Thomas Ingram,** d. 1672, 'for his eminent loyalty, suffering, and services' to Charles I and Charles II, made Chancellor of the Duchy of Lancaster. Buried below with his only child, Mary, aged twelve.

Chapel of St Edmund

(*first on entering the gates*)

A fine wooden screen, with a doorway in the centre, separates the Chapel from the Ambulatory. This St Edmund is the King of East Anglia, martyred by the Danes in 870, for refusing to give up Christianity, and not the St Edmund, Archbishop of Canterbury, 1234. St Edmund's Bury is dedicated to this King, and the connexion which existed between the two abbeys, together with the fact that King Edmund's figure is linked with that of St Edward twice in Henry VII's Chapel and once in Henry V's, leaves little doubt that this Chapel is dedicated to him. It was looked upon as next in degree of

sanctity to the Chapel of St Edward, and was used as a burial-place for relations of the sovereigns.

William de Valence, Lord of Pembroke and Wexford (d. 1296), was a half-brother of Henry III, being son of Hugh de Lusignan, Comte de la Marche (d. 1249), by Isabella of Angouleme, King John's widow. Valence near Lusignan was probably his birthplace. William in addition to his French lordships, acquired vast estates in England and Ireland by his marriage with Joan, daughter and in her issue heir of Warin de Munchensy, Lord of Swanscombe, whose first wife Joan was in her issue a coheir of the Marshals, Earls of Pembroke; but William de Valence was never created Earl nor invested with the earldom. The tomb is of great interest because it is the only existing example in England having Limoges champlevé enamelwork. The effigy and the chest on which it lies are of oak, and both were once covered with enamelled copper plates. Most of these have been lost from the tomb-chest but the five small shields on round plates should be noted. The decoration on the figure is more complete, and the finely diapered cushion under William's head and the large shield at his side are especially remarkable. William's arms, as on the great shield, occur on the pillow, on small shields powdering the surcoat and on one of the roundels on the tomb-chest. The stone base bears the arms of England, Valence and Valence dimidiating Clermont-Néelle, commemorating the first marriage of William's son Aymer (see page 53). His daughter Margaret (d. 1276) and his son John (d. 1277) are buried in Edward the Confessor's Chapel.

Edward Talbot, 8th Earl of Shrewsbury, d. 1618, and **Jane,** his wife, daughter of Cuthbert, 7th Lord Ogle, who erected this fine Jacobean tomb, with the recumbent figures of herself and her husband; the effigy of their little girl is kneeling near her father. The monument, which was once protected by an iron grate, is by *Maximilian Poultrain* or Colt of Arras.

Sir Richard Pecksall, d. 1571, kneels between his two wives; Master of the Buckhounds to Queen Elizabeth, a post he inherited from his mother, who was the heiress of the Brocas family. The four small kneeling figures are his daughters by his first wife.

Sir Bernard Brocas, d. 1396. The man commemorated here is the father of the Sir Bernard Brocas who was

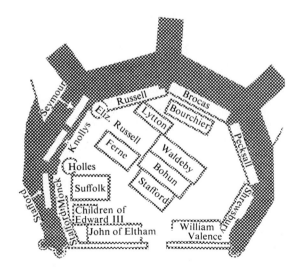

---

[1] *See W. R. Lethaby, 'Medieval Paintings at Westminster'* (Proc. Brit. Academy, *vol. xiii, 1927) and F. Wormald, 'Paintings in Westminster Abbey'* (Proc. Brit. Academy, *vol. xxxv, 1949*).

Shield from brass of Eleanor, Duchess of Gloucester

Effigy of John of Eltham

executed in 1400 for conspiring to reinstate Richard II. The inscription now above the tomb is of the eighteenth century and is erroneous. The head rests on a helmet surmounted by his crest, a crowned Moor's head. The story of his cutting off the King of Morocco's head, mentioned by Addison, is a legend of later days. This Sir Bernard Brocas, like his son, held office at the Court of Richard II. He became Hereditary Master of the Royal Buckhounds in right of his wife, the daughter and heiress of Sir John de Roche. The monument was painted all over about the middle of the eighteenth century, and the recumbent figure is probably a restoration. The brass inscription is original and fine.

Sir Humphrey Bourchier, d. 1471, killed fighting for Edward IV at the Battle of Barnet. He was the son of one John, Lord Berners, and his own son, John, Lord Berners (d. 1533) was Chancellor of the Exchequer to Henry VIII and is well known as the translator of Froissart's *Chronicles*. The brass effigy in armour has disappeared from the low altar tomb, but the helmet, with Saracen's head crest, shields and heraldic badges remain.

Edward Bulwer-Lytton, 1st Baron Lytton, b. 1803, d. 1873, the well-known writer, author of *The Caxtons*, *The Last Days of Pompeii*, and many other novels.

John Russell, Lord Russell, d. 1584, son of the second Earl of Bedford, died in his father's lifetime. The inscriptions in Latin, Greek, and English were composed by his wife, the learned daughter of Sir Anthony Cook and sister of Lady Burghley. Lord Russell is represented dressed in his robes, his face turned towards the spectator, and reclining on his left elbow. At his feet is the figure of his infant son, Francis. His daughter, **Elizabeth Russell,** d. 1601, called by Dean Stanley the 'child of Westminster',

was born within the precincts and christened in the Abbey (1575); Queen Elizabeth (represented by the Countess of Warwick), and Sir Philip Sidney's aunt, the Countess of Sussex (buried in St Paul's Chapel), were the godmothers, and Robert Dudley, Earl of Leicester, was godfather. She afterwards became maid of honour to her royal god-mother, and died young of consumption. The monument, put up by her sister Anne, Lady Herbert, represents Elizabeth as seated upright in an osier chair on a floridly decorated pedestal. Her finger pointing to the skull at her feet gave rise to the 'vulgar error' that she died from pricking it with a needle. Addison relates the tale of 'that martyr to good housewifery' as being told to Sir Roger de Coverley on his visit to the Abbey, and as having greatly excited the knight's curiosity. (*Spectator*, No. 329.)

Two mural tablets, the first of their kind in the Abbey – **Lady Jane Seymour,** d. 1560, aged nineteen, daughter of the Protector Somerset, and cousin to Edward VI; **Lady Catherine Knollys,** d. 1569, sister of Lord Hunsdon, and niece to Anne Boleyn. She remained with her aunt during her imprisonment in the Tower, and attended her to the scaffold.

Francis Holles, d. 1622, aged eighteen, having already served through the Flemish campaign. The monument, a seated figure in Roman armour on a pedestal, put up by his father, the Earl of Clare,[1] was much praised by Horace Walpole. *Nicholas Stone sculpt.*

Frances, Duchess of Suffolk, b. 1517, d. 1559, daughter of Charles Brandon, Duke of Suffolk, by the Lady Mary, daughter of Henry VII of England, and widow of Louis XII

---

[1] *See also the monument to Clare's brother, Sir George Holles, in St John's Chapel, page 84.*

of France. Frances married Henry Grey, Marquess of Dorset, created Duke of Suffolk, and thus became the mother of the unfortunate Lady Jane Grey. After her daughter's execution in 1553 she lived in disgrace and poverty through the reign of Mary, and only survived a year after Queen Elizabeth's accession and her own consequent return to favour and prosperity. The tomb with its recumbent figure was erected by her second husband, Adrian Stokes, whom she married during the time of her misfortunes. Her funeral service was the first Protestant service held in the Abbey after the reconstitution of the Chapter by Queen Elizabeth.

Close by lies the daughter of Frances's only sister, Lady Clifford, **Margaret, Countess of Derby**, d. 1596. She was accused of witchcraft, and imprisoned by her jealous cousin, Queen Elizabeth, in 1590, and when released forbidden to approach the Court or live with her husband. She died in obscurity; her only memorial is a portrait at Skipton Castle, with a simple inscription in praise of her virtues.

Beneath a diminutive altar tomb lie two children of Edward III, **William of Windsor** and **Blanche of the Tower**, d. 1340, both surnamed from their birthplaces, that of Blanche being the Tower of London. The alabaster effigies, for which John Orchard,[1] stonemason of London, received 20s., are only 20 inches in length; they are interesting examples of the civilian costume of the time. The sides of the Purbeck marble tomb show traces of the approach of the Perpendicular style of architecture. A brass inscription has disappeared from the ledge, and also the small figures with which the panels were adorned.

A pyramidical monument to **Nicholas Monck**, Bishop of Hereford, 1660, b. 1610, d. 1661, brother of the famous General Monck, who at the Bishop's repeated instigations undertook the restoration of Charles II. The monument was erected by his grandson in 1723. *W. Woodman sculpt.*

John of Eltham, Earl of Cornwall, d. 1337, second son of Edward II. In spite of his youth he was three times Regent of the kingdom during his brother Edward III's absence; he also took a prominent part in quelling the border raids of the Scots. He was born at the Royal Palace of Eltham, in Kent, and died, aged nineteen, at Perth, from whence his body was brought in great state to be buried in the Abbey. The alabaster effigy is probably by the same sculptor as that of his father Edward II in Gloucester Cathedral. The feet rest on a lion; two angels, which support the head cushions, are ready to bear away the soul of the deceased. The small crowned figures round the sides of the tomb represent the kings and queens to whom he was related. Those on the south side, are sadly mutilated, but those on the north are in a better state. These include John's grandparents, Edward I and his second wife, Margaret of France, and his parents Edward II and Queen Isabella. The beautiful canopy was unhappily broken down in 1776, and afterwards removed by Dean Zachary Pearce.

In the centre of the Chapel is a low altar tomb, on which is the finest brass in the Abbey, to **Eleanor or Alianore, Duchess of Gloucester**, d. 1399. She was the wife of Edward III's youngest son, Thomas of Woodstock, Duke of Gloucester (see page 94) and daughter and co-heir of Humphrey de Bohun, Earl of Hereford, Northampton, and Essex, and Constable of England. After her husband's death, the Duchess spent the re-

mainder of her life, two years only, in the nunnery at Barking. She is represented in her widow's dress, under a triple canopy; above her head is the Bohun badge, a swan, afterwards adopted by Henry V. Most of the inscription, in brass letters interspaced with heraldic devices, remains round the ledge. Near hers is the tomb of her lineal descendant, **Mary, Countess of Stafford**, d. 1694; created Countess in her own right eight years after the attainder and execution of her husband, Viscount Stafford, for alleged treason, in 1680. In the corner is a tablet to **John Paul Howard**, b. 1700, d. 1762, grandson of the above and last **Earl of Stafford**. On the south of the Duchess of Gloucester's tomb lies **Robert de Waldeby, Archbishop of York**, d. 1397, the learned friend and companion of the Black Prince. A fine brass figure under a canopy, in mitre and robes, his right hand raised in the act of giving benediction, his left holding a cross.

Under a blue slab with five shields of arms and a mitre in brass lies **Henry Ferne, Bishop of Chester**, b. 1602, d. 1662, who attended Charles I during his imprisonment, and 'whose only fault it was that he could not be angry'.

Here also is buried a naval hero, **Sir Frescheville Holles**, b. 1641, d. 1672, son of the antiquary Gervase Holles, knighted by Charles II after the victory over the Dutch off Lowestoft (1665), and killed in the bloody action of Southwold Bay.[1] Holles wrote an interesting epitaph for his gravestone, never inscribed upon it: 'Know, reader, whosoever thou be, if I had lived 'twas my intention not to have owed my memory to any other monument but what my sword should raise for me of honour and victory.'

Chapel of St Nicholas

The Chapel is separated from the Ambulatory by a fine stone screen, erected probably in the reign of Henry IV; the frieze is decorated with shields and roses. It is dedicated to St Nicholas, the youthful Bishop of Myra, and patron-saint of children. A finger of the saint and other relics were presented to the Abbey by Eleanor, Queen of Edward I. Those who attended mass at this

[1] *See page 74.*

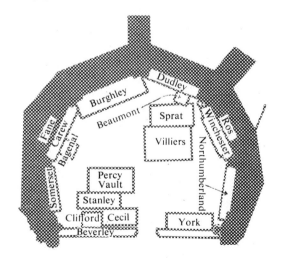

---

[1] *Also employed on Philippa's tomb, page 94.*

altar were granted indulgences of three years and sixty days. The Chapel contains many Elizabethan monuments, also the private vault of the Percy family, members of which have still a right to be interred there. The position of several of the monuments was shifted in order to make room for the new Percy vault opened in 1776.

The first tomb on the right as you enter the Chapel is that of **Philippa, Duchess of York,** d. 1431, daughter of John, Lord Mohun, and wife of Walter, Lord Fitzwalter, of Sir John Golofre (see p. 55) and of Edward, 2nd Duke of York (grandson of Edward III) successively. After the death of the Duke of York at Agincourt, his widow was allowed to hold the lordship of the Isle of Wight, which had been granted to her husband. Her body was brought from Carisbrooke Castle to be buried here, in great state. Her tomb is the earliest in the Chapel, and formerly stood in the centre. The recumbent figure is dressed in a long cloak and robes, which cover the feet; a wimple and plaited veil are on the head. An engraving is preserved of a fine triple canopy in wood, which has disappeared; it was painted with the Crucifixion on a blue ground studded with stars.

Elizabeth, Duchess of Northumberland, d. 1776, 'In her own Right BARONESS PERCY, LUCY, POYNINGS, FITZ PAYNE, BRYAN, & LATIMER Sole Heiress of ALGERNON DUKE OF SOMERSET & of the ancient EARLS OF NORTHUMBERLAND'. She married Sir Hugh Smithson, who took the name of Percy and was created Duke of Northumberland in 1766. Her funeral was the occasion of an uproar. The crowd that collected to witness it broke down the canopy of John of Eltham's tomb (page 58), an irreparable piece of damage. Several persons were injured, and the confusion which ensued was so great that the burial-service could not be resumed until after midnight. *Adam des., Read sculpt.*

Winifred, Marchioness of Winchester, d. 1586, daughter of Sir John Brydges, Lord Mayor of London, who, as Lieutenant of the Tower, had attended Lady Jane Grey on the scaffold, and had received, as a dying gift, her prayer-book, still extant in the British Museum. By her first husband, Sir Richard Sackville, Winifred was mother of **Lord Buckhurst,** the poet, whose figure kneels below, and of **Anne, Lady Dacre** (d. 1595), widow of Gregory, 10th Lord Dacre, who also kneels beneath, with her infant behind her. She bequeathed her fortune to found a hospital for sick women and children in Tothill Fields, Westminster (the Emmanuel Hospital, pulled down in 1891), schools and the pensions for poor women still called the Dacre Bequest. She married as her second husband, John Paulet, 2nd Marquess of Winchester.

Above is a portion of a monument with reclining figure which was removed to make way for the Percy vault; **Elizabeth Cecil,** d. 1591, daughter of the Earl of Rutland, *suo jure* **Baroness Ros** or Roos, a title inherited from the Rutland family, mother of Lord Ros, and wife of William Cecil, afterwards Earl of Exeter, a grandson of the great Lord Burghley.

William Dudley (also called Sutton), d. 1483, **Bishop of Durham** (1476–83) and previously Dean of Windsor (1473–8). He was the third son of John, Lord Dudley, and uncle to Edmund Dudley, Henry VII's minister. A brass of the bishop in his vestments, together with the inscription, has disappeared from the tomb which has an elaborate canopy.

A pyramid of black and white marble supports a vase containing the heart of **Anne Sophia,** d. 1605, infant daughter of the **Comte de Beaumont,** Ambassador from the French Court to James I.

Against the south wall is a large monument erected by Lord Burghley to his second wife, **Mildred Cecil,** d. 1589, and their daughter **Anne, Countess of Oxford,** d. 1588. Lady Burghley was one of the four learned daughters of Sir Anthony Cooke; she was also well known for her active benevolence. She died at Burghley House, in the Strand. The Latin inscriptions, by Lord Burghley himself, commemorate his grief for the loss of those 'who were dear to him beyond the whole race of womankind'. He is represented in the upper story, kneeling in his robes of State. He was buried at Stamford, but a grand funeral service was held here in his honour. Below, on the sarcophagus, are the effigies of his wife and daughter. Lady Burghley's son, Robert Cecil, kneels at her feet, and her three grand-daughters, Elizabeth, Bridget, and Susannah, at her head. The monument is 24 feet high, and is composed of different coloured marbles, with much gilding.

Sir George and **Lady Fane,** d. 1618, a mural monument with kneeling figures beneath a canopy occupies the altar site. It was erected by her husband 'who, as his effigy is placed near hers, so intends their ashes shall be united'.

Nicholas Carew (d. 1470), feudal Baron of Carew in Pembrokeshire, and **Margaret,** his wife (d. 1470), daughter of John, Lord Dinham. A grey marble altar tomb, from which the brass shields and inscription have disappeared.

Nicholas Bagenall, d. 1688, an infant two months old, 'by his Nurs, unfortunately overlayd', the son of Nicholas Bagenall, of the Isle of Anglesey.

Anne, Duchess of Somerset, d. 1587, widow of the Protector Somerset, sister-in-law to Queen Jane Seymour and aunt by marriage to Edward VI. She was a daughter of Sir Edward Stanhope of Rampton, Nottingham. Her eldest son, Lord Hertford, 'in this dolefull dutie carefull and diligent, doth consecrate this monument to his deere parent'. 'A mannish, or rather a devilish woman,' says Sir John Hayward, 'for any imperfectibilities intolerable, but for pride monstrous, exceeding subtle and violent.' An alabaster effigy of the Duchess in her robes lies under a recessed arch with richly decorated soffit.

Isabella Susannah, d. 1812, wife of Algernon Percy, **Earl of Beverley.** *Nollekens sculpt.*

Lady Jane Clifford, d. 1679, great-grand-daughter of the Protector Somerset.

Elizabeth Cecil, d. 1591, daughter of Lord Cobham, and wife of Sir Robert Cecil, afterwards 1st Earl of Salisbury, son of Lord Burghley. She was Lady of the Bedchamber to Queen Elizabeth. An alabaster altar tomb with black marble slab, erected by her husband, who wrote the epitaphs in rhyme on either side, recording the mutual affection of husband and wife.

In the pavement near the above monument is the brass figure of a man in plate armour. **Sir Humphrey Stanley,** d. 1505, knighted for his services by Henry VII on Bosworth Field.

In the centre of the Chapel is the altar tomb of **Sir George Villiers,** d. 1605, and **Mary (Beaumont),** his second wife, d. 1632, the parents of George Villiers, Duke of Buckingham,[1] the favourite of James and Charles I. At her son's request Lady Villiers was made Countess of Buckingham in her own right by James I in 1618. Clarendon relates the story of Sir George Villiers's ghost appearing shortly before the assassination of his

---

[1] *See page 73.*

son at the bedside of an old servant, bidding him to go to the Duke 'and tell him if he did not do somewhat to ingratiate himself to the people, or at least to abate the extreme malice they had against him, he would be suffered to live but a short time'.[1] Lady Buckingham also had so strong a presentiment of her son's end that she was quite calm on hearing of his murder, though she had taken

leave of him previously 'in the highest agony imaginable'. The white marble tomb, with recumbent figures in the costume of the time, was set up by the Countess, a year before her death, at the cost of £560. *Nicholas Stone sculpt*. The remains of Catherine de Valois, Henry V's Queen, which were moved several times, lay in the Buckingham vault for over a century.[2]

[1] History of the Rebellion, *vol. i, page 74.*

[2] *See page 94.*

CHAPEL OF HENRY VII [*See plan, page 62*]

THIS MAGNIFICENT CHAPEL was built by Henry VII in place of the old Lady Chapel,[1] which was pulled down to make way for this *orbis miraculum*, or 'wonder of the world', as it was called by Leland. Besides the original Lady Chapel of Henry III, the small Chapel of St Erasmus, built by Queen Elizabeth Woodville, was demolished. The tenement leased to the poet Chaucer also stood on this site.

When Henry VII was firmly established upon the throne he appears to have suffered from an uneasy conscience, and to have determined to try and make his peace with Heaven by founding a splendid Chapel to the Virgin, 'in whom,' he says in his will, 'hath ever been my most singulier trust and confidence . . . and by whom I have hitherto in al myne adversities ev'r had my special comforte and relief'. The King richly endowed this Chapel, in order to make provision for the celebration of masses and the distribution of alms for the welfare of his soul, 'perpetually for ever while the world shall endure', as he reiterates, little foreseeing how quickly his own son was to sweep away a great part of his work. He also desired to give lustre to the new dynasty, of which he was the founder, by providing a magnificent place of burial for himself and his family. In order to give prominence to his claim, as a descendant of John of Gaunt, to be a member of the House of Lancaster and a relation of Henry VI, by this time popularly revered as a saint, Henry VII originally intended to build a tomb in the Chapel, in which the 'bodie and reliquies of our uncle of blessed Memorie King Henry VI' might repose, and for whose canonization he applied to Pope Julius II. But the Court of Rome demanded a larger sum in return than the King's avarice was prepared to grant, so the matter was dropped, and the connexion of Henry VI with the new Chapel gradually faded away. One of its altars was subsequently dedicated to his memory, but his body was never brought here from Windsor, though a licence for its removal was obtained from the Pope, and a large sum paid to the King by the Abbey for the expenses of its transit.

'On the 24th daie of January (1503), a quarter of an hour afore three of the clocke at after noone of the same daie, the first stone of our Ladie Chapell within the monasterie of Westminster was laid, on behalf of the

[1] *The dimensions of the old Lady Chapel are believed (from the foundations which remain) to have corresponded with those of the present one, without including its aisles and eastern chapels.*

king, by the hands of John Islip, Abbot of the same monasterie . . . and diverse others.' Recent research points out that the designer of this Chapel was probably one of Henry's three master masons, Robert Vertue, whose brother, William Vertue, vaulted St George's Chapel, Windsor, *c.* 1505. The King's will and numerous indentures which remain show with what minute care he planned every detail of his new foundation, providing large sums of ready money for the building, and for the monument to himself and his wife. The total cost was about £14,000. He endowed the Chapel with estates obtained by the dissolution of other religious houses for the maintenance of the additional priests required, and for the charities established in connexion with it. The King also bequeathed crucifixes and costly services of plate for the different altars, embroidered draperies, and other ornaments, so that the interior must have presented a very rich and splendid appearance. The windows were filled with painted glass, by the hand of the famous Bernard Flower, whose designs for these were copied soon after his decease in the splendid glass now to be seen in King's College Chapel, Cambridge. The upper were filled with large figures, the lower with the Tudor badges. Some fragments of these remain in the west window and in the aisles. The royal badges recur in every part of the Chapel; prominent amongst them are the red rose of Lancaster and the white rose of York, both separately and conjoined; the portcullis of the Beauforts, which Henry VII inherited through his mother, and to which he added the motto *Altera securitas*, implying that as the portcullis gave additional security to the gate, so his descent through his mother added strength to his other titles; the root of daisies, the Countess of Richmond's especial cognizance; the leopards of England; the fleurs-de-lis; the Welsh dragon; the initials H.R. surmounted by the Crown on a bush (in memory of the King's hasty coronation on the field of Bosworth with the coronet of Richard III, which was found hanging on a hawthorn bush); the greyhound for Richmond; and a falcon within an open fetter-lock, a badge of her father, Edward IV.

The fine gates at the entrance to the Chapel are made of bronze mounted on a framework of wood. They closely resemble the screen round the founder's tomb, and are no doubt also by the same hand, of *Thomas Ducheman*. They are adorned with repetitions of the badges referred to above. The Chapel was finished about 1519, but 'in the springtime of the Reformation' it was stripped of some of its splendid fittings. The destruction of the glass, of the

Gates of Henry VII's Chape

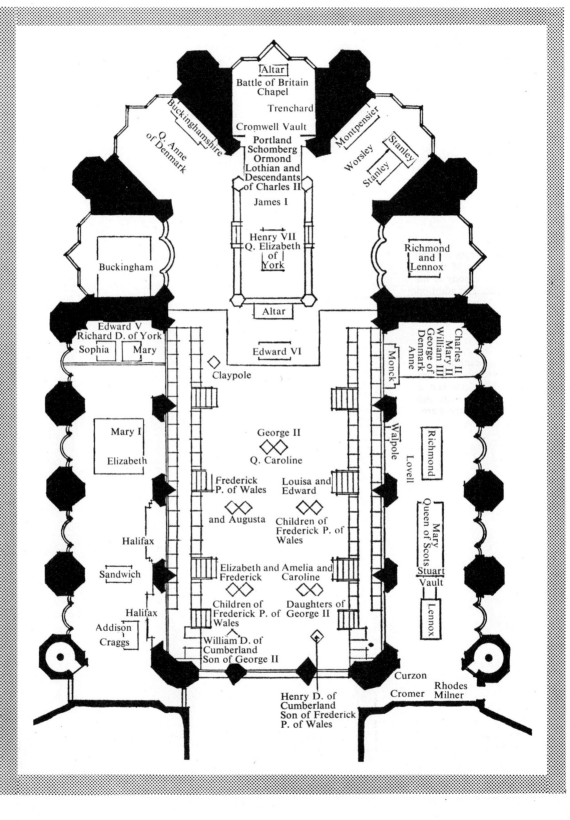

images of saints, and of the altars continued at intervals under Edward VI and Elizabeth and was probably not completed until the Civil War. In January 1540, the Abbey was surrendered to Henry VIII by Abbot Boston and was immediately dissolved, like all the other religious houses throughout the country. After the Dissolution the Chapel was used for the 'early morning prayers' which were held here and not in the Choir after 1660. The consecration of various bishops also took place here until 1708, and periodical meetings of Convocation. But unfortunately the exterior and interior of the Chapel were greatly neglected, and by 1803, the outside had become an 'almost shapeless mass of ruins'. Owing chiefly to the exertions of Dean Vincent a Parliamentary grant was obtained for its restoration in 1807, the necessary repairs were immediately set on foot, and gradually carried on until completed in 1822. Gayfere, the Abbey mason, working under the Surveyor of the Fabric, Wyatt, practically destroyed all that remained of the outside sculptures, and rebuilt the exterior.

The stalls date from different periods. Originally they occupied only three of the bays on each side, a stone screen dividing the body of the Chapel from the eastern bay of each aisle. The additional seats were added when the Chapel was fitted up for the installation of the Knights of the Bath in 1725, when the Order was re-constituted by George I, and the Deans of Westminster declared perpetual Deans of the Order. The extra canopies required for the new stalls were obtained by cutting some of the canopies on the south side in half. The banner of each knight hangs over the stall appointed for his use, to the back of which is attached a small plate of copper, emblazoned with his arms. Below the stalls are seats for the knights' esquires (there are three to each knight), with their arms engraved on copper plates. A small wooden portrait figure of Henry VI is on a ledge of the Great Master's stall. These stalls retain the misericordes of the monks, who used the Lady Chapel, and afterwards the present Chapel for the services of Our Lady. The seats are hinged in order to give support to the brethren who had to stand during the long hours of their services. They are decorated with curious carvings, which resemble the engravings by Albert Dürer and other German artists.

A range of statues of saints standing on pedestals in richly carved niches, surrounds the interior of the Chapel below the clerestory windows. There were originally 107 figures, 95 of which remain. The most wonderful part of the Chapel is the incomparable roof, with its fan-work tracery and carved pendants, hanging as it seems in mid-air, so delicate is the stonework. The interior of the Chapel, the roof and the whole of the stonework were cleaned in 1934. **In 1725 this Chapel was first used for the installations of the Knights of the Bath,** George I presided in person; from that time till 1813 the installations took place here with magnificent ceremony. No installations were held after 1813 and the banners of the knights, which hung above their stalls, fell into decay, and finally, before the re-inauguration of the Order, the tattered remnants were removed, and where possible returned to the families whose names were inscribed upon them. On 12 July 1913, after a century of neglect, the Order was re-inaugurated by King George V, and his uncle, the Duke of Connaught, was appointed Great Master.

The banners of the forty-six new knights then installed were hung over their respective stalls, and their name plates affixed to the back of each.

Further installations took place at services held in 1920, 1924, 1928, 1935, 1951, 1956, 1960, and 1964.

In 1955 Queen Elizabeth II and Queen Elizabeth the Queen Mother presented a **sword which belonged to King George VI.** It was presented to him by his father King George V when he entered the Navy, and was the sword which King George VI always wore when in naval uniform and with which he conferred the accolade of knighthood. It has been placed in a case by the Sovereign's stall.

A brass plate on the floor commemorates the presentation of the marble pavement by **Dr Henry Killigrew,** d. 1700, Prebendary of Westminster (1660–1700).

South Aisle

Evelyn Baring, 1st Earl of Cromer, G.C.B., O.M., b. 1841, d. 1917, statesman, diplomatist, and administrator, 'Regenerator of Egypt'. A white marble tablet with medallion portrait. *W. Goscombe John sculpt.*

Alfred Milner, 1st Viscount Milner, K.G., b. 1854, d. 1925, Under-Secretary of Finance in Egypt (1889–92), Secretary of State for War 1918–19. A medallion portrait inscribed 'Servant of the State'. Milner rendered great services to South Africa as High Commissioner 1897, and Governor of the Transvaal 1901. Buried at Great Wigsell, Bodiam. A memorial tablet was also placed in Canterbury Cathedral. *Ledward sculpt*

Cecil Rhodes, b. 1853, d. 1902, Imperialist and Founder of the Rhodes Scholarships.

George Nathaniel Curzon, 1st Marquess Curzon of Kedleston, K.G., b. 1859, d. 1925. Curzon was Under-Secretary of State for India 1891, and Viceroy of India from 1899 to 1905. Secretary of State for Foreign Affairs (1919–24). Chancellor of Oxford University and President of the Royal Geographical Society. *Sir Bertram McKennal sculpt.*

The first tomb is that of **Margaret Douglas, Countess of Lennox,** b. 1515, d. 1578, daughter of Margaret Tudor, the widow of James IV of Scotland, by her second husband, the Earl of Angus. She was niece to Henry VIII, and grandmother to James I through her son Lord Darnley's marriage with Mary, Queen of Scots. Lady Lennox was extremely beautiful, and was the cause of Lord Thomas Howard's imprisonment in the Tower by Henry VIII for becoming affianced to her without her uncle's consent. She too was imprisoned for a time, but on the death of Lord Thomas she was released, and married Matthew Stuart, Earl of Lennox, 6 July 1544. She died in poverty at Hackney, and was buried at the expense of her cousin, Queen Elizabeth. The alabaster effigy of the Countess, in her robes of State, lies on a marble tomb, painted and gilt; at the sides are the kneeling figures of her four daughters and four sons. Foremost of the latter is Henry, Lord Darnley, dressed in armour and a long cloak, with a crown over his head. Behind him kneels Charles, Earl of Lennox, d. 1576,[1] buried in his mother's grave.

Mary, Queen of Scots, beheaded 1587, the daughter of James V of Scotland and Mary of Guise, b. 8 December 1542, a week before her father died, broken-hearted by his defeat at Solway Moss. Mary was betrothed to the French Dauphin and educated at the French Court. Her

---

[1] *Father of Arabella Stuart.*

Misericorde Seat with Stall-Plates

young husband, Francis II, died within a year of his accession to the Crown, and Mary left France in 1560 never to return. She married Darnley in 1565, and had one child, James VI of Scotland and I of England. After Darnley's mysterious murder (1567) Mary married James Hepburn, Earl of Bothwell (d. 1578), one of the men who was suspected of having contrived his death, but was shortly after obliged to divorce him. A fervent Roman Catholic and a dangerous claimant to the English Crown, she was Elizabeth's deadliest foe. She was captured by the English in 1568, and, after nineteen years' imprisonment, executed at Fotheringay Castle, 8 February 1587. The remains of the Queen were first buried in Peterborough Cathedral with great solemnity by Elizabeth's orders, but James I afterwards had them brought to Westminster, that the 'like honour might be done to the body of his dearest mother and the like monument be extant to her that had been done to others and to his dear sister the late Queen Elizabeth'. The two Queens rest opposite one another in the aisles of this Chapel; their monuments were both erected by James I. The white marble effigy of Mary, finely sculptured, lies on a sarcophagus, under an elaborate canopy. She wears a close-fitting coif, a laced ruff, and a long mantle fastened by a brooch. At her feet sits the Scottish lion crowned.

The tomb was not completed for several years; in 1607 a royal warrant ordered the payment of £825 10s. and 'all further sums as the marble shall amount to', to Cornelius Cure, master mason of the works, and as late as 1611 a pattern for this tomb, to cost £2,000, is mentioned as ready to show the King. The grille, which originally protected it, has been replaced round the tomb. *Wm. and Cornelius Cure sculpt.*

An inscription in the floor records the burial in Queen Mary's vault of the following:

Henry Frederick, Prince of Wales, b. 1594, d. of fever 1612, the eldest son of James I. A prince of great promise, and the hope of the Puritan Party from his violent anti-Catholic opinions.

Lady Arabella Stuart, b. 1575, d. 1615, the daughter of Charles, Earl of Lennox, and Elizabeth Cavendish, stepdaughter of that Earl of Shrewsbury under whose care the Queen of Scots spent part of her long captivity. She was always looked upon as a possible claimant to the throne, and was the centre of many political intrigues. Her marriage, without permission, in 1610 with Sir William Seymour (afterwards Marquess of Hertford), a representative of the Suffolk branch of the royal family, contributed to make her doubly dangerous in the eyes of James I, who imprisoned his unfortunate cousin in the Tower,

Vaulting of Henry VII's Chapel with Banners of Knights Grand Cross of the Order of the Bath

where she lost her reason and died in a few years. Her body was brought here at midnight by river, and laid 'with no solemnity' upon the coffin of her aunt Mary.

Four children of Charles I: **Prince Charles**, d. 1629, his firstborn, an infant; the **Princess Anne**, d. 1640, 'a very pregnant lady above her age, and died in her infancy when not full four years old. Being told to pray by those about her at the last, "I am not able," saith she, "to say my long prayer (meaning the Lord's Prayer); but I will say my short one, 'Lighten mine eyes, O Lord, lest I sleep the sleep of death.'" This done, the little lamb gave up the ghost.'[1] **Henry, Duke of Gloucester,** b. 1639, d. 1660, the youngest son; he came over to England with his elder sister, **Mary, Princess Royal,** b. 1631, d. 1660, wife of William of Orange and mother of William III, of England 'to congratulate the happiness of their brother's miraculous restitution', and both died of smallpox at Whitehall Palace.

Elizabeth, Queen of Bohemia, b. 1596, d. 1662, at Leicester House, Strand. The grandmother of George I, she was the eldest daughter of James I, and wife of Frederick, Elector Palatine, the unhappy 'Winter King' of Bohemia. After his death Lord Craven, who is said,

but without foundation, to have married her, placed his London house at her disposal and this enabled her to have a peaceful end to her life 'after all her sorrows and afflictions'. Her son, **Prince Rupert,** b. 1619, d. 1682, fought for his uncle, Charles I, with much gallantry in the Civil Wars. He was Admiral of the Fleet during the Dutch wars under Charles II and James II, and founded the Hudson Bay Company, 1670. First Lord of the Admiralty 1673–9. **Anne, Duchess of York,** b. 1637, d. 1671, first wife of James II, whose accession she did not live to see. She was the daughter of Lord Clarendon, and the mother of the two Queens, Mary II and Anne. In this vault also are buried many children of **James II,** and also of **Queen Anne,** none of whom survived infancy excepting **William, Duke of Gloucester,** who died in 1700, aged eleven, 'of a fever occasioned by excessive dancing on his birthday'.

Margaret (Stanley), Countess of Richmond and Derby, b. 1443, d. 1509, best known as the Lady Margaret Beaufort and the mother of Henry VII by her second husband, Edmund Tudor, Earl of Richmond (d. 1456), the eldest son of Owen Tudor and Henry V's widow, Catherine de Valois. Margaret's third husband was Lord Henry Stafford, son of the Duke of Buckingham. She married fourthly Thomas, Lord Stanley, who deserted

---

[1] *Fuller's* Worthies.

Richard III, and crowned his stepson Henry with Richard's coronet, on the battlefield of Bosworth; he was afterwards created Earl of Derby. The Lady Margaret will always be remembered as the foundress of two colleges at Cambridge–Christ's and St John's–and a Chair of Divinity at both Oxford and Cambridge. She was a great lady, to whom the King her son owed much, and 'whose notable acts and charitable deeds all her life exercised cannot in a small volume be expressed'. She was the patroness of Wynkyn de Worde and of Caxton, whose printing-press was in the Abbey almonry, and by her protection of these two printers encouraged the development of printing in England. Lady Margaret not only contributed to the endowment of her son's new Chapel, but established charities of her own in connexion with it, one of which–a small weekly dole of 'alms and bread' to poor widows–still exists. These many fruits of her intellectual and benevolent activities are recorded in the plain and just epitaph upon her tomb, composed by Erasmus, and for which St John's College paid him 20s. In short, as her friend and confessor Bishop Fisher said in her funeral sermon, 'Every one that knew her loved her, and everything that she said or did became her'. She died (29 June 1509) at the Abbot's house, Cheyney Gates, now the Deanery. The tomb[1] resembles that of Henry VII; patterns were prepared for it by Meynnart Wewyck, a Fleming, but the execution was carried out by *Pietro Torrigiani*, who was then at work on Henry VII's monument. The greater part of the cost (£4,000) was defrayed by Margaret's executors, Sir Thomas Lovell and Bishop Fisher, and Torrigiani undertook to finish the work by 1 February 1513. The portrait effigy of Margaret in her old age is Torrigiani's masterpiece: she wears a widow's dress with a hood and long mantle, her feet rest on a hind couchant, the delicate and most characteristic wrinkled hands are raised in prayer. The effigy and canopy are of gilt bronze, as are the coats of arms arranged within flowered wreaths, like those on the tomb of Henry VII; the tomb itself is of black marble. The iron grate or grille has been replaced, after having been lost for over ninety years. In 1823 the surveyor of the fabric, Wyatt, sold this and other grates on behalf of the Dean and Chapter for about £100. The pieces of two of these were put away in a country residence, those of Margaret and Mary, Queen of Scots being mixed up together, until they were discovered and disentangled by a London dealer. The National Art Collections Fund purchased Margaret's grate in 1915 and presented it to the Dean and Chapter, by whom it was re-erected in its original position. It was constructed by an English smith, Cornelius Symondson, and the cost was defrayed by St John's College, Cambridge, and paid in instalments; it was finished and gilded in 1529. Originally the whole, which was made of Bilbao iron, was elaborately painted and decorated with coats of arms, crests, fleurs-de-lis, and other ornaments. The stone supports were made by Raynold Bray, Citizen and Freemason of London, and cost £2 13s. 4d.

On the wall close by is a bronze relievo bust, enclosed in a modern frame, presented to the Dean and Chapter, 1903, by Sir J. C. Robinson. The bust, which is by *Torrigiani*, represents his patron, **Sir Thomas Lovell**, d. 1524, Chancellor of the Exchequer, a lover of art, and a great builder, and was originally over the gateway of

Lovell's country house, East Harling Manor, Norfolk. Lovell was at one time Speaker of the House of Commons, and High Steward of both Universities, a benefactor also to Caius College, Cambridge, and to Lincoln's Inn. As executor to Henry VII and to Lady Margaret, he superintended the erection and design of their tombs.

Catherine, Lady Walpole, (d. 1737), daughter of John Shorter of Bybrook, Kent, first wife of the great Whig Minister. The statue, copied from a Roman figure of Modesty, was erected to his mother by Horace Walpole, in 1754, who also wrote the inscription. *Valory sculpt.*

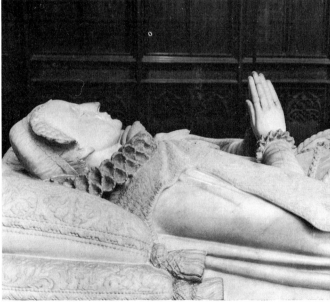

Effigies of Lady Margaret Beaufort (above) *and Mary, Queen of Scots* (below)

---

[1] *See R. F. Scott, 'On the contracts for the Tomb of the Lady Margaret Beaufort' etc. (Archaeologia, vol. lxvi, 1915).*

Tombs of the Countess of Lennox (foreground) *and Mary, Queen of Scots* (behind)

In the royal vault below are buried:

Charles II, b. 1630, d. 1685. The magnificence of his coronation (23 April 1661) is described by Pepys and Clarendon. 'It is impossible,' says Pepys, 'to relate the glory of this day, expressed in the clothes of them that rid (in the procession) and their horses and horsecloths.' It contrasted strangely with his funeral, for 'he was very obscurely buried at night without any manner of pomp, and soon forgotten after all his vanity'.

Queen Mary II, b. 1662, elder daughter of James II, died of smallpox at Hampton Court, 28 December 1694. She was crowned here with her husband, William of Orange,[1] in 1689. The short King and tall Queen walked side by side, as joint Sovereigns, carrying the sword between them. The Queen's funeral, 5 March 1695, was attended by both Houses of Parliament, the Lords 'robed in scarlet and ermine, the Commons in long and black mantles. No preceding Sovereign had ever been followed to the grave by Parliament; for till then Parliament had always expired with the Sovereign.'[2] Purcell wrote special anthems and Archbishop Tenison preached the sermon.

William III, d. 1702, born at The Hague, 1650, the grandson of Charles I, by his daughter Princess Mary's marriage with William of Orange. 'The least popular, but, by his public acts, one of the most deserving of monarchs', was buried here with great simplicity. William founded Greenwich Hospital in memory of his wife. Both added much to Hampton Court Palace.

Queen Anne, b. 1665, d. 1714, the second daughter of James II by his first wife, Lady Anne Hyde. She was married to **Prince George of Denmark** (d. 1708, youngest son of Frederick III, King of Denmark) at Whitehall in 1683. Ten days only elapsed between the funeral of William III and Anne's coronation, to which ceremony, owing to gout, she was carried from St James's Palace. The Queen, her husband and their many infants rest in the vault below.

George Monck ('General Monck'), b. 1608, d. 1670, created **1st Duke of Albemarle** by Charles II, in whose restoration to the throne he played a leading part. He first distinguished himself when a captain in many actions against the Dutch Fleet, under their famous admirals de Tromp and Van Ruyter, in the English Channel and the North Sea. Under the Commonwealth he was appointed General-in-Chief of the Forces on land and Admiral of the Fleet at sea. He retained both these posts after the Restoration by the King's wish. But at the end of his career disaster overtook the successful admiral; in June 1667 the Dutch broke the chain laid by his orders across the Medway, burnt eight great warships, and captured Monck's flagship, the *Royal Charles*. From this time Monck took little part in naval battles, an old wound received in the Civil War tormented him, he became increasingly infirm, and died 3 January 1670, 'standing upright in his chair like a Roman soldier, his chamber like a tent, open with all his soldiers about him'. His funeral was delayed for three months, owing to the King's dilatoriness, he having offered and failed to pay the expenses. It finally took place 30 April 1670, with great pomp, in the North Aisle of Henry VII's Chapel. Charles himself attending as chief mourner. His son **Christopher, 2nd Duke of Albemarle**, b. 1653, d. 1688, was buried in the same grave. Monck's funeral armour is in the Museum.

The monument was not put up till 1720, the expenses defrayed by the bequest of Monck's son. *Kent des., Scheemakers sculpt.*

The Nave

William Augustus, Duke of Cumberland, b. 1721, d. 1765, third son of George II, for some time Commander-in-Chief of the British Forces; notorious as 'the Butcher' of Culloden.

Caroline Elizabeth, b. 1713, d. 1757, and **Amelia Sophia Eleonora,** b. 1711, d. 1786, unmarried daughters of George II. **Frederick Louis, Prince of Wales,** b. 1707 at Hanover, d. 1751 at Leicester House, eldest son of George II, and father of George III. He was buried without anthem or organ, 13 April. 'Here lies Fred who was alive and is dead. . . . There's no more to be said' his only epitaph. His wife, **Augusta of Saxe Gotha, Princess of Wales,** d. 1772, married to him at St James's Palace, 1736. She lived to see her son George III on the throne. Five of their other children are also buried here: **Elizabeth Caroline,** d. 1759, his second daughter. **Louisa Anne,** d. 1768, his third daughter. **Edward Augustus, Duke of York,** d. 1767, his second son, brought home to be buried from Monaco. **Henry Frederick, Duke of Cumberland,** d. 1790, his fourth son. **Frederick William,** d. 1765, his fifth son.

George II, born at Hanover, 1683, d. 25 October 1760, at Kensington Palace; and crowned here with Caroline in 1727, 'with all the pomp and magnificence that could be contrived'. His funeral (11 November) which was also very stately, and 'absolutely a noble sight', is graphically described by Horace Walpole, who 'walked as a rag of quality' in the procession.[3]

Queen Caroline of Anspach, b. 1683, d. 1737, Consort of George II, married at Hanover in 1705. Her husband, as a last proof of that unalterable attachment to her which he testified so strangely, directed that his wife's remains should not be separated from his own in death. 'Accordingly the two coffins were placed in a large black marble sarcophagus inscribed with their joint names, and with their sceptres crossed, and one side of each of the wooden coverings withdrawn.'[4] Handel's anthem, 'When the ear heard her, then it blessed her', was composed for her funeral.

Buried at the head of his grandfather Henry VII lies **Edward VI,** b. 1537, d. 1553, son of Henry VIII and Jane Seymour. The Burial Service of the English Prayer Book was used for the first time over a Sovereign at his funeral, where 'the greatest moan was made for him as ever was heard or seen'.[5] He was laid beneath the altar at the head of Henry VII's tomb, and masses were to be said there for his soul 'perpetually and for ever'. This altar was broken down in an outbreak of iconoclastic zeal at the beginning (1643) of the Civil Wars, and an oak table used in its place. Sir Gilbert Scott constructed a cedarwood altar in 1870, which was used for sixty years. The marble frieze of the original altar, with the Renaissance carving by *Bernadette de Rovezzaro,* or by *Torrigiani* himself, was found by Dean Stanley during his search for James I's coffin in the vaults below, and two of the original pillars were afterwards discovered in the Ashmolean Museum at Oxford and incorporated in Sir Gilbert Scott's black

---

[1] *The Coronation Chair made for Mary is now in the Undercroft.*   [2] *Macaulay.*

[3] *Walpole's* Letters *(ed. Toynbee), vol. iv, pages 455–7.*
[4] *Stanley's* Memorials, *page 167.*   [5] *Grey Friars'* Chronicle.

Edward the Confessor and St Vincent: medallion on Henry VII's tomb

marble altar. Three strange fragments were inserted into the back of this altar by Stanley's instructions, a sacred stone from an Abyssinian altar brought from Magdala in 1868, a fragment of jasper from the Norman altar of Canterbury Cathedral, destroyed by fire in 1174, and a piece of mosaic from the Greek Church at Damascus. **A new altar** in the Renaissance style was presented as a gift from some of the Knights of the Bath, and reproduces the original sixteenth-century altar as depicted in engravings. It was designed by *Sir Walter Tapper, R.A.* (see page 107) in 1935. Torrigiani's two pillars with two reproductions support the marble table. The Italian work

on the frieze has been lengthened and reproduced with the addition of the Badge and Star of the Order of the Bath.

In the centre of this altar is an Italian picture of the Virgin and Child by Bartolommeo Vivarini (late fifteenth century), presented by Lord Lee of Fareham, G.C.B.; above is a canopy resting upon four decorated Corinthian columns.

Beyond the altar is the tomb of the founder and his Queen.

Henry VII, b. 1456, d. 1509, the son of Edmund Tudor, Earl of Richmond, and Margaret Beaufort, the descendant of John of Gaunt and Catherine Swynford. Tradition says that Richard III's crown was placed on Henry's head on the victorious field of Bosworth (1485); he was crowned again in the Abbey, but without much ceremony, his marriage with Elizabeth of York a few months afterwards being by far the greater pageant of the two. The first person to be buried in her husband's Chapel was his wife, **Elizabeth of York,** b. 1465, d. 1503, eldest daughter of Edward IV, and the last of the House of York to wear the English Crown. She died in the Tower about a month after the ceremony of laying the foundation-stone of the Chapel and was temporarily buried in one of the side chapels until the new building was sufficiently advanced for her grave to be made in it. The magnificent funeral given her by the avaricious Henry was considered a great proof of his affection. Her body was brought through the city in a gorgeous hearse, on which lay her effigy in Royal robes, with 'hair dishevelled' and with her crown and sceptre.[1] Eight ladies on white horses followed behind, and 'a grand procession of the religious, and the Mayor and Commonalty of London, amidst an innumerable quantity of torches, that everywhere illuminated the streets as they passed and made a glorious appearance'. At Charing Cross the procession was met by the Abbots of Westminster and Bermondsey and escorted to the Abbey.

The King in his will gave minute directions for the monument to himself and his wife, and for innumerable masses to be said for their souls; he also directed that his obsequies should have respect 'somewhat to our dignitie Roial, eviteng alwaies dampnable pompe and outeragious superfluities'. His funeral was, however, performed with great, if not with 'outeragious', magnificence. He died at Richmond, and his body was carried in state to the Abbey, where it rested on a splendid hearse all night, and was buried with much ceremony the following day. The agreements between the executors of Henry VII and the Florentine artist Pietro Torrigiani for the construction of the tomb still exist. It was to cost £1,500, and appears to have been finished by 1518. The recumbent portrait effigies of the King and Queen, executed with fine simplicity in gilt bronze, lie side by side, as directed by the will. The black marble tomb has a beautifully carved frieze, and is adorned with medallions in copper gilt, representing the Virgin and Henry's ten patron saints; amongst them are St Michael and St George, St Christopher carrying the infant Christ, St Edward the Confessor, and St Barbara with her tower. At either end the King's arms are supported by brass cherubs. A small altar where precious relics, such as the leg of St George and a piece of the true Cross, are kept, used to stand at the foot of the tomb. The fine screen or 'closure' of bronze was partly erected before Henry's death. The upper part of it has gone, and some of the statues have disappeared from the niches, but on it may be seen the badges of Henry VII, the Welsh dragon, the greyhound for Richmond, and the Tudor roses. Elegiac verses, by Skelton, Poet Laureate to Henry VIII, on 'parchment tables' used to hang on this screen.

James I, b. 1566, d. 1625, the son of Mary, Queen of Scots and Henry, Lord Darnley. He succeeded to the Scottish throne as James VI and upon the death of Elizabeth I in 1603 united both countries under the English Crown. He was crowned by the new title of 'King of Great Britain, France, and Ireland'. His exact burial-place in the Abbey was unknown until Dean Stanley in 1869 brought to light the huge coffin, resting in the vault below, beside those of Henry VII and his Queen. James died at his country palace, Theobalds, 27 March 1625, and his funeral took place on 5 May. Dean Williams preached the sermon, his eldest son and successor, Charles I, attended in state as chief mourner, and a grand hearse with the late King's effigy upon it was placed in the Abbey before the ceremony.

Five small chapels form the apse of Henry VII's Chapel. On the south side is the tomb of **Ludovic (Stuart), Duke of Richmond and Lennox,** b. 1574, d. 1624, cousin to James I, and his **Duchess,** d. 1639, **Frances** (widow of Edward Seymour, Earl of Hertford), who erected this huge monument, with enormous bronze figures of Hope, Truth, Charity and Faith supporting the canopy. Against the east wall, an urn, mounted on a pyramid, contains the heart of **Esmé (Stuart), Duke of Richmond and Lennox,** who died in Paris, aged eleven, 1660. In the vault below lie: Esmé's father, **James (Stuart),** b. 1612, d. 1655, **4th Duke of Lennox,** created **1st Duke of Richmond** by James I, and other members of the family. These include **Charles Stuart,** b. 1639, d. 1672, **Duke of Richmond and Lennox,** the last of the House of Lennox, and his widow, **Frances Theresa,**[2] b. 1647, d. 1702, whose wax effigy stood here till the nineteenth century. When the titles and honours of this family became extinct they were transferred by Charles II to one of his illegitimate children, **Charles,** son of the Duchess of Portsmouth, who thus became **Duke of Richmond and Lennox:** he died 1723, and was buried in this vault.

Arthur Penrhyn Stanley, b. 1815, d. 1881, Dean of Westminster 1864–81. The ideal for which he laboured unceasingly was to make the Abbey a national church. His *Memorials of Westminster Abbey* (1868), a companion volume to his *Memorials of Canterbury*, laid the foundations for this guide-book. His *Life of Dr Arnold* of Rugby is well known. *Boehm sculpt.*

The coffin of Stanley's wife, **Lady Augusta,** b. 1822, d. 1876, daughter of Thomas (Bruce), 7th Earl of Elgin, rests beneath his in the vault below. She was lady-in-waiting first to the Duchess of Kent, and afterwards to her daughter, Queen Victoria, who was much attached to her and personally attended the funeral.

Antoine Philippe, Duc de Montpensier, d. 1807, when an exile in England, younger son of Philippe Egalité, 5th Duke of Orleans and brother to Louis Philippe, afterwards King of France, who erected this monument. The Latin inscription was written by Dumouriez, the exiled general, who was famous for his scholarship. *Westmacott sculpt.* The remains of Queen Louise of Savoy, d. 1810, wife of Louis XVIII, rested in this vault for a time after her death at Hartwell, but were afterwards removed to Sardinia.

R.A.F. Chapel

Battle of Britain Memorial Window. In 1947 the easternmost Chapel was dedicated to the memory of the men of the Royal Air Force killed in the Battle of Britain (July–October 1940). The principal part of the Memorial is a stained and painted glass window designed and made by

---

[1] *The head of this effigy is preserved in the Museum (see page 113).*

[2] *See her wax effigy, page 115.*

Hugh Easton: The lower lights contain the badges of the fighter squadrons that took part in the battle. In four panels are shown visions which symbolize the Redemption, while above these are the Heavenly Seraphim with hands outstretched. At the foot of the window are the words from Shakespeare's *Henry V*: 'We few, we happy few, we band of brothers'. Below the window, in the stonework, is a hole now covered with glass, which was made by a fragment of a German bomb during the Battle of Britain in September 1940. The Altar, designed by Sir A. E. Richardson, R.A., is of English walnut. Below are sculptured figures of King Arthur and St George by Mr A. F. Hardiman, R.A. The Cross, candlesticks, candelabra, and chapel rails are of silver designed by Mr J. Seymour

Battle of Britain Window

Lindsay. The carpet was made in Tabriz about one hundred years ago. In the adjoining Chapel is a Roll of Honour on parchment and bound in blue leather. It contains the names of 1,495 pilots and air crew killed or mortally wounded in the battle. The names include men from the United Kingdom and the Colonies, Canadians, New Zealanders, Poles, Australians, Czechoslovaks, South Africans, Belgians, and one American.

The Memorial was unveiled by H.M. King George VI and dedicated on 10 July 1947.

Here is buried **Hugh M. Trenchard, 1st Viscount Trenchard**, b. 1873, d. 1956, Marshal and 'Father' of the R.A.F.

A stone in the pavement of the Chapel records the burial here of **Oliver Cromwell** and of some of the regicides and several of Cromwell's family. After the Restoration the bodies of Cromwell, Ireton, and Bradshaw were dug up and dragged to Tyburn, where they were hanged and decapitated, the heads being set on Westminster Hall. The others were re-interred on the north-east of the Abbey, near the house which had belonged to Archbishop Laud. The remains of **Elizabeth Claypole**, Cromwell's favourite daughter (d. 1658), were left undisturbed north of Henry VII's tomb.

Among the bodies ejected was that of **Isaac Dorislaus**, of Leyden, d. 1649, a Judge of the Court of Admiralty, who had helped to draw up the legal document containing the charge of treason against Charles I. He was sent as Parliamentary envoy to The Hague, and murdered there by the instigation of his Royalist enemies. His body was buried near Queen Elizabeth I's monument.

The chief of those buried in 'Oliver's Vault' were:

Oliver Cromwell, born at Huntingdon, 1599, died 3 September 1658 of a tertian ague. Cromwell was installed Lord Protector in the Court of Chancery, Westminster Hall, 1653, 'amid great shoutings of the people'. Several accounts remain of his death and state funeral. The body of the Protector lay in state at Somerset House, from thence it was escorted to the Abbey by an immense train of mourners, including the City Companies with their insignia draped in black, through streets lined with soldiers. 'The effigy or statue of the dead, made most lifelike, in royal robes, crown on head, in one hand the sceptre and in the other globe, was laid out on a bier richly adorned, and borne hither in a coach made for the purpose, open on every side and adorned with many plumes and banners.' Little more than two years elapsed before his body was exhumed.

The bodies of the following were also removed after the Restoration and thrown into a pit on the north green.

General Henry Ireton, b. 1611, d. 1651, the Protector's son-in-law. He died in camp while with the forces in Ireland, and was brought here for burial.

John Bradshaw, b. 1602, d. 1659, and his wife, **Mary (Marbury)**. He was President of the tribunal which condemned Charles I and died in the Deanery which had been granted to him as a residence.

Elizabeth Cromwell, d. 1645, mother of the Protector. **Jane Desborough**, d. 1656, sister of the Protector and wife of the Parliamentary general. **Anne Fleetwood**, probably grandchild of the Protector.

General and Admiral Richard Deane, b. 1610, d. 1653, cut in two by a cannon ball in a decisive naval engagement with the Dutch off the East Coast. His body lay in state at Greenwich, and received the honour of a public funeral here by order of Cromwell.

Colonel Humphrey Mackworth, d. 1654, a member of Cromwell's Council, and Governor of Shrewsbury during the Civil War.

Sir William Constable, Bt (1611); d. 1655, received knighthood in Ireland, when a young man, from Elizabeth's favourite, the Earl of Essex; at Edgehill he fought under his first commander's son, and afterwards was made Governor of Gloucester. He signed his name to the King's death warrant, and his estates were especially exempted from the general pardon after the Restoration.

Robert Blake, Admiral and General of the Parliamentary forces on land and at sea, born at Bridgwater 1599, died of wounds, 17 August 1657, as his ship was entering Plymouth Harbour, after destroying the Spanish West Indian Fleet at Santa Cruz. He had previously fought many engagements with the Dutch under Van Tromp in the Channel. Nelson honoured his memory in the words: 'I do not consider myself equal to Blake'. He reformed the pay of the sailors and made it a fixed rate which continued till the mutinies of 1797. Cromwell caused him to be buried in Henry VII Chapel, 'amongst the Kings with all the solemnity possible'.[1] In 1945 a tablet to his memory was placed in the south aisle of the Choir (see page 35).

Dennis Bond, d. 1658, one of Cromwell's Council, who took part in the King's trial.

After the ejection of the above, the vault was used as a place of burial for **James Butler, 1st Duke of Ormond**, b. 1610, d. 1688, and his family, as well as for various noblemen whose names are inscribed on the slab, including several of Charles II's illegitimate descendants, **Charles, Earl of Doncaster**, d. 1674, son of the Duke of Monmouth; **Charles Fitzroy, Duke of Cleveland and Southampton**, d. 1730; **Charles Fitz-Charles, Earl of Plymouth**, d. 1681. Besides these, **William Bentinck, 1st Earl of Portland**, b. 1649, d. 1709, the faithful friend of William III, whom he accompanied to England from Holland, and his descendants; also **Meinhard Schomberg, 3rd Duke of Schomberg**, b. 1641, d. 1719, who rose to the rank of general in the English army, like his father, who was killed at the Battle of the Boyne, 1690. The remains of the famous **Duke of Marlborough** were interred in this vault with much solemnity, 9 August 1722; they were removed to the chapel at Blenheim twenty-four years afterwards.

In the north-eastern chapel is the monument of **John Sheffield, 1st Duke of Buckinghamshire**, b. 1648, d. 1721, only son of the 2nd Earl of Mulgrave, early distinguished for his political and military services under Charles II, and James II. He took the oath of allegiance to William and Mary, by whom he was created successively Marquess of Normanby and Duke of Buckinghamshire. He ended his days in political disgrace in consequence of having plotted for the return of the Stuarts in the reign of Queen Anne, whose suitor he had been in her youth. Sheffield is also remembered as a man of letters, the friend of Pope and Dryden, to whom he erected monuments in Poets' Corner. His own productions earned him a place in Johnson's *Lives of the Poets*, where, however, he is spoken of as 'a writer that sometimes glimmers but rarely shines'. He built Buckingham House for himself on the site of the present palace in St James's Park. Pope wrote an epitaph for him which was never inscribed on the monument; the concluding lines of the Latin one by himself are striking – the following is a contemporary translation

---

[1] *Clarendon's* History of the Rebellion.

of them: 'I lived doubtful but not dissolute; I died un-
resolved, not unresigned. Ignorance and error are incident
to human nature; I trust in an Almighty and all-good
God. Oh thou Being of Beings, have compassion on
me!'

The monument was erected by his widow, **Catherine,
Duchess of Buckinghamshire**,[1] d. 1743, who is also buried
here. She was the illegitimate daughter of James II by
Catherine Sedley. She always insisted on being treated
with royal state, and on the anniversary of the 'martyrdom
of her grandfather, Charles I, received Lord Hervey in the
great drawing-room of Buckingham House, seated in a
chair of state, attended by her women in like weeds in
memory of the royal martyr'.[2] She settled every detail for
her own funeral ceremony, and quarrelled with Pope over
the epitaph which she wrote and he corrected, but which
was not inscribed here. Her ladies were made to promise
that if she should become insensible at the last they
would stand up in her presence till she was actually dead.
The Duke is represented in Roman armour, the Duchess
in the ordinary costume of her time. The principal figures
are by *Scheemakers*, the allegorical by *Delvaux*.

With the above are buried their four children, three of
whom Time is represented as bearing away. The fourth,
Edmund, 2nd and last **Duke of Buckinghamshire**, d. 1735,
in Rome, aged nineteen.[3]

In the same chapel lies **Anne of Denmark**, b. 1574, d.
1619, Queen of James I, and daughter of Frederick II,
King of Denmark and Norway. She died at Hampton
Court, declaring herself 'free from Popery'.

In this Chapel are kept, except when in use, **the Chairs
and Faldstools** presented to the Abbey in 1949 by the
Canada Club for the use of the Sovereign and Consort
when they attend divine service at the Abbey. The Chairs
are made of Canadian birch, stained and polished to a dark
tone and have on them the royal arms in enamel. On the
Faldstools are the arms of Canada. They were used by the

[1] *See her wax effigy, page 114.*   [2] *Walpole's* Reminiscences.
[3] *See his wax effigy, page 114.*

Effigy of Elizabeth I

King and Queen for the first time on Dominion Day 1949
when the Chairs were dedicated by the Dean.

The next chapel is filled by the tomb of **George Villiers,
1st Duke of Buckingham**, b. 1592, d. 1628, the powerful
favourite of James I and Charles I, fourth son of Sir
George Villiers (see page 59). Clarendon says of his rapid
rise to power, 'his ascent was so quick that it seemed
rather a flight than a growth. . . . And as if he had been
born a favourite, he was supreme the first month he came
to Court.' The effects of his rash and disastrous counsels
soon made him as increasingly unpopular with the nation
as he was dear to the King. On the eve of leading an
expedition for the relief of La Rochelle, he was assassinated (23 August 1628) at Portsmouth by a discontented
soldier named John Felton, who believed 'he should do
God good service if he killed the Duke'. Charles I buried
his friend in the Chapel of Henry VII, hitherto reserved
for those of royal descent, but the funeral was performed
with little ceremony for fear of a popular uproar. The
monument, by *Le Sueur*, was erected by the **Duchess**,
formerly **Lady Katherine Manners**, d. 1643, daughter of
the Earl of Rutland. She afterwards married the Marquess
of Antrim. The small statues, by *Nicholas Stone*, represent
their children, some of whom were buried in their father's
vault, including the youngest, **Lord Francis Villiers**, b.
1629, d. 1649, a posthumous child, 'a youth of rare beauty
and comeliness of person', killed in a skirmish with the
Parliamentary forces near Kingston-on-Thames. **George
Villiers**, b. 1628, d. 1687, the only surviving son, succeeded
his father, as 2nd Duke of Buckingham, and left no heir;
he was pilloried by Dryden as 'Zimri' in *Absalom and
Achitophel*.

North Aisle

The small enclosure to the left on entering, erroneously
called 'the Oratory', was probably used as a sacristy or
vestry by the additional priests for the services of Henry
VII's Chapel.

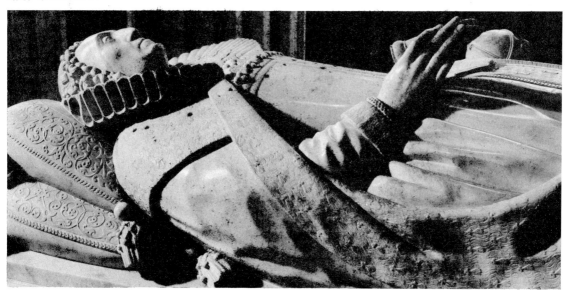

A large vault at the head of Queen Elizabeth's tomb contains amongst others the coffins of General Monck (see page 68) and his family.

The graves of: **Joseph Addison**, d. 1719 (page 44); and **James Craggs**, d. 1721, Addison's successor as Secretary of State (page 23).

Charles Montagu, 1st Earl of Halifax, K.G., b. 1661, d. 1715, a great Parliamentary orator, he was a brilliant financier as well as statesman; the founder of the Bank of England. A munificent patron of literature and science, he was the friend of Addison, and of Sir Isaac Newton. Buried in Monck's vault.

Edward Montagu, 1st Earl of Sandwich, K.G., b. 1625, d. 1672, one of the promoters of the Restoration. A naval commander of great courage, blown up with his ship in the fight with the Dutch called the Battle of Sole (Southwold) Bay. The friend and patron of Samuel Pepys, who was his secretary and was also his cousin (see page 94).

George Saville, Marquis of Halifax, b. 1633, d. 1695, 'the Trimmer', Lord Keeper of the Privy Seal for some time in the reigns of three Kings–Charles II, James II, and William III. 'A man of very great and ready wit, full of life, and very pleasant, much turned to satire, but with relation to the public he went backwards and forwards and changed sides so often that in conclusion no one trusted him.'[1]

The white marble tomb of **Queen Elizabeth I**[2] was erected by James I. She was born at Greenwich 7 September 1533, and died at Richmond 24 March 1603, crowned 15 January 1559, amidst the enthusiastic rejoicings of the people. On 'the 14th day of January, the Queene, with great majestie, rode through London to Westminster, against which time the Lord Mayor and citizens of London had furnished the streets with stately pageants, sumptuous showes and devices; the next day she was crowned by Dr. Oglethorpe, Bishop of Carlisle', as the See of Canterbury was vacant and the Archbishop of York refused to officiate. Oglethorpe was assisted by Abbot Feckenham and the service was read partly in Latin and partly in English. Queen Elizabeth was the Foundress of this Collegiate Church (1560), and her long reign was one of the most brilliant in English history. Her death was an occasion of universal mourning: 'The 28 day of Aprill being her funeral day at which time the citie of Westminster was surcharged with multitudes of all sorts of people in their streets, houses, windows, leads, and gutters, that came to see the obsequie, and when they beheld her statue or picture lying upon the coffin set forth in Royall robes, having a crown upon the head thereof and a ball and sceptre in either hand, there was such a general sighing, groning, and weeping as the like hath not beene seene or knowne in the memory of man, neither doth any history mention any people, time, or state to make like lamentation for the death of their Sovereign.'[3] The funeral train was composed of sixteen hundred mourners.

The monument is plainer and less sumptuous than that of Mary, Queen of Scots; it was finished long before hers, in 1606, and cost less, only £765. The recumbent figure of the Queen is fine, and resembles her later portraits. Her crown has disappeared, as also most of the other accessories. A grate which formerly enclosed the tomb was removed in 1822. The Latin epitaph calls Elizabeth 'the mother of this her country, the nurse of Religion and Learning, for perfect skill of very many languages, for glorious endowments as well of mind as of body, a Prince incomparable'. In the Abbey Museum is a gold ring, with a sardonyx cameo, upon which is carved a portrait of the Queen. This ring is traditionally the same which Elizabeth gave the Earl of Essex, and which should have been sent her from him as an appeal for pardon when under sentence of death. The ring through a mischance never reached her and the Earl was executed. It was presented to the Dean and Chapter in 1927. *Maximilian Poultrain* (alias Colt) *and John de Critz.*

Beneath the coffin of Elizabeth rests that of her half-sister **Queen Mary,** b. 1516, d. 1558, the first occupant of this aisle, interred without any monument or other remembrance. The stones from the broken altars were piled upon Mary's grave during the whole of her sister's reign. The hearse, upon which lay an effigy of the Queen in her royal robes, was a very grand one, adorned with wax angels and escutcheons. White, Bishop of Winchester, and Feckenham, Abbot of Westminster, preached funeral sermons upon her in the Abbey; 'The best is, the Protestants of that age cared not how many (so it be *funeral*) sermons were preached for her.'[4] At Mary's funeral was performed the last requiem mass said in the Abbey, by the last abbot, excepting that in honour of the Emperor Charles V, ordered by Elizabeth a few days later. The striking words of the Latin inscription include both sisters. 'Consorts both in throne and grave, here rest we two sisters, Elizabeth and Mary, in the hope of one resurrection.'

At the eastern end of the aisle, called by Dean Stanley 'The Innocents' Corner', are two small monuments of children of James I. **Princess Sophia,** d. 1606, aged three days, is represented as lying in a cradle, 'wherewith vulgar eyes, especially of the weaker sex, are more affected (as level to their cognizance more capable of what is pretty than what is pompous) than with all the magnificent monuments in Westminster'.[5] Her sister **Princess Mary,** d. 1607, aged two years, reclines on her elbow on a small altar tomb. Of her, 'King James the Protestant was wont pleasantly to say that he would not pray to the Virgin Mary, but he would pray for the Virgin Mary, meaning his own daughter.'[6] *Maximilian Poultrain,*[7] the sculptor of both monuments, received £140 for the 'Lady Sophia's' tomb. A small sarcophagus against the east wall contains the bones found at the foot of a staircase in the Tower, and placed here by order of Charles II in 1674, who presumed them to be the bones of **Edward V,** b. 1470, created Prince of Wales, 1471, and his brother **Richard, Duke of York,** b. 1472, the sons of Edward IV, supposed to have been murdered by order of their uncle, Richard III, in 1483. Edward V may be called the child of Westminster, having been born in the Abbot's house, where his mother Queen Elizabeth Woodville, took refuge in 1470.

Against the south wall are three Morris tapestries. These represent: St Edward the Confessor, giving his ring to: St John the Evangelist, in the garb of a pilgrim, the gift of Mr H. Yates Thompson; and Henry III, given by Mr and Mrs A. Murray Smith. The figures of the two kings are copied from the painted portraits on the north and south of the sedilia (pages 53, 55).

---

[1] *Burnet's* History of his own Time.
[2] *See her wax effigy, page 115.*   [3] *Stow's* Chronicle.

[4] *Fuller's* Church History.   [5] *Fuller's* Worthies.
[6] *Speed's translation.*   [7] *Known also by the name of Colt.*

THE CHAPELS AND NORTH AMBULATORY [*See plan, page 52*]

The North Ambulatory

AT THE FOOT OF the steps leading to Henry VII's Chapel: **Edward Hyde, 1st Earl of Clarendon,** b. 1609, d. 1674, statesman and historian of the Civil Wars and Restoration. For two hundred years he lay beneath a nameless stone, till, in 1867, the present inscription was cut. Clarendon was created Lord Chancellor by Charles II at Bruges, 1658, and, scarcely ten years after, was removed from his post, impeached, and banished. He died in exile at Rouen, and his body was brought over to England and buried, 4 January 1675, in the Abbey, where twenty of his relatives and descendants, among them his royal granddaughters, Queen Mary and Queen Anne, now lie. His mother, Mrs Mary Hyde (d. 1661), and his mother-in-law, Lady Aylesbury (d. 1661), her daughter Frances, his second wife (1667), and three young sons are buried in this vault.

William Pulteney, 1st Earl of Bath, b. 1684, d. 1764, popularly called 'Patriot Pulteney', was an orator and statesman of considerable note. For many years a staunch Whig, in 1721, he quarrelled with his party, and went over to the Tory Opposition and became the chief opponent of Walpole who said that he 'feared Pulteney's tongue more than other men's swords'. After his elevation to the peerage his political career practically ceased, and, in Pope's words, he 'foams a Patriot to subside a Peer'. Buried in the Islip Chapel. The funeral took place at night, and, as often happened on the occasions of any ceremonial in the Abbey, the mob outside broke into the building, and, mixing with the mourners, a scene of indescribable confusion ensued. In the tumult the wooden canopy over Edward I's tomb was destroyed, for some of the gentlemen took their stand upon the top of the steps leading into the Confessor's Shrine, and defended themselves against the pressure of the crowd with their drawn swords and the broken rafters. *Wilton sculpt.*

Rear-Admiral Charles Holmes, d. 1761, Commander-in-Chief of the fleet at Jamaica. One of the last monuments in the Abbey in which an English seaman was dressed as a Roman soldier. *Wilton sculpt.*

Sir John Wyndesore, d. 1414, nephew to William, Lord Wyndesore, who was a famous man in the reign of Edward III, and Lord Lieutenant of Ireland. Sir John 'had been a soldier in his youth, and was a great commander in the wars in Ireland, and the battle of Shrewsbury with Henry IV, but, repenting him of his bloodshed, finished his life in piety'.[1] All that remains is the Latin verse inscription. The body of **John Pym,** b. 1584, d. 1643, the leader of the popular party in the Long Parliament, was laid with great pomp and ceremony under Sir John Wyndesore's gravestone, 15 December 1643, both Houses of Parliament following him to the grave. The Royalists nicknamed him 'King Pym', for 'he seemed to all men to have the greatest influence upon the House of Commons of any man, and in truth I think he was at that time (1640),

and some months after, the most popular man, and the most able to do hurt, that hath lived in any time'.[2] Pym's body was disinterred in 1661, and flung, with those of the other Parliamentarians, into a pit outside the Abbey walls.

Close by rested, till it shared the same fate, the body of **William Strode,** d. 1645, the 'Parliament Driver', one of the five members demanded by Charles I when he made his memorable entry into the House of Commons with an armed force in 1642.

Brian Duppa, b. 1588, d. 1662, Dean of Christ Church, Oxford, successively Bishop of Chichester, Salisbury, and Winchester, and tutor to Charles II. 'He was ev'ry way qualified for the tuition of the Prince and for the conservation of the distress'd King, who when prisoner at Carisbrooke Castle, was much reliev'd by that divine conversation, and whose exemplary conduct had rais'd such reverence for him in his Royal Highness Charles II that the day before his death that Prince came to Richmond, and at the bedside asked his blessing on his bended knee.' He was a generous benefactor to Christ Church and to All Souls College, Oxford; he also founded a hospital at Greenwich, where he was born, with this inscription over the door: 'A poore Bishop vow'd this House, but a great and wealthy one built it.'[3] The Latin inscription records his love for Richmond, where 'he lay concealed in the troublesome times, and afterwards breathed forth his pious soul'. Buried close by. Tablet now on west wall of Islip Chantry Chapel. *Burman sculpt.*

John Theophilus Beresford, d. 1812, a young lieutenant in the 10th Foot, who was mortally wounded by the explosion of a powder magazine during Wellington's famous siege and capture of Ciudad Rodrigo. Buried at Almeida.

Field Marshal John, 1st Earl Ligonier, b. 1680, d. 1770. A French refugee, who served as a soldier of fortune under Marlborough, and fought at the battle of Blenheim. He afterwards became one of Anne's generals, and wound up a long military career at the lost battle of Val (1747), where he checked the advance of the French, but was taken prisoner and led before Louis XV, who complimented him on his brilliant charge. He afterwards became General of the Ordnance, and lived till the middle of George III's reign. Medallion heads of the four British sovereigns whom he served and the names of the chief battles in which he took part are on the monument. He put up a tablet in the Cloisters to his brother Francis (d. 1746), who lost his life at Falkirk Muir, through leaving his sick bed to rally Hawley's dragoons, and died of pleurisy afterwards. *Moore sculpt.*

General James Wolfe, b. 1727, d. 1759. He entered the army when only fourteen, and, after a brilliant career, was killed at the age of thirty-three. His last and greatest exploit, the capture of Quebec, the capital of French Canada, established the English ascendancy in that province. At the head of his troops he scaled the Heights of Abraham, above Quebec, and fell, mortally wounded, in the moment of victory as he was cheering on his men.

---

[1] *Dart, vol. ii, page 18.*

[2] *Clarendon, vol. vi, page 438.*   [3] *Dart, vol. ii, page 10.*

He was carried behind the ranks. 'Yet fast as life ebbed out, his whole anxiety centred on the fortune of the day. He begged to be borne nearer to the action, but his sight being dimmed by the approach of death, he entreated to be told what they who supported him saw. He was answered that the enemy gave ground. He eagerly repeated the question, heard the enemy was totally routed, cried: "I am satisfied," and expired.' Buried at Greenwich. This colossal monument, erected by the King and Parliament, in 1772, at the cost of £3,000, was *Joseph Wilton's* first public work. Esteney's and Harpedon's tombs were moved to make way for it, and a worse sacrilege was contemplated, but fortunately not carried out.[1] The group is a fanciful representation of Wolfe's death; on the bronze bas-relief, by *Capizzoldi*, is the scene of the landing of the British troops, and their ascent of the Heights of Abraham. During the First World War a number of Canadian regiments deposited their Colours in the keeping of the

[1] *See page 53.*

Dean and Chapter, and they were arranged in a picturesque group upon Wolfe's monument. After the Peace was signed, the different regiments fetched their colours, but the Canadian Government ordered two flags to be placed on the monument as a perpetual reminder of Canada's help to the Mother Country in her need.

Sir John Harpedon, d. 1438, fifth and last husband of the celebrated Kentish heiress Joan de la Pole, Lady Cobham. Her fourth husband was Sir John Oldcastle, the Lollard leader, called the 'Good Lord Cobham', who was executed in 1417. Lady Cobham died in 1434, and lies in Cobham Church, Kent. His tomb was once raised 4 feet from the floor, and formed, with Esteney's, part of the screen of St John's Chapel, but was removed to make way for Wolfe's monument. The brass represents a knight; his feet rest on a lion, his head on a helmet, its crest a hind's head issuing from a coronet.

John Esteney, d. 1498, Abbot of Westminster from 1474 till his death. He was Millyng's successor, and like him had the guardianship of Elizabeth Woodville, when

Detail of monument of Edmund Crouchback, Earl of Lancaster

she and her daughters took sanctuary for the second time (1483). 'During the Queen's stay here this church and monastery was enclos'd like a camp, and strictly guarded by soldiers . . . and none were suffer'd to go in or out without special permission, for fear the Princesses should convey themselves over the sea, and baulk Richard the III's designs.'[1] The obligation for each new abbot to go to Rome to be confirmed by the Pope was remitted in Esteney's time. Esteney was Caxton's patron, and it was he who enabled Caxton to set up his press within the Precincts, first in 1476 in a shop outside the Chapter House and then in 1483–4 in larger premises in the Almonry (see page 101); several of Caxton's early books have 'In the Abbey of Westminster' printed on the title page. Esteney continued his predecessor's work on the building of the church, the Nave was completely roofed, the vaulting of the west end, all but three bays, was completed and the great window set up: 'The Abbot seems to have been much set on the work, for he kept it always in his own direction, which before Millyng's time had been committed to the care of some one of the monks.'[2] As we have seen, Esteney's screen was destroyed and his tomb moved and mutilated, in the eighteenth century. The brass effigy represents an abbot in mass vestments under a triple-headed canopy, one hand raised in blessing, the other holding the crozier. A label proceeds from the mouth with the words: '*Exultabo in Deo Jhu Meo*'. The tomb was once surrounded by an iron railing; it also had a canopy, through the arch of which St John's Altar could be seen. It has been twice opened, in 1706 and again in 1772, when the Abbot's body was found entire, 'lying in a chest quilted with yellow satin, he had on a gown of crimson silk girded to him with a black girdle; on his legs were white silk stockings, and on his face, which was black, a clean napkin doubled up and laid cornerwise' (Dart).

In the floor are two slabs, once containing brasses. Two monks of the Abbey–**Thomas Brown** (d. 1513–14) and **Robert Humphrey** (d. 1509)–lie beneath one. The other was originally raised on a grey marble tomb, but is now level with the floor. Beneath it lies **Sir Thomas Parry**, d. 1560, Treasurer of the Household and Master of the Courts of Wards and Liveries to Queen Elizabeth. All that remains are four shields which for better preservation are fixed to the base of a neighbouring Purbeck marble column.

Five naval officers, all killed in the bloody but victorious engagement with the Dutch off Lowestoft, 3 June 1665 are buried here. Three were captains: **James Ley, 3rd Earl of Marlborough; Charles MacCarthy, Viscount Muskerry;** and **Charles Berkeley, Earl of Falmouth,** created a peer at the Restoration for his services to the royal family. Also his younger brother, **Admiral Sir William Berkeley,** aged only twenty-seven, to whose remains the Dutch paid a rare tribute. They carried his body on his own ship, the *Swiftsure*, to Holland, embalmed it, and placed it in the cathedral at The Hague, whence it was sent, by desire of the family, for interment in the Abbey. The fifth, **Sir Edward Broughton,** survived three weeks, and died at his own house here. Imprisoned in the Gatehouse during the Commonwealth, he had married the Gatehouse Keeper's widow, Mrs Aquila Wyke, and succeeded to this post.

Three French Protestant ladies are buried in the same vault in this Ambulatory. **Mme Hester Hervart,** d. 1697, widow of a French banker, who patriotically placed his funds at the disposal of Louis XIII, and thus enabled him successfully to repulse the invasion of Alsace; her daughter, **Esther, Marquise de Gouvernet,** d. 1722, aged eighty-six, widow of a distinguished French Protestant, the Marquis de la Tour de Gouvernet, and her granddaughter **Esther, Lady Eland,** d. 1694, aged twenty-eight, widow of Henry Saville, Lord Eland, eldest son of the Marquess of Halifax. After Hervart's decease, his vast estates were confiscated on the revocation of the Edict of Nantes, and his widow took refuge in England with her son and daughter, both of whom were afterwards naturalized. The son became Ambassador at Geneva under William III. Madame de Gouvernet lived for thirty years in the same house in St James's Square, and was a well-known figure in English society. In 1704 she put up a mural monument by the French sculptor *Nadauld* in memory of her daughter Lady Eland, which used to stand near the vault against Queen Eleanor's tomb. In the nineteenth century the monument was divided, the inscription placed above the door inside St John the Baptist's Chapel, and the sculptured figure of Lady Eland hidden away. This interesting example of eighteenth-century French sculpture has been reunited to the marble base, and is now in the Triforium.

Chapel of St Paul   [*See plan, page 78*]

This, the first of the northern chapels, corresponds to St Nicholas's, the last on the south side; the place of the altar is taken by a tomb (the Countess of Sussex), and the wall arcading destroyed and hidden by monuments. The screen has completely lost its original character, the eastern half forming part of the Robessart tomb, while the western was destroyed to make way for Pulteney's[3] monument. Dedicated to St Paul, it contained, among other relics, the cloth in which the saint's head was wrapped after execution, presented by Edward the Confessor.

Sir Lewis Robessart, K.G., d. 1431, a native of Hainault, created **Lord Bourchier** after his marriage with Elizabeth *suo jure* **Baroness Bourchier** who is buried in her husband's tomb. Robessart was made the King's Standard Bearer for his exploits at the battle of Agincourt; and on Henry V's marriage with Catherine of Valois he was attached to the Queen's personal household. He afterwards became Chamberlain to the young King, Henry VI. The monument forms part of the screen, which is carried over it, and the whole was once richly gilt and painted, the upper part covered with coats of arms and mottoes; the text, *Non nobis Domine non nobis sed Nomini tuo da gloriam*, on the cornice is still partly legible, but few traces of anything else remain.

James Watt, b. 1736, d. 1819, Civil engineer and craftsman, the improver of the steam engine. Buried at Handsworth, near Birmingham. The statue[4] of Carrara marble by *Chantrey*, cost £6,000, the amount raised by subscriptions, the inscription is by Lord Brougham. The introduction of the monument into this little chapel was

---

[1] *Dart, vol. ii, page 34.*   [2] *Widmore, page 118.*

[3] *See page 75.*

[4] *Removed Dec. 1960 to the Transport Commission's Museum at Clapham and replaced by a bronzed plaster bust presented by the Institution of Mechanical Engineers.*

a work of some difficulty; the pedestal, divided into three pieces, was dragged in over Robessart's tomb, destroying the ancient coffin lid. The statue was forced through the door, but the vaulting gave way beneath its weight disclosing 'rows upon rows of gilded coffins', and, had not the area been planked over, 'workmen and work must inevitably have fallen in and joined the dead in the chamber of death'.[1]

Francis Cottington, created **Baron Cottington,** of Hanworth, b. 1578, d. 1652. He was twice Ambassador to Spain. His career there began as a young man, when he was sent by Robert Cecil as English agent. Later he accompanied 'Baby Charles' and 'Steenie', as the Prince's secretary, to Madrid on their famous journey to negotiate the Spanish match. By using all his influence with James I against the project he incurred Buckingham's enmity;[2] he was disgraced at Court, and was not restored to favour till after the Duke's murder. He openly opposed Laud at the Council, but retained the confidence of the King, and was made Lord Treasurer at Oxford, where he joined him on the outbreak of the Civil War, 1643. For his faithful adherence to the Royalist cause he was ruined and obliged to fly abroad, where he soon joined Prince Charles, and was sent by him as Ambassador to Madrid, 1649, in company with Hyde (afterwards Lord Clarendon). His mission was a failure, his enemies procured his fall, and he finally returned to Spain, and died at Valladolid, having become a Roman Catholic for the second time. 'He raised himself by his natural strength, without any artificial advantage; having his parts above his learning, his experience above his parts, his industry above his experience, and (some will say) his success above all.'[3] 'A very wise man, whose greatest fault was that he could dissemble and make men believe that he loved them very well when he cared not for them. . . . He was heartily weary of the world, and no man was more ready to die, which is an argument that he had peace of conscience. He left behind him a greater esteem of his parts than love for his person.'[4] His remains were brought to England in 1679 by his nephew, who raised this monument, which is

[1] *Cunningham's Handbook, page 24.*
[2] *Clarendon, vol. i, pages 30, 58.*
[3] *Fuller's Worthies, vol. iii, page 329.*
[4] *Clarendon, vol. iv, pages 405–7.*

of black and white marble, in severe Renaissance style, by *Fanelli,* a one-eyed Florentine sculptor. The upper part, to his wife **Anne** (d. 1634), daughter of William Meredith, was put up by Lord Cottington himself; the bust is metal, enclosed in a metal wreath, the sculptor *Hubert le Sueur,*[5] a pupil of John of Bologna.

Frances Sidney, Countess of Sussex, d. 1589, aunt to Sir Philip Sidney; second wife of Thomas Ratcliffe, Earl of Sussex and Lord Deputy of Ireland, who was Leicester's rival in Elizabeth's favour. She founded the College of Sidney Sussex, Cambridge, which restored her monument in the nineteenth century. 'A woeman whyle she lyved adorned with many and most rare guifts both of mynde and bodye. Towards God trulie and zelouslie religious: To her frends and kinesfoulke most liberall: to the poore, to prisoners, and to the ministers of the worde of god, allwaies most charitablie' (epitaph). This monument takes the place of St Paul's Altar. *Rudolf Symors,* the architect of the college, may also have designed the tomb.

Dudley Carleton, b. 1574, d. 1632, created **Viscount Dorchester** and Secretary of State by Charles I. He was the last English Deputy who sat on the States-General of the Netherlands (1615–26)–a privilege the English Crown had possessed from the middle of Elizabeth's reign. He seems to have understood very well all that related to foreign affairs, 'but was utterly unacquainted with the government, laws, and customs of his own country, and the nature of the people'.[6] Carleton and his first wife **Anne,** daughter of Sir Henry Savile (d. 1627), are buried here in the same grave. The monument was erected about 1635. *Nicholas Stone,* the sculptor, says he received £200 in money for it, and also 'an old monument that stood in the same place sett up for his lady some eight years before'.[7]

Giles Daubeny, created **Baron Daubeny** (b. 1452, d. 1508) and **Elizabeth,** his wife (who survived her husband), daughter of Sir John Arundelle. He was Lord Lieutenant of Calais, Lord Chamberlain 'unto the noble King Henrie the Seventh', as stated in a Latin inscription which Camden gives and translates, but of which all trace has now disappeared. He was raised to the peerage in 1486 in recognition of his services during Henry VII's exile. An altar tomb of Purbeck marble surmounted by alabaster effigies. The knight is in plate armour, and wears the full insignia of the Garter; at his feet are little crouching figures of bedesmen with rosaries in their hands. The whole tomb was restored in 1889, and a modern iron grille replaces the ancient one, which had long disappeared.

Sir Thomas Bromley, b. 1530, d. 1587, succeeded Sir Nicholas Bacon as Lord Keeper. He presided at the trial and sentence of Mary, Queen of Scots, and never got over the responsibility, but died two months after her execution. Dart gives and translates the Latin inscription, which is now illegible: 'When he had for eight years delivered Equity with singular Integrity and Temper of Mind, being snatch'd hastily away to the grief of all good men, was here buried.' His son erected the monument, which is of Lydian marble and alabaster. The effigy represents the Chancellor in his robes; in front kneel his eight children; at the back is the official purse, supported

[5] *The sculptor of the equestrian statue of Charles I at Charing Cross.*
[6] *Clarendon, vol. i, page 114.*
[7] *Walpole's Anecdotes of Painting.*

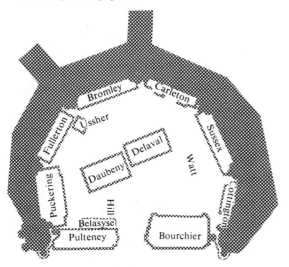

Tomb of Sir John and Lady Puck

IVRISPRVDENTIA, PIETATE CONSILIO QVI
TISQ. ALIIS VIRTVTIBVS INSIGNIS IOANNES
PVCKERING MILES A SERENISSIMA
ELIZABETHA ANGLIÆ REGINA IN
SECRETVS CONSILIVM AC SVMMVM MAGNI
SIGILLI ANGLIÆ CVSTODIS MVNVS
ASCITVS, CVM QVATVOR ANNIS SINGVLARI
FIDE ET ÆQVITATE IVS DIXISSET PLACIDE
IN DOMINO OBDORMIENS HIC SITVS EST
VIXIT ANNOS 52 OBIIT 30 APRILIS 1596

CAVSARVM IMPERII ET CVRARVM
PONDERE FESSO
VIVERE PŒNA FVIT MORS MIHI
SOMNVS ERAT

by winged boys; above in the spandrels are the figures of Fame and Immortality, bearing trumpets.

Sir James Fullerton, d. 1631, First Gentleman of the Bedchamber to Charles I. 'A firme Pillar to yᵉ Cõmon Wealth, a faithful Patron to yᵉ Catholiq Church; a faire Patterne to yᵉ British Court: He lived To yᵉ welfare of his Country; To yᵉ Honour of his Prince; To yᵉ Glory of His God: He dyed Fuller of Faith then of Feares: Fuller of Resolučon, then of Paienes; Fuller of Honour then of Dayes' (epitaph). Buried in the Ambulatory. His wife's effigy is here, but there is no record of her burial in the registers, and the space for her inscription on the monument is left vacant. The effigies are of alabaster, recumbent on a marble altar tomb. Fastened to the lady's girdle is a miniature of her husband.

Close to the tomb of Fullerton, his schoolmaster in Dublin, lies the Irish Archbishop, **James Ussher,** b. 1581, d. 1656. He lived at Westminster during the troubles in Ireland, and for a time, while Dean Williams was in the Tower, had the use of the Deanery. Ussher was honoured by both parties. He attended Charles I at Oxford, and later on won his way into Cromwell's favour. He was buried here by the Protector's orders, and at his expense. Ussher's funeral was the only occasion on which the

Entrance to Chapel of Our Lady of the Pew

Liturgical service was read in the Abbey during the Commonwealth. The inscribed stone was laid above his grave by desire of Dr Salmon, then Provost of Trinity College, Dublin, in 1905; the inscription is mainly from the pen of Dr Gwynn, who was Regius Professor of Divinity at that time.

Sir John Puckering, b. 1544, d. 1596, a parliamentary lawyer, twice Speaker of the House of Commons; he took an active part in the trial of Mary, Queen of Scots, and by Queen Elizabeth's wish, unfairly prosecuted his secretary Davison, for obtaining her signature to the death warrant. Puckering succeeded Sir Christopher Hatton as Keeper of the Great Seal. Dart translates the Latin verse on the monument thus:

> The Public Care and Laws engag'd my breast,
> To live was toilsome but to die is rest,
> Wealth, Maces, Guards, Crowns, Titles, Things that fade
> The Prey of Time, and sable Death were made.

The tomb of different kinds of marble was erected by Puckering's widow, who added her own statue. The effigies and the children's statues are alabaster. Above are figures of a Purse and a Mace Bearer, in costumes of the period. Notice behind Puckering's tomb (from the Ambulatory) remains of the ancient wall arcading, with a small figure probably of St Anne.

Sir Henry Belasyse, of Brancepeth, d. 1717, who claims in his epitaph to be descended from Belasius, one of William the Conqueror's generals. He was himself Lieut.-General of William III's forces in Flanders. Buried in this Chapel. *Scheemakers sculpt.*

Sir Rowland Hill, b. 1795, d. 1879, the inventor of penny postage, buried close by. *Bust by Keyworth, junior.*

Chapel of Our Lady of the Pew

The Chapel of St John is now entered through a double vestibule. But in its original form the outer of these vestibules was a self-contained rectangular recess about 5 feet square, hollowed out of the thickness of the wall. The painted vaulting of this recess with its carved boss of the Assumption dates from the second half of the fourteenth century and in the back wall of the recess, facing the Ambulatory, is a shallow niche with a bracket on which stood an image of Our Lady, presumably the one presented by the Countess of Pembroke, the widow of Aymer de Valence and foundress of Pembroke College, Cambridge. The hooks which secured the image still remain, and the painted background still shows a shadow outline of the figure. The walls of the recess were elaborately painted and are studded with hooks evidently for votive offerings. The outer doorway with its painted wooden half-gates and iron bracket for an alms box are also original. In this form the Chapel of Our Lady of the Pew (i.e. a small enclosure) remained until about 1502, when it was enlarged to contain an altar dedicated to St Erasmus. At the same time the bracket with its image was moved back a few feet and placed in the new north wall of the enlarged Chapel. Finally Bishop Ruthall's tomb (1524) having blocked the original entrance to St John's Chapel, a new entrance had to be made with the result that this Chapel of the Pew and of St Erasmus became the present vestibule leading into St John's Chapel.

On the wall just outside this Chapel two tablets commemorate **Juliana Crewe** (d. 1621), daughter of Sir

Ranulph Crewe and her sister-in-law **Jane** (d. 1639), daughter of Sir John Pulteney and wife of Sir Clipesby Crewe. She is depicted on her deathbed with her family round her. *Epiphanius Evesham sculpt.*

St John the Baptist's Chapel

A wooden screen with a doorway in the centre originally divided this Chapel from the Ambulatory until it was displaced by the stone tombs, first of Abbot Fascet, then, in 1514, of Bishop Ruthall, when the new passage-way through the little chapel above mentioned was made. The aumbries, where the sacramental plate was kept, still remain in the north-east wall, but Lord Hunsdon's monument takes the place of the altar, and only an elevation in the pavement marks the altar step.

A monument with a kneeling figure to **Mrs Mary Kendall**, b. 1677, d. 1709, whose many virtues 'Render'd Her every way worthy Of that close Union & Friendship, In which She liv'd, with The Lady Catherine Jones'.

George Fascet, Abbot of Westminster for only two years, 1498, till his death in retirement about 1500. An altar tomb and canopy of freestone with a Purbeck slab; grated with iron on the Ambulatory side; in the panels at the sides are the arms of Fascet and of the Abbey; on the frieze, his name in a cipher.

Thomas Millyng, d. 1492, **Bishop of Hereford**, Abbot of Westminster 1469–74. In Millyng's time Elizabeth Woodville first took sanctuary, and her eldest son, Edward V, was born and baptized in the Abbot's house, with no ceremonial service, like 'any poure man's child', the Abbot and Prior standing as godfathers.[1] In 1468, when Prior, Millyng had started a continuation of the Nave, the work on which had ceased under Henry VI. He now roofed in another bay of the Nave with the money, £520, which the grateful King, Edward IV, his Queen and the young prince gave him. Edward rewarded Millyng for his protection of the Queen with the Bishopric of Hereford in 1474. He died at Hereford, but was buried in the centre of this chapel. A stone coffin, said to be that of Millyng, was formerly in this Chapel but is now in the Ambulatory.

Thomas Ruthall, d. 1523, **Bishop of Durham**, private secretary to Henry VII, and Privy Councillor to Henry VIII. He is said to have died of grief from having sent an inventory of his own wealth, which amounted to £100,000, instead of a volume of State papers, to Henry VIII. Wolsey discovered the mistake, but, having a grudge against the Bishop, gave the book to the King with the remark that 'he knew now where a man of money was in case he needed it'. Shakespeare uses this incident in the play of *Henry VIII*, but applies it to Wolsey. Ruthall had made good use of his wealth, helping to build the great bridge at Newcastle-on-Tyne, and 'intended many more benefactions had not death surprised him'. 'Some years after,' says Anthony Wood, 'was a fair tomb built over his grave, with his statue mitred and crested, and a small inscription on it, but false (1542) as to the year of his death.' The tomb and effigy are of freestone, much decayed; only a few fragments, set up at the head of the tomb remain of the canopy.

William de Colchester, d. 1420, succeeded Litlyngton as Abbot of Westminster in 1386. The work on the re-

building of the Nave, which had commenced under his predecessor, continued to progress during Colchester's abbacy, with the help of gifts of money from Richard II, and from Henry V, who was a generous benefactor. The Abbot was concerned in a plot to restore Richard II, and committed to the Tower for a short period in 1400 after the accession of Henry IV. But the chroniclers' story[2] that he was so distressed by the discovery of the conspiracy that he fell 'into a sudden palsie and shortly afterwards ended his life', is untrue although Shakespeare followed the legend:

The Grand Conspirator, Abbot of Westminster,
With clog of conscience and sour melancholy
Hath yielded up his body to the grave.[3]

In fact Colchester lived for twenty years after the conspiracy, was restored to the favour of Henry V and was sent on various important embassies during his reign, notably to the Council of Constance in 1414. An altar tomb and portrait effigy of freestone, the canopy of which has long disappeared; the whole has been painted and renovation has restored the brilliant colours of such paint as remains; the vestments were very rich, the gloves and mitre ornamented with jewellery.

Above is a tablet to the gallant young officer **Lieut.-Colonel Charles Macleod**, who fell at the siege of Badajos, 1812. *Nollekens sculpt.*

Henry Carey, 1st Baron Hunsdon, b. 1525–6, d. 1596, cousin and Lord Chamberlain to Queen Elizabeth. He was Governor of Berwick and suppressed the Northern rebellion in 1570. During the alarm of the Spanish Armada he had charge of a bodyguard enrolled expressly to guard the Queen. He was 'a fast man to his prince and firme to his friends and servants . . . of an honest, stout, heart, and such a one that upon occasion would have fought for his prince and country, for he had the charge of the Queene's person both in the Court and in the camp at Tilbury',[4] and 'a valiant man and lover of men of their hands; very choleric, but not malicious'. It is said that the old man's last illness was caused by the delay of his long-expected promotion to the earldom of Wiltshire. 'When he lay on his deathbed the Queen gave him a gracious visit, causing

---

[1] *Page 74.*

[2] *Hall and Holinshed and a French Chronicle.*
[3] Richard II, *Act V, Sc. 4.*
[4] *Naunton's* Court of Queen Elizabeth.

his patent for the said earldom to be drawn, his robes to be made, and both to be laid down upon his bed; but this lord (who could dissemble neither well nor sick), "Madam," said he, "seeing you counted me not worthy of this honour whilst I was living, I count myself unworthy of it now I am dying."[1] The monument was erected by his son against the east wall, where the altar formerly stood, and is 36 feet high, the highest in the Abbey. Buried in Hunsdon's vault are his daughter-in-law **Elizabeth,** wife of George, 2nd Baron Hunsdon, who married after her first husband's death Ralph, 3rd Lord Eure and died in 1618. Spenser dedicated his poem *Muiopotmes* to her; and **Alice, Countess of Carbery** (d. 1689) (daughter of John Egerton, 1st Earl of Bridgwater), an incident in whose early life led to the production of Milton's *Comus.*

Thomas Carey, d. 1649, son of Henry, 2nd Earl of Monmouth. He was Gentleman of the Bedchamber to Charles I, and is said to have died of grief at his master's fate; the only mention of Charles I's execution in the Abbey is on this tablet. He lies in Lord Hunsdon's vault.

Near the wall is the small tomb of **Hugh** and **Mary de Bohun,** d. 1305, children of Humphrey de Bohun, Earl of Hereford and Constable of England, by Elizabeth, fourth daughter of Edward I. This tomb was originally in St Nicholas's Chapel but was moved to St John's Chapel at some date between 1532 and 1600. The material is grey Purbeck marble, and, perhaps, was once coloured; round the sides runs a trefoiled arcade; there is no other tomb like this in the Abbey, but it resembles Archbishop Theobald's in Canterbury Cathedral.[2]

Colonel Edward Popham, b. 1610 (?), d. 1651, and **Anne,** his wife (daughter of William Carr, Groom of the Bedchamber to James I). 'A principal officer of the Parliament in their fleets at sea, and of a passionate and virulent temper, of the Independent party.'[3] He was buried in the North Ambulatory, on the evening of the day (24 October) of thanksgiving for the Royalist defeat at Worcester (3 September), and Cromwell and many of the Parliamentary members attended his funeral. His body was disinterred at the Restoration; but, instead of being flung into the pit with the rest, his friends were allowed to carry it away; and the monument was suffered to remain on condition that the inscription was erased. Keepe says that by the intervention of Anne Popham's relations, the Carrs, 'who had eminently served his Majesty, the stone was only turned whereon the inscription was insculpt'; but this story has no historical authority.

Sir Thomas Vaughan, d. 1483. Private treasurer to Edward IV, who created him Chamberlain to his son Edward V, as stated in a Latin inscription in brass letters round the verge of the tomb, little of which now remains. Vaughan was beheaded soon after Edward IV's death by order of the Duke of Gloucester, at Pontefract Castle. Shakespeare mentions his arrest and death without a trial, in the play of *Richard III.* The tomb has possibly been removed from some other place, but nothing authentic is known either of its original position or of the date when it was placed here. The tomb is of grey Purbeck; on the slab is the brass figure of a knight in plate armour, his

hands joined in prayer; under his head is a helmet, the crest a unicorn's head; the feet and brass shields are gone.

Thomas Cecil, b. 1542, d. 1623, and his first wife, **Dorothy Nevill,** d. 1609. He was the eldest son of William, 1st Baron Burghley, and was created **Earl of Exeter** by James I. He took an active part in the suppression of the Northern rebellion of 1569, and distinguished himself in the Low Countries. Elizabeth made him Governor of Hull as a reward for his services. He founded a hospital at Liddington, Rutland, and was a benefactor to Clare College, Cambridge. The inscription erroneously states that his second wife, Frances Brydges, for whose effigy a vacant space was left, is buried here; but she died forty years after her husband, and lies in Winchester Cathedral. An altar tomb of black and white marble, with recumbent effigies in the centre of the Chapel; round the sides are shields of arms enclosed in laurel wreaths.

Robert Devereux, Earl of Essex, b. 1591, d. 1646, son of Elizabeth's unfortunate favourite, 'The most popular man in the kingdom, and the darling of swordsmen', he did good service for Charles I, but in 1642 sided with Parliament, and became General-in-Chief of the Parliamentarian army. The Independents gave him a magnificent funeral, but that same night 'some rude vindictive fellows' broke into the Abbey and mutilated the Earl's hearse, which was standing near the Communion table, defacing Camden's monument in passing. The original intention had been to remove the General's remains to Henry VII's Chapel, and raise a monument over him; but the enthusiasm of the moment passed away, and his body was left here, and overlooked at the Restoration. Dean Stanley placed the present inscription over the vault.

The Islip Chantry Chapel

This chapel was fitted up by Abbot Islip[4] as a Jesus Chapel, and his name and rebus–an eye within a slip or branch of a tree grasped by a hand, and a man slipping from the branch 'I-slip'–are repeated many times in the elaborate carving both on the frieze and inside the

---

[1] *Fuller's* Worthies, *vol. ii, pages 47, 49.*
[2] *For an account of the opening of this tomb in 1937 see* Archaeologia, *vol. xciii (1949),* 'On some Recent Discoveries in Westminster Abbey', *by Sir Charles Peers and L. E. Tanner.*
[3] *Clarendon, vol. v, page 68.*

[4] *H. F. Westlake,* Westminster Abbey. The Last Days of the Monastery as shown by the Life and Times of Abbot John Islip (*Philip Allan, 1921*).

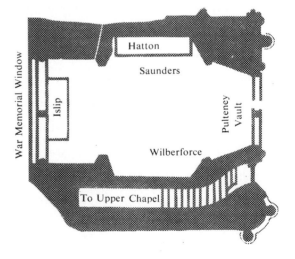

Chapel, and were also painted on the window. Horace Walpole says he saw two panes of glass purloined from Islip's Chapel in the Bishop of Rochester's Palace (1752). It is separated from the Ambulatory by a stone screen, part of which was cut away to form a new doorway when the old door inside the Chapel was walled up. Two Jesus altars, where masses were said for the Abbot's soul, formerly stood here, one in the Chantry Chapel above, and one in the Chapel below. At the back of each was a representation of the Crucifixion; the red and white damask frontals bore the Abbot's arms.

The remains of Islip's tomb are now in the Upper Chantry Chapel; it was originally in the centre of the Lower Chapel, and consisted of two slabs of black marble; the upper one supported by brass pilasters, formed a canopy to the lower one, upon which was an alabaster figure of the Abbot in his vestments. **John Islip**, elected Abbot 1500, called 'the great builder', was born (10 June 1464) at Islip, Oxfordshire, the Confessor's birthplace, whence he took his surname. He was a favourite with two Kings, Henry VII and Henry VIII, and a Privy Councillor. Although a friend of Cardinal Wolsey, he was not involved in Wolsey's disgrace. Under his rule Henry VII's Chapel was built, the Abbot laying the foundation stone with his own hands (1503). In his time the Nave was completed, the great west window set up by Esteney was glazed, and the Abbot himself superintended the erection of the western towers as far as the roof, filling the niches outside with statues of kings that had been benefactors. He also added the Jericho Parlour and the rooms above it to the Abbot's Lodgings, and the gallery in the Nave called the 'Abbot's Pew'. Lastly, he planned to build a lofty central tower and lantern, with a chime of bells; but the pillars were found too weak to support the tower and the design was never carried out. Islip died eight years before the dissolution of the monastery, at his Manor House of Neyte, 12 May 1532, whence his body was brought with much ceremony to his own little chapel. The funeral lasted two days, and was conducted 'after a very pompous manner'. It is illustrated in the famous Islip Roll, a brief announcing his death – intended to be sent round to the other chief monasteries – which was restored to the Dean and Chapter by the Society of Antiquaries in 1907, to whom it had been lent by Dean Thomas in the eighteenth century. The roll was never completed, probably on account of the Dissolution. It consists of pen drawings attributed to Gerard Hornebolt, which represent: the Abbot on his deathbed; the hearse standing before the High Altar; and Islip's Chapel, showing the paintings on the walls, which included a Crucifixion, with a figure of the Abbot praying beneath it.

Anne Mowbray, b. 1472, d. 1481, daughter and heiress of the last Duke of Norfolk, of that name, who had been married (1477) in childhood to Richard, Duke of York, son of Edward IV, the bridegroom's age being only five years. She was originally buried in the old Lady Chapel and, when that was pulled down to make way for Henry VII's Chapel, it was believed she was re-buried here. In 1964, however, her coffin was found on the side of a medieval nunnery near St Clare St., Stepney.

The Altar has been restored. Until a few years ago its site was covered by the monument of the younger **Sir Christopher Hatton**, d. 1619,[1] created Knight of the Bath

by James I, kinsman and heir to Lord Chancellor Hatton, and **Alice,** his wife, daughter of Thomas Fanshaw.

Admiral Sir Charles Saunders, b. 1713 (?), d. 1775, First Lord of the Admiralty, without whose co-operation when commander-in-chief of the fleet, Wolfe could not have captured Quebec, is also buried in this Chapel.

A tablet in memory of three generations of the Wilberforce family: **William Wilberforce** (1759–1833), the Emancipator (see page 37); **Samuel Wilberforce** (1805–73), Dean of Westminster and Bishop of Oxford; **Basil Wilberforce** (1841–1916), Canon and Archdeacon of Westminster.

In 1948 a window, executed by *Hugh Easton*, was presented by Dr Alan Don (Dean of Westminster 1946–59) as a thank-offering for the deliverance of Westminster Abbey and St Margaret's Church from the perils of the Second World War and in remembrance of John Islip, sometime Abbot, and of Paul de Labilliere, sometime Dean.[2]

The Islip Upper Chantry Chapel now the Nurses' Memorial Chapel

A flight of steps leads to the Upper Chantry Chapel of Abbot Islip which in 1950 was furnished as a Memorial Chapel containing a Roll of Honour with the names of those of the nursing and midwifery professions who died during the Second World War. For this purpose Abbot Islip's tomb slab on its original gilt bronze colonnettes was removed from the Lower Chapel and re-erected against the east wall and on it has been placed the Roll of Honour and two gilded bronze candlesticks presented by Her Majesty the Queen in 1950. Above on the wall is a Crucifix in bronze. This Crucifix, which is slightly larger than life-size, is a duplicate of the original by Giovannida Bologna (1524–1608) which is in the Church of SS. Annunziata at Florence. The Memorial Window was designed by *Hugh Easton*.[3] The remainder of the Memorial was designed by *S. Comper, F.R.I.B.A.*

Chapels of St John the Evangelist, St Michael and St Andrew

Formerly three separate chapels, divided from each other and the Transept by richly painted and carved screens with doorways opening into the North Transept. A fifteenth-century screen, given by Abbot Esteney, 'finely carved, gilt, and adorned with arms of several of our nobility', stood till about 1772 between St John's Chapel and the Ambulatory; a fragment, including the doorway, still remains on the Transept side. St Michael's screen was destroyed to make way for the tomb of the old Duke of Newcastle, and St Andrew's, which had been enriched by Abbot Kyrton, was removed for John Holles, the Duke's son-in-law's enormous monument. Queen Maud, Henry I's wife, presented relics of St John's cell and garments to the monastery, and Edward the Confessor gave the bones and part of the cross of St Andrew, who is said to have been crucified in Achaia. In the time of the Stuarts the Lower House of Convocation held its sittings here, while the Upper House sat in Henry VII's Chapel. Keepe, writing in 1681, says: 'This chappel (St Michael), with part of the Chappels of St John the Evangelist and St Andrew, are now taken up and the monuments almost covered by

---

[1] *Buried at the entrance to Our Lady of the Pew's Chapel. The monument was removed to the Triforium in 1950.*

[2] *See page 32.*   [3] *See page 119.*

the scaffolds placed here, being made use of at present for the Lower Convocation House.'

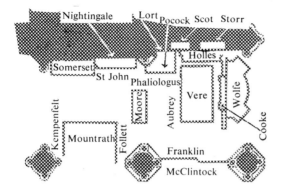

St John's Chapel

Sir Francis Vere, b. 1560, d. 1609, son of Geoffrey Vere, brother of John, 16th Earl of Oxford. A famous soldier in Elizabeth's reign, who 'brought more glory to the name of Vere then he took of blood from the family of Oxford'. Commander-in-Chief of the English forces in the Netherlands, he gained honour by his courage at the battle of Nieuport, and by his brave defence of Ostend for five months against the Spanish army. 'A gentleman of singular character, both for arms and letters; of the first, his being train'd up from his youth to the camp, being thirty years in the States' service and twenty years the Queen's general over the English, are sufficient proofs; and for the second, his learned and excellent commentaries do witness.'[1] The inscription has gone, but the following is an epitaph upon Vere given in Pettigrew's collection:

> When Vere sought death, arm'd with the sword and shield,
> Death was afraid to meet him in the field.
> But when his weapons he had laid aside
> Death, like a coward, struck him, and he died.

Vere's brother, **Horace, 1st Baron Vere of Tilbury**, b. 1565, d. 1635, who served with his brother and took over the command of the English Army in Holland lies in the same tomb. The monument was erected by Francis Vere's widow, in imitation of the tomb of Engelbrecht II, Count of Nassau, at Breda. It consists of two slabs of black marble; upon the lower lies the effigy, in white marble, of Sir Francis Vere, with his cloak wrapped round him like a Roman toga. Upon the upper slab, which is supported by four kneeling knights, are laid pieces of his armour to show that he died in his bed and not upon the field of battle. It is said that Roubiliac, while superintending the erection of the Nightingale monument was found one day by Gayfere, the Abbey mason, standing with his arms folded and his looks fixed upon one of the supporting knights. 'As Gayfere approached, the enthusiastic Frenchman laid his hand on his arm, pointed to the figure, and said in a whisper, "Hush! hush! he vil speak presently".'[2]

Aubrey de Vere, 20th and last **Earl of Oxford** (b. 1627, d. 1703) of that name lies with his family in the vault north of his ancestor's tomb. He was an ardent Royalist imprisoned during the Commonwealth, and after the Restoration made Lord Lieutenant of Essex, but he opposed James II's policy, and fought against him at the battle of the Boyne. He was made Lieut.-General of the forces under William III.

Sir George Holles, d. 1626, brother of John, 1st Earl of Clare. Major-General of the forces in the Netherlands, where he served under his uncle Sir Francis Vere, and distinguished himself at the battle of Nieuport (1600), which is represented on the bas-relief. *Nicholas Stone* received £100 from Holles's brother the Earl of Clare,[3] for executing this monument. The alabaster statue stands 'on the site of the altar once dedicated to the Confessor's favourite saint – the first in the Abbey that stands erect; the first that wears not the costume of the time but that of a Roman general; the first monument which, in its sculpture, reproduces the events in which the hero was engaged' (Stanley). The right eye is black, probably in allusion to some defect in the eyesight, or to a wound.

Captain Edward Cooke, b. 1772, d. 1799, whose capture of a French frigate in the Bay of Bengal was an event of great importance to British trade in India. He died of the wounds received in this action, and the East India Company erected the monument to him. *Bacon, jun., sculpt.*

Clement Saunders, d. 1695, Carver in Ordinary to three kings – Charles I, James II, and William III – a man 'well known and beloved by many of the nobility and gentry'. He was buried in the Abbey by his own desire, and left several bequests solely on that condition.

Admiral Sir George Pocock, K.B., b. 1706, d. 1792, served under Wager (page 19), and Watson (page 20), whom he succeeded in the chief command of the fleet. In 1762 he commanded the naval forces which captured Havana from the Spaniards, but on the return voyage many of the ships were wrecked and the crews perished from sickness and famine. Pocock himself resigned his command and retired into private life having amassed a large fortune. *Buried at Twickenham. Bacon sculpt.*

Grace Scot, b. 1622, d. 1646; both her husband, Colonel Thomas Scot, and her father, Sir Thomas Mauleverer, were regicides; the latter died 1655, before the Restoration, but the former was executed at Charing Cross in 1660. Epitaph by her husband:

> Hee that will give my GRACE but what is Hers
> Must say, her Death hath not
> Made only her Deare SCOT,
> But, Vertue, Worth, & Sweetnesse, Widowers.

Sir John Franklin, b. 1786, d. 1847, the Arctic explorer, lost with all his crew when completing the discovery of the North-West Passage. Epitaph by Tennyson:

> Not here: the White North has thy bones; and thou,
>   Heroic sailor-soul,
> Art passing on thine happier voyage now
>   Towards no earthly pole.

Noble sculpt.

Admiral Sir Leopold McClintock, d. 1907, Arctic explorer, who discovered the relics of Franklin's expedition, and so learnt the fate of his former chief twelve years after his loss.

---

[1] *Dart, vol. ii, page 2.*   [2] *Cunningham's Handbook, page 2.*

[3] *See statue of the Earl of Clare's son, page 57.*

Chapel of St Michael

Catherine, Baroness St John of Bletso, wife of John, 2nd Baron St John of Bletso and daughter of Sir William Dormer, d. 1615, a stiff effigy of a lady in Elizabethan dress, reclining on her elbow. The tomb has gone through several vicissitudes; not only was it once broken to pieces and put together again, but when the Nightingale monument was erected it was removed to St Nicholas's Chapel and placed on the Bishop of Durham's monument. Dean Stanley restored it to its original position, and placed it upon a modern pedestal.

Theodore Phaliologus, d. 1644. He was almost certainly the eldest son of Theodore Paleologas (d. 1636) on whose monument in the church at Landulph, Cornwall, is set out in full his claim to be directly descended from the brother of Constantine Paleologus the 'last Christian Emperor of Greece'. Their son, Theodore, served as lieutenant in the Parliamentary regiment commanded by Oliver, 1st Earl of Bolingbroke.

Lady Elizabeth Nightingale, d. 1731,[1] daughter of Washington, 2nd Earl Ferrers and wife of **Joseph Gascoigne Nightingale** (d. 1752), both buried in the North Ambulatory. The monument, of white marble, was erected by her son in 1761. Death is represented starting from beneath it, and aiming his dart at Lady Elizabeth, who shrinks back into her husband's arms. At the time of its erection there was great enthusiasm for this 'epigrammatic conceit'. Horace Walpole, however, styled it 'more theatric than sepulchral', and Allan Cunningham, while praising the anatomy of the figures, says: 'The Death is meanly imagined; he is the common dry-bones of every vulgar tale. It was not so that Milton dealt with this difficult allegory. We are satisfied with the indistinct image which he gives us. . . . The poet saw the difficulty, the sculptor saw none.' It is said that a robber, who broke into the Abbey one night, was so terrified by Death's figure in the moonlight that he dropped his tools and fled from the building. Roubiliac himself, while engaged upon the work, frightened his serving boy one day at dinner by dropping his knife and fork and starting forward, his eyes fixed on vacancy with an expression of intense fear. *Roubiliac sculpt.*

Sarah, Duchess of Somerset, d. 1692, daughter of the celebrated physician Sir Edward Alston,[2] and wife of John (Seymour), Duke of Somerset (d. 1675). She devoted the greater part of her fortune to charitable bequests in Oxford, Cambridge, Wiltshire, and Westminster. Buried near the Norris monument. Her tomb took the place of St Michael's Altar; behind it are part of the ancient reredos and the altar slab, which was found in the floor of the North Transept in 1872, and placed here in 1876.

Rear Admiral Richard Kempenfelt, b. 1718, d. 1782, in his youth fought under Vernon at the capture of Portobello; nearly forty years later he won honour by routing a French squadron and capturing twenty prizes. Only a year after this exploit his flagship, the *Royal George*, was resting at anchor off Spithead, Kempenfelt himself was writing in his cabin and the decks were crowded with the friends of the crew, when the vessel suddenly heeled over and about 800, including the brave old admiral, were drowned. Buried at Alverstoke.

His sword was in its sheath,
His fingers held the pen:
When Kempenfelt went down,
With twice four hundred men.[3]

Bacon, jun., sculpt.

St Andrew's Chapel

On the floor is the indent of a lost brass to **Edmund Kyrton,** d. 1466, Abbot of Westminster from 1440 till his resignation in 1462. He was Prior of Gloucester Hall, now Worcester College, Oxford, a college set apart for Benedictine scholars, from 1421 to about 1427. The tomb was originally raised from the floor, forming part of St Andrew's screen, which Kyrton had ornamented with 'carved birds, flowers, and cherubim, and with the arms, devices and mottoes of the nobility'.[4]

Mrs Anne Kirton, d. 1603, wife of James Kirton of Castle Carey, Somerset. Tears are descending from a large eye and covering the tablet.

Thomas Telford, b. 1757, d. 1834, celebrated in his time as the first engineer in Europe. He was one of the founders, in 1818, of the society which became the Institute of Civil Engineers. He was its first President and in 1828 procured for it a charter of incorporation. The Menai Bridge, the Caledonian Canal and the Inland Navigation of Sweden are among his best known works. Buried near Stephenson. *E. H. Baily sculpt.*

Lieut.-General William Anne Villettes, b. 1754, d. 1808, Governor and Commander-in-Chief of the forces in Jamaica.

Dr Matthew Baillie, b. 1761, d. 1823, physician and anatomist, brother of Joanna Baillie, the poetess. *Bust by Chantrey.*

Sir Humphry Davy, Bt., b. 1778, d. 1829, scientist. President of the Royal Society. The inventor of a famous safety-lamp for use in the mines. Buried at Geneva.

Dr Thomas Young, b. 1773, d. 1829, whose mathematical and hieroglyphical discoveries have outshone his medical fame. Buried at Farnborough, Kent. Inscription by Hudson Gurney. *Medallion by Chantrey.*

Mrs Sarah Siddons, b. 1755, d. 1831, the great actress. Buried in Paddington Cemetery. A statue by *Chantrey* after Reynolds's picture of her as the Tragic Muse. Macready defrayed the expense. And her brother, the celebrated actor, **John Kemble,** b. 1757, d. 1823, represented as Cato. The statue was moved here in 1865 from the North Transept. Buried at Lausanne. *Flaxman des., Hinchcliffe sculpt.*

Sir James Young Simpson, Bt., b. 1811, d. 1870, the discoverer of the anaesthetic properties of chloroform. Buried at Edinburgh. *Brodie sculpt.*

A tablet with a long inscription to **Susannah Jane Davidson,** only child of William Davidson, a wealthy merchant of Rotterdam and London, died in Paris, aged twenty, January 1767. Her father, d. 1794, survived thirty years, but never got over her loss. Both he and Susannah were painted by Sir Joshua Reynolds, the girl with a large lamb on her lap. *Richard Hayward sculpt.*

John William Strutt, 3rd Baron Rayleigh, O.M., b. 1842, d. 1919. President of the Royal Society, 1905–8, Chancellor of the University of Cambridge, 1908–10. A distinguished

---

[1] *Date 1734 on monument incorrect.*
[2] *Died 1669. President of the College of Physicians 1635–66.*

[3] *See Cowper's well-known lines on 'The Wreck of the Royal George'.*   [4] *Widmore, page 115.*

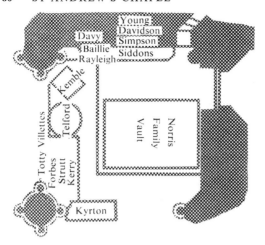

physicist. Medallion portrait head. *Derwent Wood sculpt.*

Henry, 1st Baron Norris, b. 1525, d. 1601, and his wife, **Margaret,** d. 1599, daughter of Lord Williams of Thame, the 'keeper of Queen Elizabeth while in restraint under her sister and civil unto her in those dangerous days. Thus Queen Elizabeth beheld them both not only with gracious but grateful eyes.'[1] She sent Norris as Ambassador to France, and created him Baron Norris of Rycote on his return, 1572. The Queen used to call Lady Norris 'her own dear crow', either from her swarthy complexion, or from the Norris crest, a raven. Lord Norris acquired Rycote, in Oxfordshire, by his marriage, and he and his wife are buried there. Round the parents kneel their six sons, 'a brood', as Camden calls them, 'of martial-spirited men', for the 'Norrises were all *martis pulli* (men of the sword), and never out of military employment'. Four were knighted; four died in battle, or from wounds; the second son, Sir John, died of disappointment at losing the Lord-Lieutenancy of Ireland, 'his death went so near the heart of the lord, his ancient father, that he died soon after'. One alone, Sir Edward, survived his father and brothers, and while the rest are represented praying with bowed heads he looks cheerfully upward. The monument erected by their kindred 'in honourable remembrance of their noble acts, true valour, and high worth'.[2] It is made of coloured marbles, the effigies and figures of alabaster. *Monument by Isaac James.*[3]

---

[1] *Fuller's* Worthies, *vol. iii, pages 15, 16.*

[2] *Neale, vol. ii, page 199.*

[3] *See* Country Life *(17 February 1950), 'A Westminster Abbey Puzzle', where Mrs K. Esdaile proves the sculptor to have been Isaac James.*

Monument of Lady Elizabeth Nightingale

CHAPEL OF ST EDWARD THE CONFESSOR OR THE CHAPEL OF THE KINGS [*See plan, page 52*]

IN MOST OF THE great churches of the Middle Ages immediately behind the High Altar there is a 'shrine' containing the relics of the Patron Saint, or of a great benefactor to the church. In Westminster Abbey this shrine encloses the body of Edward the Confessor whose great benefactions to the Abbey were so largely responsible for the pre-eminent position it subsequently occupied. St Edward's shrine and the five kings and three queens whose bodies lie round it make this Chapel the most sacred part of the Abbey. It is entered by a flight of steps from the North Ambulatory. In the centre of the Chapel is the Confessor's tomb; at the east end is the Chantry Chapel of Henry V. Where this Chantry now stands the relics were originally kept, but after its erection they were moved to a chest placed between the tomb of Henry III and the shrine, and there remained till they were scattered and destroyed at the dissolution of the monastery. The most precious among them were: the Virgin Mary's Girdle, presented by Edward the Confessor; a stone marked with the print of Christ's foot at the Ascension; His blood in a crystal vase; and a piece of the Cross, set in jewels, brought from Wales, and given by Edward I; the skull of St Benedict, brought from France and presented by Edward III.

Very few of the original inscriptions round the verge of the tombs remain; those in Roman letters are of a much later period, and generally have the date incorrect. Wooden tablets, upon which were Latin verses with English translations, probably those noticed in the sixteenth century by the chronicler Fabyan, used to hang from iron chains by each of the royal tombs. These epitaphs were long supposed to have been the work of the poet Skelton, who, when Poet Laureate, wrote those affixed to the tombs of Henry VII and his mother, but all the early ones have been found in a chronicle written by a Westminster monk late in the fourteenth century. They must therefore have been contemporary verses and are of great interest. In Keepe's time (late seventeenth century) some were still existing, and they are copied in his book.

Edward the Confessor

Edward the Confessor, b. between 1002 and 1005, reigned 1042–66;[1] he was a prince of extreme piety, caring little for State affairs, but worshipped as a saint by his people. Driven from his kingdom by the Danes, after his father Ethelred's death, Edward vowed to make a pilgrimage to St Peter's grave at Rome if he returned in safety. But once on the throne he found it impossible to leave his subjects, and the Pope released him from his vow on condition that he should found or restore a monastery to St Peter. This led to the building of a new church in the Norman style to replace the Saxon church of the Benedictine monastery on Thorneye (see page 10).

The work took fifteen years, and the church was consecrated on Innocents' Day, 1065, but the royal founder was dying and unable to be present at the service. He died 5 January 1066, and was buried before the High Altar in his own new church. Tradition marks Edward as the first king who touched for the 'King's Evil' (a skin disease), and after his death many miracles were said to have been worked at his grave. Wulstan, the Saxon Bishop of Worcester, when required to resign his see at the Conquest, appealed for help to the dead King, and struck his staff into the tomb, where it stood upright, and could be displaced by no one but Wulstan himself. On hearing of this miracle William the Conqueror allowed Wulstan to retain his bishopric, and raised a costly stone tomb, sparkling with gold and jewels, over the Confessor's remains. In 1102 the tomb was opened by Abbot Gilbert in the presence of Henry I; and a Norman chronicle relates how the body was found entire, the joints as flexible as if it were 'a body asleep'. Gundulph, Bishop of Rochester, 'who is very bold, strokes the yellow beard whence he wishes to draw an hair, but he cannot draw it from the beard'. Two attempts were made to canonize Edward. The first (in 1140) failed, but the second was successful, and on 13 October 1163, the saint's body was transferred to the shrine prepared for it by Henry II, in the presence of the King and of Thomas Becket, Archbishop of Canterbury. The robes in which the body was wrapped were made into three copes, and Abbot Laurence drew St John's famous ring off the finger and deposited it among the relics. After that the corpse remained undisturbed for nearly a hundred years till Henry III pulled down that part of the church, and removed the old shrine containing the Saint's body to another part of the church, while a new tomb was prepared for it. Abbot Ware brought the workmen and porphyries for the pavement from Italy, and the ancient inscription gives the name of the chief artist, Peter, a Roman citizen. Only the basement now remains of Henry's magnificent fabric; the material is Purbeck marble, decorated with glass mosaic. Above this marble and mosaic base was the golden shrine enclosing the Confessor's coffin. The shrine was decorated with eleven small gold images of kings and saints; amongst them were St Edmund with the church in one hand, St Peter trampling on Nero, and a king, probably Henry III himself, holding a model of the shrine; besides these were many great jewels and cameos. At the sides, upon two pillars, were golden statues of St Edward and St John the Evangelist; at the west end was an altar, which was destroyed at the Dissolution, and used to be replaced at coronations by a table called St Edward's Altar. A permanent altar was placed here at the coronation of King Edward VII, upon which are the silver candlesticks given by the Duke and Duchess of York (later King George VI and Queen Elizabeth) to commemorate their marriage in the Abbey. In the lower part of the shrine are the recesses in which sick persons were often left during the night to be cured by the Saint. Round the verge was an inscription 'formed by bars of blue glass set in gold

---

[1] *Confessor means a martyr without bloodshedding – a man who had led a pious life and been persecuted but not killed.*

mosaic'. All the glass has long been picked out, but traces of letters can be seen in places under the plaster. On 13 October 1269, the wainscot chest which contained the Confessor's body was brought in solemn procession to its new resting-place; Henry III, his brother, Richard, King of the Romans, and his two sons, bore the coffin on their shoulders. This day, 13 October, the date of the two translations, was kept yearly with great ceremony in the Abbey; processions resorted to the shrine from all the religious bodies in London, and the steps are worn away by the knees of the pilgrims. On St Edward's Day Roman Catholic worshippers still make pilgrimages to his mutilated shrine. A special service now marks the day as one to be remembered in the Abbey services here. Proofs of the veneration in which the Saint was held by our early kings may be found in every reign. But in 1540 came the dissolution of the monastery; the shrine was despoiled of its treasures, the relics were buried beneath it, and the gold images and jewels carried off, while the body of the Saint was removed and buried in some obscure place. Under Mary the coffin was restored to its place, and the shrine was repaired by Abbot Feckenham, who added the present wooden erection (1557) above the cornice, and painted an inscription over the ancient one, the Queen presenting fresh jewels and images to replace the stolen ones. Later on the shrine again suffered, losing its images and jewels, but was not destroyed. Soon after James II's coronation (1685) a golden cross and chain were taken out of the Confessor's coffin by Taylor, 'one of the singing men, who, as the scaffolds were taken down after his Majesty's Coronation, espying a hole in the tomb and something glisten, put his hand in and brought it to the Deane, and he to the King',[1] receiving a bounty of £50. Through the hole Taylor saw the Saint's head, 'solid and firm, the upper and lower jaws full of teeth, a list of gold round the temples', and 'all his bones and much dust in his coffin'. King James had the old coffin enclosed in one strongly clamped with iron, where it has remained undisturbed till this day.

The **Lady Edith** or Eadgyth, d. 1075, wife of Edward the Confessor, was buried near her husband's tomb, in the old church, before the High Altar; there is no record of the traditional removal of her coffin to the north side of the new shrine. Edith was the daughter of Earl Godwin of Wessex. Not only was she very beautiful, and 'a lady of singular piety and sweet modesty', but renowned for her learning. 'Her breast,' says one writer, 'was a store house of all liberal science.' Estranged from her husband and immured in a nunnery after his quarrel with her father (1052), she returned to Court after their reconciliation and nursed the Confessor in his last illness.

Close to Edith lay the Confessor's great-niece **Maud**, or as she was first called Edith, the wife of Henry I; there is no reason to believe in the removal of her coffin to the south of the shrine.[2] 'She was,' says an old chronicler, 'the very mirror of piety, humility, and princely bounty,' and her marriage with Henry I united the Saxon and Norman lines, and went far to reconcile the two peoples. 'This Queen would every day in Lent walk from her Palace to this Church, barefoot and barelegged, and wearing a garment of hair. She would wash and kiss the feet of the poorest people, and give them alms.'[3] She would also often lie for days and nights 'in prayer and in penance' before the shrine. The Latin epitaph which used to hang near her grave, speaks of 'her goodness and probity, if we should go about to tell all, the day would be too short'. Two lamps in memory of these two queens used to hang before the High Altar in the early days of the monastery, the one to Queen Maud was kept burning by the Sheriffs of London.

The heart of **Henry d'Almayne**, son of Richard, King of the Romans, and nephew of Henry III, was long preserved in a golden cup either within, or, more probably, near, the shrine of the Confessor. He was murdered by the sons of Simon de Montfort, in the cathedral at Viterbo, 1271. Dante mentions the fact of the preservation of the heart 'on the banks of the Thames',[4] and places one of the murderers up to his chin in a river of blood because the fatal blow was struck during the elevation of the Host.

Edward I

Edward I, surnamed 'Longshanks', b. 1239, d. 1307, has been fitly called the English Justinian. He succeeded his father Henry III in 1272. 'A worthy Prince he was . . . equally fortunate in drawing and sheathing the sword, in war and peace. . . . In a word, as the arm of King Edward I was accounted the measure of a yard generally received in England, so his actions are an excellent model, and a praiseworthy platform for succeeding Princes to imitate.'[5] He was the first king crowned in Henry III's new church—the first coronation in the Abbey as it now appears; and he and Eleanor were the first sovereigns who were jointly crowned there. Edward continued his father's benefactions to the Abbey Church, and the shrine of St Edward, after whom he was called, received special tokens of his veneration. Here he raised splendid tombs to his father and his wife; here he deposited the stone of Scone and the Scottish regalia; and it was before the shrine that his little son, Alphonso, hung the golden coronet of Llewellyn, last native Prince of Wales, and, dying shortly after, was buried by his father's wish close by the Saint. Edward died on 7 July 1307, at Burgh-on-the-Sands, a little village on the Solway Firth, on his way to Scotland. His body was carried with great funeral pomp to Waltham Abbey, where it lay for about fifteen weeks by the side of King Harold. The parliament, which met in August at Northampton, gave orders that it should be removed to Westminster Abbey 'with all the honours befitting so great a monarch'. In the following October the King's body was taken to London, and after resting for three nights successively in the Churches of Holy Trinity, St Paul's, and the Friars Minors, was brought in an open chariot, attended by a great concourse of nobles, to the Abbey (27 October), where it was interred on St Simon and St Jude's Day, 28 October 1307. He lies in an altar tomb composed of five blocks of grey marble upon a freestone basement: 'a plain monument for so great and glorious a King'. It has been suggested that the tomb was left in this unfinished state so that the body could be taken out at any time, in fulfilment of the 'famous pact which the dying King required of his son that his flesh should be boiled, his bones carried at the head of the

---

[1] See L. E. Tanner, 'The Quest for the Cross of St Edward the Confessor' (Journal of the British Archaeological Association, vol. xvii, 1954).
[2] See Westlake's Westminster Abbey, vol. ii, pages 455–6.

[3] Monumenta Westmonasteriensia, page 139.
[4] Inferno, vol. xii, pages 119–20.
[5] Fuller's Church History, page 92.

Shrine of Edward the Confes

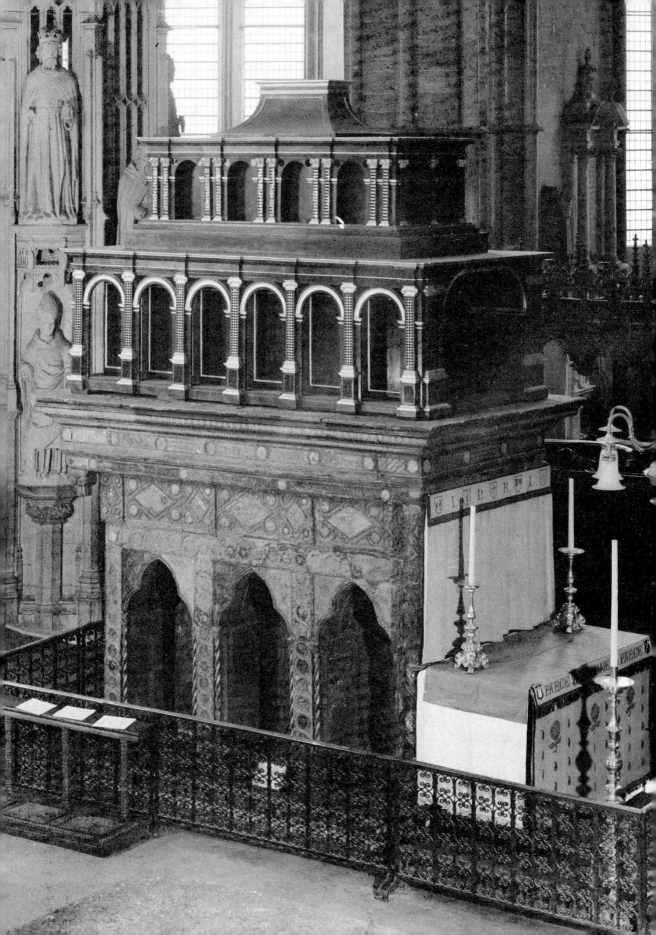

Tomb of Henry III from the Ambulatory

Tomb of Henry III from the Confessor's Chapel

English army till Scotland was subdued, and his heart sent to the Holy Land'. It seems that the cerecloth was kept waxed till the deposition of Richard II. The marble was painted and gilt, and an embroidered pall covered its sides. Over it was a wooden canopy broken down in the riot at Pulteney's funeral, and it was protected from the Ambulatory by an iron grille. On the north side are the words *Scotorum Malleus* (the Hammer of the Scots) and *Pactum Serva* (Keep troth), which belong to the same period as the other painted inscriptions, and were probably placed on the tombs by Abbot Feckenham. In 1744 the tomb was opened; the covering stone was found quite loose and uncemented; within was a Purbeck marble coffin. The King's body was wrapped in a large waxed linen cloth, the head covered with a face cloth of crimson sarsenet. Beneath this were the royal robes, a tunic of red silk damask with gold tissue work, and a mantle of crimson velvet; a piece of rich cloth of gold laid loosely over them. In the right hand was a sceptre, in the left a rod surmounted by a dove and oak leaves, in white and green enamel; a gilt crown was upon the head. The corpse was found almost entire, the innermost cover being another waxed cloth fitting closely to the face and limbs; the length of the body was 6 feet 2 inches.[1] The tomb was fastened down with strong cement before the spectators left the spot, and, says Horace Walpole, 'they (the Dean and Chapter) boast now of having enclosed him so substantially that his ashes cannot be violated again'.

[1] *See account in* Archaeologia, *vol. iii, by Sir Joseph Ayloffe.*

Henry III

Henry III, b. 1207, d. 1272. He succeeded his father King John in 1216 and was the builder of the greater part of the present church. He was a Prince 'rather devout than wise . . . as appears from his hearing mass three times a day, at the same time as he refused to hear any complaints made against his court parasites'. 'Quiet King Henry, our English Nestor (not for depth of brains but length of life), who reigned fifty-six years, in which terme he buried all his contemporary Princes in Christendom twice over.'[2]

Henry was recklessly extravagant. He built the Abbey at the expense of fines and exactions laid upon the people, and with the spoils of other churches, till at last, 'having neither coin nor credit', he was driven to pawn the jewels with which he had himself enriched St Edward's shrine. Henry was taken ill at Bury St Edmunds, while he was performing his devotions, and carried to his new palace at Westminster, where he died, 16 November 1272. The funeral took place on St Edmund's Day, and was concluded with great magnificence. The body, borne by the Knights Templars, whom Henry had first introduced into England, was temporarily laid before the High Altar, in the coffin which had contained the Confessor's bones, and nineteen years after removed to the splendid tomb prepared for it by Edward I in St Edward's Chapel. The heart was at the same time (1291), according to Henry's will, delivered to the Abbess of Fontevrault, 'to be en-

[2] *Fuller's* Church History, *page 73.*

shrined in the Norman Abbey where his mother Isabella, his uncle Richard I, his grandfather Henry II, and his grandmother Eleanor were buried'. The tomb is Italian in design; the mosaics and the workmen came, like those for the shrine, from Italy. It consists of a double marble tomb, once sparkling with jewels and glass mosaic. Below, upon the inner side, are three recesses which in all probability contained the reliquaries of saints. Above is a second mosaic tomb. The slabs of porphyry, inserted at the side, were brought from abroad in 1280 by Edward I. Upon it lies *William Torel's* bronze effigy, which is an idealized portrait of the King. The account for payments speaks of it as made 'in the likeness of King Henry'. In the garment are holes which once contained jewels. An iron grate, by *Master Henry of Lewes*, formerly protected the tomb, and the plain wooden canopy was gilt and decorated with paintings. Some of the original Norman-French inscription round the verge still exists, but only a few letters of the later Latin inscription, painted in Feckenham's time on the north side, now remain.

Princess Elizabeth Tudor, d. 1495, daughter of Henry VII. Although she died at the age of three years and two months her obsequies were celebrated with great pomp; her body was brought in a black 'chair' drawn by six horses from Eltham, where she died, received at the gate of the Abbey by the Prior, and borne with great ceremony into the church. The tomb is a small one of Lydian marble. The gilt effigy and inscriptions have disappeared.

Eleanor of Castile

At the feet of her father-in-law lies **Queen Eleanor of Castile,** d. 1290, first wife of Edward I and mother of Edward II. She was Edward's constant companion during the thirty-six years of their married life. Fearless of danger, she accompanied him on his Crusades, saying, when he tried to dissuade her: 'The way to heaven is as near from Palestine as from England'. While in the Holy Land, it is said that she saved her husband's life at the risk of her own by sucking the poison from a wound given him by an assassin's dagger. She was crowned with him at Westminster on their return (1274), and died in November 1290, at Harby in Nottinghamshire. Edward brought her body in state to Westminster, erecting memorial crosses of which only three, at Northampton, Geddington, and Waltham, remain – to mark the places where the procession rested from Lincoln to Charing Cross, 'that passengers reminded might pray for her soul'. The body was embalmed and laid in a coffin 'full of spices', the heart given to the Preaching Friars. The funeral service was performed by the Bishop of Lincoln, as a quarrel between the Archbishop of Canterbury and the Abbot of Westminster prevented their meeting. Three tombs were raised over her remains: one at Lincoln, which was destroyed in the Civil Wars; another, over her heart, in the Blackfriars Monastery, which disappeared at the Dissolution; and the third, the only one now remaining, at

Effigy of Eleanor of Castile

Westminster. This was erected about the time that the tomb of Henry III was approaching completion. *William Torel*, Citizen and Goldsmith of London, cast (1291) the effigies of both Eleanor and her father-in-law. Traces of a painting perhaps by Master Walter of Durham still remain on the Ambulatory side of the tomb. This shows an armed knight, Sir Otes (or Otho) de Grandison, kneeling before the Virgin and Child and four pilgrims praying before the Holy Sepulchre. Sir Otes, who died in 1328, was a close friend of Edward I and accompanied him to the Holy Land. A more reliable tradition names him rather than Queen Eleanor as the person who sucked the poison from Edward's wound. Above is the tomb itself of Purbeck marble decorated with panels enclosing coats of arms. Upon it is Torel's fine effigy, which is an ideal likeness of the Queen; it is made of gilt bronze, originally set with jewels. The garment consists of two long dresses and a cloak; the right hand once held a sceptre, the left is closed over the string of the cloak. William Sprot and John de Ware furnished the metal, and sundry gold florins for the gilding were brought from Lucca. Thomas de Hokyntone did all the woodwork, which included a canopy painted by Walter of Durham, but the latter was probably destroyed when Henry V's Chantry was erected, and the present plain Perpendicular one substituted. On the Ambulatory side is a curved iron grille of exquisite workmanship,[1] by an English smith, Master Thomas of Leighton Buzzard. 'She hathe,' says Fabyan, 'ij wexe tapers brennynge upon her tombe both daye and nyght, whyche so hath contynued syne the day of her buryIng to this present day.' Besides that a hundred wax tapers were to burn round her grave in the Abbey every St Andrew's Eve. Round the copper verge is a Norman-French inscription, partly hidden from sight by Henry V's Chantry: ICI GIST ALIANOR IADIS REYNE DE ENGLETERE FEMME AL REY EDEWARD FIZ LEREY HENRY EFYLLE AL REY DE ESPAYGNE ECONTASSE DE PVNTIV DEL ALME DELI DEV PVR SA PITE EYT MERCI AMEN.[2]

Henry V

Henry V, b. 1388, d. 1422, surnamed of Monmouth, the place of his birth. He was the eldest son of Henry IV, by Mary de Bohun, and succeeded his father in 1413. The hero of Agincourt went 'commonly with his head un-covered; the wearing of armour was no more to him than a cloak'; he was fortunate 'in fight and commend-able in all his actions, verifying the proverb that an ill youth may make a good man'.[3] Henry was actually ruler of France and heir to the French king after the Treaty of Troyes (1420). Inflexible in justice, with strong religious principles added to personal charm, Henry was long remembered as a popular hero. Shakespeare describes the last scene in Westminster Abbey, when the nobles standing round the hearse express the nation's grief for their King's untimely death:

Hung be the heavens with black, yield day to night!

. . . .

King Henry the Fifth, too famous to live long!
England ne'er lost a King of so much worth.

(*Henry VI*, Act I, Sc. 1.)

Henry had, like his predecessors, a great veneration for the Abbey. A Te Deum service for the victory of Agincourt, fought on St Crispin's Day, 25 October 1415, was held before the shrine, and the King contributed 1,000 marks yearly towards the rebuilding of the Nave, besides other gifts of money; he also restored a ruby ring, originally given by Richard II, to St Edward's Shrine. He died at Vincennes, in his thirty-fourth year (August 1422), and his body was embalmed and deposited for a time in Rouen Cathedral. It was then laid on an open chariot drawn by four horses, and 'above the corpse was placed a figure made of boyled hides or leather, represen-ting his person, and painted to the life. Upon whose head was set an Imperial diadem of gold and precious stones, on his body a purple robe, furred with ermine';[4] in one hand he held a sceptre, in the other a golden globe. The clergy attended the corpse, singing funeral services as they went; round the car a hundred torches were carried by men in white robes; behind came the household and nobility, and the Queen followed at the distance of a league. At Dover the great bishops and ecclesiastics met the procession and accompanied it to London, where the body was placed in state in St Paul's Cathedral. Thence it was taken in procession to the Abbey, 7 November 1422, and interred with much pomp among the kings, James I, King of Scots, attending as chief mourner. Behind the effigy of the King, which was carried on the funeral car instead of exposing the embalmed body, his three chargers were led up to the altar, and his banners were borne by great nobles. Henry's will directed that a high Chantry Chapel should be raised over his body, and the eastern end of St Edward's Chapel was accordingly cleared out in order to carry out his wishes. This structure,[5] which was planned by John of Thirske, who was also the architect of the Nave at that period, encroaches on the Ambulatory and on the tombs of Eleanor and Philippa. The tomb, which was not finished until about 1431, is beneath the arch, and the Chantry Chapel, with the Altar of the Annunciation dedicated to the Virgin, where prayers were said for the King's soul, is over it. Above this altar is an Annunciation and the patron saints of England and France, St George and St Denis, and two kings, the Confessor and St Edmund, on either side. The centre niche, which probably contained a representation of the Trinity, is vacant. In the niches are smaller statues. On a wooden bar above are a shield and saddle, purchased for the funeral, and a tilting helmet which by tradition was worn by the King at Agincourt. On the Ambulatory sides, north and south, are representations of the homage and crowning at Henry V's coronation – the heads of the King are undoubtedly portraits – on the north is his figure on horseback leaping a stream with the tents of his soldiers behind. Among the devices on the frieze and cornice are heraldic badges of a cresset, a collared antelope, and a swan also collared, chained to a beacon; the swans were the Bohun family's emblems. The Purbeck marble tomb has lost its ancient splendour; the figure is now a block

---

[1] *Taken down in 1822, but replaced by Sir Gilbert Scott.*

[2] *'Here lies Eleanor, sometime Queen of England, wife to King Edward, son of King Henry, daughter of the King of Spain, and Countess of Ponthieu, on whose soul God in His pity have mercy. Amen.'*

[3] *Fuller's* Church History, *page 169.*

---

[4] *Sandford, page 280.*

[5] *See* Archaeologia, *vol. lxv, pages 139–186.*

Chantry Chapel of Henry

of oak; the head, sceptre, and other regalia, all of silver, and the plates of silver gilt which covered the body, were stolen in 1546. The iron railings, painted red and blue, which guarded the treasure, are broken, but the gates, by a London smith, Roger Johnson, put up in the ninth year of Henry VI, still remain. Henry V's tomb was always one of the sights of the Abbey. Sir Philip Sidney speaks of going to Westminster to see Harry the Fifth, and readers of Addison will remember that Sir Roger de Coverley's anger was roused by the lost head: 'Some Whig, I'll warrant you. You ought to lock up your Kings better; they'll carry off the body too if you don't take care.'

Catherine of Valois, b. 1401, d. 1437, Henry V's Queen, daughter of Charles VI of France. After Henry's death she married Owen Tudor, a Welshman, who traced his descent from Cadwalladr. Edmund, Earl of Richmond, the father of Henry VII, was one of Catherine's sons by this marriage, and she thus became the ancestress of the Tudor line. Catherine died in the monastery at Bermondsey, and was buried, 10 February 1437, with much pomp and cere- mony. The painted funeral wooden effigy (now much dilapidated and without any garments) was 'fully robed in a satin mantle, surcote, and tunic, all furred with ermine; crown, sceptre, and rings silver gilt' and was carried on a magnificent hearse. Her son, Henry VI, and his Queen attended the funeral in state, in the Lady Chapel. When Henry VII pulled down the old chapel he removed his grandmother's body and it was ultimately placed above ground in an open coffin of loose boards by Henry V's tomb. There it remained for over two hundred years, and Pepys, writing in 1669, boasts that he saw, 'by particular favour, the body of Queen Catherine of Valois, and I had the upper part of her body in my hands, and I did kiss her mouth, reflecting upon it that I did kiss a Queene, and that this was my birthday 36 years old that I did kiss a Queene'. In the eighteenth century the bones were still 'firmly united, and thinly cloth'd with flesh, like scrapings of tann'd leather'. In 1776 the Queen's body was at last hidden from sight beneath the Villiers monument (page 59). It was removed in 1878 by Dean Stanley and placed beneath the ancient altar slab in the Chantry Chapel of Henry V.

In an unmarked grave immediately in front of the North Turret of Henry V's Chantry Chapel is buried **Richard Courtenay, Bishop of Norwich,** who accompanied Henry V to France and died at the siege of Harfleur in 1415. He was buried here by the express command of the King.

Philippa of Hainault

Philippa, b. 1314, d. 1369, Edward III's queen, and daughter of William, Count of Hainault. She was married in 1328, and crowned with Edward at Westminster in the same year. 'She was a woman of great honour and virtue and a firm friend to England', sometimes accompanying her husband on his foreign expeditions, as on the occasion of the well-known anecdote of her intercession for the lives of the burgesses of Calais. At other times, in his absence, she defended the kingdom against the Scots.

Throughout their long union of forty-two years Philippa had great influence over the King, and the scene at her deathbed, as described by Froissart, is most touching. Holding the King's right hand in hers, she told him her last wishes, and, above all, entreated that 'when it should please God to call you hence you will not choose any other sepulchre than mine, and that you will lie beside me in the cloister at Westminster'. She was the reputed foundress of Queen's College, Oxford, which was really founded by her chaplain in her honour. The tomb is an altar tomb of black and white marble, of Flemish design, and the King spent immense sums – about £3,000 – upon its erection; the name of the artist is *Hennequin de Liége*, a famous sculptor, working in Paris under Pepin de Huy. Round the sides were once 'thirty sweetly carved niches, wherein have been placed as many little images',[1] representing the thirty illustrious persons with whom Philippa was connected. None of these re- mained, and the tomb was quite bare till Sir Gilbert Scott discovered some of the alabaster tabernacle work in a museum in 1857, and replaced it on the south side of the monument. He also unearthed two of the figures and niches which had been built into the Chantry Chapel, but scarcely had he replaced them when one of them, an angel with wings of gilt metals, was stolen. The other figure, a lady holding a monkey, is now protected by a grille. The effigy is white marble, enriched with paint and gilding; the features are undoubtedly a portrait. It was finished in 1369. The Queen held the string of her cloak in one hand, but the sceptre has gone and the hands are broken; the columns at the sides enclosed little figures, and the holes were filled up with glass mosaic. A wooden canopy covers the tomb, and it formerly was protected by an iron railing, bought by the King for £600 from the custodian of St Paul's, where it had covered the tomb of Michael, Bishop of London. It appears from the inpen- tures that seventy figures in all were included in this tomb; 'divers images in the likeness of angels' being made by John Orchard, bronze-worker, of London, who also put up and repaired the grate.[2]

Close by lies **Thomas, Duke of Gloucester**, b. 1355, d. 1397, called 'of Woodstock' from the place of his birth. He was the youngest son of Edward III and Philippa of Hainault, the only one of her children present at Philippa's deathbed. It is recorded that the famous relic, the Girdle of the Blessed Virgin, was sent for on two occasions when the Queen was expecting the birth of her children, the last time when her son, Thomas, was born. He married one of the co-heiresses of Humphrey de Bohun, Earl of Hereford and Constable of England. Richard II sum- moned him to Parliament by the title of 'the King's dearest uncle', and created him Duke of Gloucester (1385). But Thomas presumed 'on the old maxim "Patruus est loco parentis" (an uncle is in the place of a father). He observed the King too nearly and checked him too sharply'.[3] He was accused of conspiring against the Crown. The King went himself and arrested the Duke at his castle of Pleshy, and had him conveyed to Calais and there he was smothered under a feather bed. The Duke was first buried in St Edmund's Chapel, but his body was after- wards removed by Henry IV, to its present position, and placed beneath a fine brass with figures of himself and his relatives upon it. Unfortunately the brass has now entirely disappeared.

---

[1] Monumenta Westmonasteriensia, *page 149.*
[2] English Medieval Architects *by John Harvey, page 199.*
[3] *Fuller's* Worthies, *vol. iii, pages 9, 10.*

Edward III

Edward III, b. 1312, reigned 1327–77, son of Edward II and Isabel, daughter of King Philip the Fair, and through her King Edward III laid claim to the Crown of France. Edward was crowned in the Abbey on his father's deposition, and the shield and sword of State, still kept near the shrine, were then first carried before the sovereign. The early part of his reign was taken up with achievements in France and Scotland. 'He conquered both before his face and behind his back, whence he came and whither he went–north and south, one in his person, the other by his substitutes in his absence. . . . Herein he stands without a parallel that he had both the kings he fought against, John de Valois of France, and David, the King of Scotland, his prisoners at one time, not taken by any cowardly surprise, but by fair fight in open field.'[1] But the end was in gloomy contrast to the beginning. After Philippa's death his 'fortunes seemed to fall into eclipse', and the death in 1376 of the Black Prince was the final blow. At last the King, old before his time and overcome with grief for his son's death, was 'forced to forsake the world as the world had forsaken him'. He died, deserted, it is said, and robbed even to the rings off his fingers, by his favourites and servants, at his Palace of Sheen, 21 June 1377, attended only by one poor priest, 'a perfect example of this world's vanity'.[2] His body, with the face uncovered, carried by four of his sons, and followed by his surviving children, was deposited

either in Philippa's tomb, or where now stands the monument erected to him by his grandson, Richard II. This monument was designed by *Henry Yevele*. It consists of an altar tomb of Purbeck marble; round the sides are niches in which were once little bronze images of twelve of the fourteen children of Edward and Philippa.[3] Only six–those on the south side–remain. These are from left to right: The Black Prince, b. 1330, d. 1376; Joan of the Tower; Lionel, Duke of Clarence; Edmund, Duke of York, the founder of the House of York; Mary of Brittany; and William of Hatfield. Their coats of arms were on little enamelled shields at the feet, only four of which are left. On the basement of the Ambulatory side are four large enamelled shields with the arms of England and St George. The King's effigy, by *John Orchard*, of gilt bronze, lies on the tomb. Round the verge, in brass letters, runs a Latin rhyming inscription. Tradition says that the face was modelled from a cast taken after death, and, although the hair and beard are conventionalized, the features no doubt resembled the King. The beautiful and elaborate wooden canopy over the tomb is by *Hugh Herland*.

Princess Margaret, d. 1472, sixth daughter of Edward IV, who died at the age of nine months. A little tomb of grey marble, probably moved here from somewhere else, perhaps from the old Lady Chapel. The brass effigy and inscriptions have been torn off.

---

[1] *Fuller's* Church History, *page 110.*   [2] *Sandford, page 175.*

[3] *Two, whose statues were among these–William of Windsor and Blanche of the Tower–have a little tomb in St Edmund's Chapel, page 58.*

Effigy of Edward III

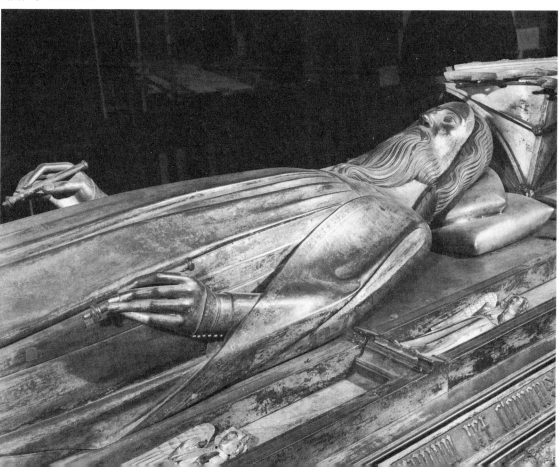

Richard II

Richard II, b. 1366, d. 1400, reigned 1377 to 1399, called of Bordeaux, the place of his birth, son of Edward the Black Prince and Joan, the 'Fair Maid of Kent'. Also his first wife, **Anne of Bohemia,** b. 1366, d. 1394, daughter of the Emperor Charles IV, and sister of King Wenceslaus IV. The King and Queen were married in the Abbey, January 1382, the first and only reigning sovereigns whose marriage took place here. Anne was crowned two days later by Archbishop Courtenay. Richard was devoted to Westminster; his coronation at the Abbey is said to have been more splendid than any that had gone before, and was distinguished by the creation of the 'Knights of the Bath', who from this time for four hundred years took part in the coronation ceremony. He partly rebuilt Westminster Hall, and also the great northern entrance of the Abbey, as well as some bays of the Nave; his badge, 'The White Hart', used to be in the glass of the window near the West Cloister door. The Hart can be seen painted on the wall of the Muniment Room and traces of it on the roof of the Chapel of Our Lady of the Pew. Richard had a special veneration for the Confessor; he impaled the arms assigned to the Confessor with his own; ' "by St Edward" was his favourite oath' and he and his Queen appeared in the Abbey, crowned, with sceptres in their hands, on St Edward's Day. In 1381, Richard, then a boy of fifteen, quelled a dangerous rebellion by his personal courage and tact. After hearing Mass in the Abbey in the morning he rode out and encountered the

rebels at Smithfield; while he was parleying with them, their leader, Wat Tyler, was struck down and slain by the King's followers. For a moment the fate of the royal party wavered in the balance, but Richard, crying to the rebels, 'Gentlemen, what are you about? Have me for your captain', placed himself at their head, led them to Islington, and by granting the required charter, induced them to disperse to their homes. Richard, though in many ways an accomplished and enlightened prince, was a weak and unsuccessful ruler. Eventually, in 1399 he was deposed by his cousin Henry of Lancaster, and was murdered or starved himself to death at Pontefract Castle. A body, purporting to be his, covered with lead all but the face, was 'placed on a litter covered with black, and having a canopy of the same' (Froissart), and taken to St Paul's where it lay exposed to public view for three days, and was then obscurely buried at Abbot's Langley, in Hertfordshire. In 1413 the body was disinterred by Henry V's orders, and removed to Westminster Abbey, 'with great honour, in a chair Royal', the King and his nobility following. There he was buried in the tomb which Richard had himself raised over the remains of his beloved first wife, Anne. She died at the Palace of Sheen, and the King loved her so passionately that he not only abandoned and cursed the place where she died, but pulled down the building. Her funeral was 'magnificently done. Abundance of wax was sent for from Flanders, to make flambeaux and torches, and the illumination was so great on the day of the ceremony that nothing like it was ever before seen' (Froissart). Richard's tomb is similar to Edward III's,

Tomb of Richard II and Anne of Bohemia from the Ambulatory

...b of Edward III from the Ambulatory

and fills up the whole large end bay. The names of the master masons, *Henry Yevele*[1] and *Stephen Lote*, and the coppersmiths, *Nicholas Broker* and *Godfrey Prest*, all citizens of London, have been preserved; by the indentures the tomb was to be completed in 1397; it cost £670, £279 being for the marble work only. The effigies are of mixed metal, gilded all over, and are undoubtedly portraits. By the King's own wish he was represented holding the Queen's right hand in his, but both arms have been stolen. He is attired in the coronation robes, his hair curls, and he wears a pointed beard. The cape to his mantle is bordered with the royal badges of the broompod of the Plantagenets. The effigies are stamped all over with badges and patterns, among them the well-known white hart, and the sun burst, besides the two-headed eagle and the lion of Bohemia. The Queen's bodice was set with precious stones; the table beneath the figures is fretted with fleurs-de-lis, lions, eagles, and leopards. There used to be twelve gilt images of saints and eight angels round the tomb, besides enamelled coats of arms. Upon the inside of the wooden canopy over the tomb are painted a representation of Christ in Majesty and the Coronation of the Virgin, and Queen Anne's coats of arms. The painter was one John Hardy. Round the edge is a Latin rhyming inscription like the one upon Edward III's tomb. Through a hole in the wooden case visitors to the Abbey used to put in their hands, and in 1776 a Westminster schoolboy removed the King's jawbone, which was restored by his descendants in 1906.

Coronation Chair

Coronation Chair–The Coronation Chair was made for Edward I to enclose the famous stone of Scone, which he seized in 1297, and brought from Scotland to the Abbey, where he placed it under the Abbot's care. The Scots made repeated and vain efforts to induce Edward to give it back.[2] Tradition identifies this stone with the one upon which Jacob rested his head at Bethel–'And Jacob rose up early in the morning and took the stone that he had put for his pillows, and set it up for a pillar, and poured oil upon the top of it' (Genesis xxviii, 18). Jacob's sons carried it to Egypt and from thence it passed to Spain[3] with King Gathelus, son of Cecrops, the builder of Athens. About 700 B.C. it appears in Ireland, whither it was carried by the Spanish King's son Simon Brech, on his invasion of that island. There it was placed upon the sacred hill of Tara, and called Lia-Fail, the 'fatal' stone, or 'stone of destiny', for when the Irish kings were seated upon it at coronations the stone groaned aloud if the claimant was of royal race, but remained silent if he was a pretender. Fergus II (d. 501), the founder of the Scottish monarchy, and one of the Blood Royal of Ireland, received it in Scotland, and King Kenneth (d. 860) finally deposited it in the monastery of Scone (846). Setting aside the earlier

myths it is certain that it had been for centuries an object of veneration to the Scots, who fancied that 'while it remained in the country, the State would be unshaken'. Upon this stone their kings, down to John Balliol, were crowned, and it is said that the following distich had been engraved upon it by Kenneth:

> Ni fallat fatum, Scoti quocunque locatum
> Invenient lapidum regnare tenentur ibidem.[4]

A prophecy which was fulfilled at the accession of James VI of Scotland and I of England. Edward had a magnificent oaken chair made to contain it, painted by Master Walter (one of the artists of the Painted Chamber in Westminster Palace), and decorated with patterns of birds, foliage, and animals on a gilt ground, and this is the chair which remains. The figure of a king, the Confessor or Edward I, his feet resting on a lion, was painted on the back. The gilt lions below were added later. Upon this chair and stone, which are moved into the Sanctuary at coronations, all the sovereigns of England, except Edward V and Edward VIII, have been crowned. A portion of the mosaic pavement, by Peter the Roman, which covered the whole Chapel can be seen round the chair. The only State occasion upon which the chair has been taken out of the Abbey was when Oliver Cromwell was installed upon it as Lord Protector in Westminster Hall. In Addison's time the chair was unguarded by railings, but the guides exacted a forfeit from every person who sat down on it. The eighteenth-century contempt for ancient relics is illustrated by the number of names and initials carved on the chair and by Goldsmith's Citizen of the World, who 'saw no curiosity either in the oak chair or the stone; could I indeed behold one of the old kings of England seated in this, and Jacob's head laid upon the other, there might be something curious in the sight'.[5]

Close by are the **Sword** and **Shield** of Edward III, which were, it is said, carried before the King in France. The sword is 7 feet long and weighs 18 lb.

The Screen

The ancient fifteenth-century stone screen which closes the west side of this Chapel was completed in 1441. Upon the frieze are sculptured the principal events, real and imaginary, of Edward the Confessor's life.[6] The subjects are (beginning on the left):

1. The nobles swearing fealty to Queen Emma in the name of her unborn son.

2. The birth of Edward the Confessor, which took place at Islip, in Oxfordshire in 1004.

3. His coronation (1043). On each side of the King are the Archbishops of York and Canterbury.

4. King Edward is alarmed by the appearance of the devil dancing on the casks which contained the danegeld. The danegeld was a tax imposed by his father Ethelred on the people to bribe the Danes to leave the country, but it was remitted by Edward after this vision. The figure of the demon has been broken off.

---

[1] *Yevele was master mason here for many years and probably designed the new Nave, also the tombs of Edward III and Langham, see* English Medieval Architects, *by John Harvey, pages 312–20, pages 171–3 (for Stephen Lote).*

[2] *Length of stone 26¾ inches, width 16¾, depth 10¾, weight 458 lb.; it is fixed into the Chair by iron clamps.*

[3] *According to Scottish lore, Pharaoh's daughter, Scota, carried it to Albion, and Moses foretold that victory should follow the stone.*

[4] *'If Fates go right, where'er this stone is found*
   The Scots shall monarchs of that realm be crowned.'

[5] *For the Coronation Chair see W. Percival-Prescott,* The Coronation Chair (*London, Ministry of Works, 1957*).

[6] *These sculptures resemble the pictures in a MS. Life of the Confessor, in Trinity College Library, Cambridge.*

5. Edward warns a scullion, who is stealing his treasure, to escape with his booty before the return of Hugolin, the Royal Chamberlain. The King is represented in bed, the thief kneeling at the chest.

6. The appearance of our Saviour to Edward when at mass.

7. Edward sees in a vision the shipwreck of the King of Denmark, who was drowned on his way to invade England. In front is a small boat, and an armed figure falling into the sea; behind is a ship, and at the top are falling towers, supposed to represent the failure of the expedition.

8. The quarrel between Harold and Tostig, Earl Godwin's sons, from which the King prophesies their future feuds and unhappy fate. The boys are in the foreground; at the back, Edward, Edith, and the Earl sit at a table. Tostig was killed at Stamford Bridge, and Harold at Hastings, within a few days of each other (1066).

9. Edward's vision of the Seven Sleepers of Ephesus, who had taken refuge in a cave from their heathen persecutors about A.D. 250. He sees them turn from their right sides to their left – a portent of misfortune during the seventy years in which the sleepers were to lie in their new position. The King's messengers are represented arriving at the cave and verifying the vision.

10. St John the Evangelist in the guise of a pilgrim asks alms of the King, who, finding his purse empty, gives him a valuable ring off his finger.

11. Blind men restored to sight by washing in the water used by Edward. The King is in the foreground, washing

his hands; at the side an attendant presents the water to the blind men.

12. St John the Evangelist restoring Edward's ring to two pilgrims in Palestine, bidding them announce to the King his approaching end.

13. The pilgrims[1] giving the ring and message to the King shortly before his death. This is the famous ring which was kept among the relics, but has been lost for centuries.

14. The subject is uncertain but is generally said to be the dedication of the Abbey Church on 28 December 1065.

South of Edward I's tomb is a large grey slab with an imperfect brass to **John of Waltham,** d. 1395, **Bishop of Salisbury.** Richard II made him Master of the Rolls, Keeper of the Great Seal, and finally Lord Treasurer. So great was Richard's affection for him that 'he caused him to be buried, though many muttered thereat, in the Chapel of the Kings, and next to King Edward I'. There was great indignation at such an intrusion into the Royal Chapel, 'many men envying him the honour'; but the Abbey authorities were compensated by the present of two splendid copes and a large sum of money from the King and the Bishop's executors. The brass represents the Bishop in his Mass vestments, with his pastoral staff; within the crook and down the front of the chasuble are representations of the Virgin and Child.

---

[1] *The pilgrims are said to have come from Ludlow, where there is a representation of the story in the window of St Lawrence's Church.*

DEAN'S YARD AND THE PRECINCTS

DEAN'S YARD WAS FORMERLY in the centre of the monastic buildings, and under the name of 'The Elms' formed part of the Abbot's garden. The approach from the Broad Sanctuary is now beneath a gateway built by Sir Gilbert Scott. The column (also designed by Scott) erected in memory of the Old Westminsters, who fell in the Crimean War, and in the Indian Mutiny, is opposite this entrance. It stands on part of the site of the old Gatehouse, pulled down in 1776, where Sir Walter Raleigh spent the night before his execution in the company of Dean Tounson, who was with him on the scaffold (29 October 1618). John Hampden, Sir John Eliot, Richard Lovelace, the Cavalier poet, who wrote the lines: 'Stone walls do not a prison make, nor iron bars a cage',[1] and Lilly, the astrologer, were some of the notable persons imprisoned here. The Sanctuary Tower stood to the north. It contained two chapels, where those who had taken sanctuary were expected to attend service. Close beside it was the Belfry Tower, 'whose ringings, men said, soured all the drink in the town'. The right of sanctuary had been a privilege belonging to the monastery from the earliest times, but the Sanctuary area gradually became a gross scandal to the neighbourhood, where all the thieves, murderers and vagabonds took refuge from the law. The sanctuary rights were therefore much restricted under

Queen Elizabeth, and finally abolished by James I. Standing further back, behind the Chapter House, is the **Jewel Tower,** which was built, probably by Richard II, on a site purchased from the monastery by his grandfather, Edward III. Here for many years the regalia and other Crown jewels were kept; later on the Acts of Parliament were lodged here, until in 1864 these were removed to the Victoria Tower. The building is interesting architecturally both within and without; in shape it is oblong, with a square addition to the south-east, and on the north is a newel staircase, which gave access to the top floors. The upper story has a fine timber roof, and the bosses on the ribs of the ceiling on the ground floor are carved with human heads, foliage, dragons, birds, etc.

On the east side of Dean's Yard the Canons' and School houses incorporate much of the 14th century monastic Guest House and Cellarer's quarters. Other monastic buildings filled up much of the square now known as Dean's Yard, and it was not until 1756 that these together with the monks' granary, then practically a ruin, were pulled down, and the materials used to construct the Terrace. But a row of ancient buildings still blocked up the 'Green', and it was not till 1815 that these were cleared away, the space in the centre sown with grass, and railings added. The pump, which formerly supplied the School with water, was left in its place opposite the Head Master's house till 1872, although it had been dry

---

[1] *In the lyric* To Althea from Prison.

over twenty years before. The original use of the Green as a playground for the boys of Westminster School was somewhat modified as the numbers increased, and it is now only occasionally used for this purpose.

During the Second World War the precincts of the Abbey suffered grievously as the result of air raids, although the damage to the fabric of the Abbey Church itself was slight.

On an October night in 1940 a bomb fell outside the House of Lords, destroying much of the glass in Henry VII's Chapel, causing one of the pendants of the roof of that chapel to fall and pitting the outside walls of the east end of the church.

Far more serious, however, was the damage caused by incendiary bombs on the night of 10 May 1941. The roof of the church was set alight but fortunately the fire was extinguished before it got too firm a hold – not, however, before the roof of the Lantern (over the central space between the Choir and the Sanctuary) had crashed to the floor beneath. There the fire burnt itself out, doing very little damage except to the roof itself and to the pews below. At the same time further incendiary bombs set fire to part of the Deanery, and to some of the houses round the Little Cloister, together with the College 'Dormitory', the great Hall ('School') and the seventeenth-century Busby Library of Westminster School. All these were completely gutted and only the Abbey Library, which had also been set on fire, was saved.

Westminster School

From the earliest times there was a school for novices within the monastic precincts, but it was not till Abbot Litlyngton's time, in the late fourteenth century, that mention is made of the 'almonry boys', who had a separate school, called the Sophouse, which formed part of the Almonry, on a site near the junction of Victoria Street and Great Smith Street. About a century later some of these scholars, called the grammar school boys, were moved to a house (No. 19 Dean's Yard, formerly the Head Master's residence) which then formed part of the Guest House, and a lay headmaster was appointed. The almonry boys were still taught by a monk, probably in the West Cloister. Both these schools were absorbed into one under Henry VIII, and re-endowed in 1561 by Queen Elizabeth, who is revered as the foundress of what has become a great public school. The connexion between the scholars and choristers was not finally severed till 1848, when a separate Choir House was built. Westminster School has remained in close association with the Abbey ever since its foundation. The Dean is *ex officio* chairman of the Governing Body; a daily service for the School is held in the Choir, and the Queen's Scholars (wearing white surplices) and the boarders attend services on Sundays. Since the accession of James II the King's (or Queen's) Scholars are present in the Abbey at every coronation and have the right to be the first to acclaim the sovereign on entry into the church.

Little Dean's Yard

In Little Dean's Yard are grouped the principal school buildings, which have gradually replaced the monastic offices. Thus at first the second master was lodged in a tower, close to the present entrance into this yard, over a gateway which was adjacent to the Monastic Granary. The granary itself, a long room built on stone arches, was used as a dormitory for Queen Elizabeth's forty scholars and remained in the scholars' occupation for nearly 200 years. By the end of the seventeenth century the room was practically in ruins and, before Queen Anne's death, Dean Atterbury, in conjunction with Sir Christopher Wren (himself an Old Westminster) planned a new dormitory, and collected a sum of money which he added to a legacy left by an Old Westminster, the Queen's oculist Sir Edward Hannes, for the same purpose. The present site in the College Garden was chosen but, owing to the opposition of the Head Master, Dr Freind, and of some of the prebendaries, the building was not completed till after the deaths of the architect (1733) and of the Dean (1731) who was in exile for his political opinions.

In 1936 part of the east side of Little Dean's Yard was reconstructed, and a new wall erected with an ornamental gate of wrought-iron opening into the College Garden. At the same time the cement which had covered the wall of the adjoining Dormitory was removed and the original brickwork revealed through the generosity of the Pilgrim Trust in commemoration of the Jubilee of King George V (1935).

The Great Hall or 'School'

At the foot of the steps leading to School is a stone gateway erected in 1734 probably from the design of Lord Burlington. School itself formed part of the monks' dormitory, but was adapted for the use of the School about 1600. From that date until 1884 when extra form rooms were built, the entire School was taught in this room. It had an exceptionally fine sixteenth-century hammer-beam roof which was unfortunately destroyed by an incendiary bomb in 1941. At the same time the panelling with its painted coats of arms and the whole of the interior was gutted and only the walls remained. It was rebuilt, with a modern roof, etc., after the war and formally reopened by Queen Elizabeth II in November 1960 as part of the Quatercentenary Celebration of the refounding of the School by Queen Elizabeth I in 1560. In the rebuilding the opportunity was taken to restore the semi-circular apse, at the north end which, formerly known as the Shell, gave its name to the form taught in front of it and was subsequently adopted as the name for a form by many other schools. New panelling was also put up on which has been painted the coats of arms of famous Old Westminsters, but it was not possible to restore the many hundreds of names which were formerly painted on the walls.

The lower portion of the walls of School and some of the windows date from the late eleventh century, but much of the walling was altered and rebuilt by Wyatt about 1814. The room is roughly divided by an iron bar from which used to hang a curtain which separated the upper from the lower school. It is over this bar that, by an ancient custom, the College cook tosses a pancake on Shrove Tuesday. It is scrambled for by a boy selected from each form, and the boy who retrieves the largest portion of it receives a guinea from the Dean.

The Head Master's Chair is traditionally said to have been presented to the famous Head Master, Dr Busby, by King Charles II. In front of it is the Rod Table also dating from this time, and two ancient chairs which were used by the masters from the reign of Henry VIII to that of Queen Victoria. At the south end of the room is an organ with a seventeenth-century case formerly used in the Abbey, and also the memorial to those Westminsters who lost their lives in the two World Wars. This replaces a Memorial in the form of an oak screen designed by the late *Sir Robert Lorimer, R.A.* in 1921 to commemorate the First World War.

The **Busby Library,** which adjoins the School, was 'built and fitted' by Dr Busby at his 'own great coste and charges' between 1660 and 1680. It had an elaborate domed ceiling surrounded by wreaths of fruit and flowers. The bookcases were also of the same period. The Library was completely destroyed by an incendiary bomb in 1941. It was rebuilt after the war, and it was found possible from photographs exactly to reproduce the ceiling, bookcases, etc., so that the room has very much its original appearance. The valuable collection of books was fortunately saved.

The Scholars' Dormitory

The College Dormitory is situated on the west side of the College Garden. It was originally designed by Sir Christopher Wren and the foundation-stone was laid in 1722. It was not, however, completed until about 1730 under the direction of the Earl of Burlington who somewhat altered the original design. The façade towards the Garden is of Bath stone, and the Dormitory was internally a copy of the Old Dormitory in Dean's Yard which had once been the Monks' Granary. The boys were lodged in one long room which filled the whole of the first floor, while the vaults beneath the old Granary were represented in the new Dormitory by an open cloister giving on to the Garden. From about 1730 to 1938 the Dormitory was the scene of the annual Latin play, a custom which dated from the reign of Queen Elizabeth I who had ordained that such a play should be acted annually at Christmas by the scholars for 'the encouragement of good elocution'. Before 1730 it was acted in the College Hall. The Dormitory was remodelled in 1846 when the Cloister was closed in and converted into living-rooms for the boys.

The interior of the Dormitory was gutted by an incendiary bomb in 1941, but the original façade survived. The Dormitory was then rebuilt internally on a different plan, and was formally reopened by King George VI in June 1951.

Ashburnham House

This beautiful seventeenth-century house is on the north side of Little Dean's Yard and incorporates part of the Prior's house, which seems to have been built and added to at various times from the twelfth to the sixteenth centuries. It contained a large hall erroneously identified with the monks' Misericorde. The Refectory was situated behind this hall, and the wall which separated it from the South Cloister still exists. Embedded in it are remains of the eleventh and fourteenth-centuries' work and a thirteenth-century doorway leads into the Cloister. Southwest was the 'Misericorde', an upper chamber resting on vaults, where the monks were allowed to eat meat, and where the grammar school boys had their meals.

After the Dissolution and during the ten years (1540–50)

when there was a Westminster bishopric, the Bishop[1] lived in the Deanery and the Prior's house was occupied by the Dean (Benson). It was afterwards let to various persons of note connected with the Court in the reigns of Queen Elizabeth and the first Stuart kings. The house is said to have been rebuilt or remodelled by Inigo Jones, when Sir Edward Powell, Master of Requests under Charles I, was the tenant (1630–40). A later and less trustworthy tradition assigns the rebuilding to Webb, Inigo Jones's pupil, after the house had passed into the hands of Colonel William Ashburnham (1662), a noted Royalist and personal friend of Charles II. In 1730 his descendant, Lord Ashburnham, leased it to the Crown, and the King's and Cotton Libraries were kept there until, in 1731, a disastrous fire broke out, when the precious books and MSS were rescued with great difficulty. The beautiful staircase and panelling, which belong to the Inigo Jones period, fortunately remained intact. In 1739 the house was bought back from the Ashburnhams by the Dean and Chapter, and divided into two prebendal houses. In one of these Milman (Canon of Westminster, 1835–49, Dean of St Paul's, 1849) wrote his *History of Latin Christianity*.

After the Public Schools Act of 1868 the School was empowered to purchase three houses from the Dean and Chapter when they next became vacant. These were: Ashburnham House, then occupied by Lord John Thynne (page 37), Sub-Dean of the Abbey; the part already divided from it, where the Abbey organist (1841–82), James Turle, was living; and 18 Dean's Yard, which is said to have been the Monk Bailiff's house.

The beautiful seventeenth-century rooms on the first floor of Ashburnham House then became, and have since remained, the School Library.

The College Hall

The College Hall in the Abbot's or Deanery Courtyard was built by Abbot Litlyngton in the late fourteenth century (1369–76), and was the Abbot's state dining-room. Shields with the Abbot's arms can be seen held by the angels which support the fine timbered roof. The Minstrels' Gallery at the west end dates from Tudor or Jacobean times. Until the middle of the nineteenth century the room was warmed by an open fire in the centre of the Hall, the smoke escaping through a louvre or lantern in the roof, which still exists. According to tradition it was in this hall that Elizabeth Woodville and her daughters, with the boy Prince, Richard of York, 'sat alow on the rushes all desolate and dismaied' when she claimed the Abbot's protection in 1483 for the second time. The tables of oak are traditionally supposed to have been made from the ships of the Spanish Armada, which were wrecked on our shores. The wainscoting dates from the middle of the eighteenth century, when the Hall was 'beautified and adorned', and new paving added. In earlier times the walls were hung with tapestry. Above the High Table are the arms of the College (i.e. the Abbey) of Westminster, the two colleges with which the School is closely connected (Christ Church, Oxford, and Trinity College, Cambridge), and the Order of the Bath, the Dean being *ex officio* Dean of the Order. The Tudor ships in each corner were inserted by Dean Robinson, High

[1] *Thirlby.*

Almoner to the King, and represent the Seal of the Royal Almonry. After the Dissolution the Hall became the College Hall and is now used by the Queen's Scholars and some of the other boys of Westminster School for their meals.

The Latin play was acted here until 1730, when it was moved to the new Dormitory. The stage was under the gallery, and dresses were hired from the office of the Revels and brought here in barges. The expenses of two plays 'plaied by the Children of the Grammar School in the Colledge of Westminster before the Queene's Majesty' in 1564 have been preserved among the Abbey Muniments. Elizabeth must have been well pleased, as she came again the following year.

The Abbot's House or Deanery

Entering the Cloisters from Dean's Yard, a dark arch on the left leads into a small courtyard. Facing the entrance are some sixteenth-century rooms built by Abbot Islip, including the Jericho Parlour, which leads into the Jerusalem Chamber; on the left is the College Hall, on the right is the other part of the Abbot's house, used since the dissolution of the monastery as the Dean's residence. The Abbot's lodging as it was called, has been added to and altered at various times, but much of the original house, dating from Litlyngton's time, still remains. Part of a wall of a much earlier date runs along one side of the Abbot's Long Room, which has a western window overlooking the Dean's Yard entrance. The eastern portion of the Long Room has a fine fourteenth-century window and was no doubt the Abbot's private chapel; below the modern floor are fragments of tiles, of the same style as those in the Chapter House. The Abbot's house was also known at one time as Cheyney Gates Manor. Elizabeth Woodville lived in the Abbot's

Entrance to the Abbot's Courtyard

house, while her husband, Edward IV, fled into temporary exile at the return of Henry VI, and here in 1470 her eldest son, Edward (afterwards Edward V), was born. In 1483 the widowed Queen again took refuge here, with her younger children, and while in sanctuary was persuaded to give up her second son, Richard, to his uncle, the Duke of Gloucester. In 1486 she appears to have leased the Abbot's house, and lived here again for a time. In 1640 the Irish Archbishop Ussher[1] inhabited the Deanery when he came to attend the Long Parliament. During the Commonwealth John Bradshaw,[2] President of the Council, leased the Deanery and died in the house. In the Triforium is a little room which is traditionally called Bradshaw's Room, where he is supposed to have kept his books and retired to study.

The Jerusalem Chamber

The approach to this historic Chamber is through a smaller room, added with the apartments above it by Abbot Islip in the early sixteenth century; it is known as the **Jericho Parlour** and contains some fine linen-fold panelling. In the vestibule is a little niche which once held a lamp, and there are remains of paintings and inscriptions on the wall. **The Jerusalem Chamber** itself formed part of the Abbot's house or lodgings and is of late fourteenth-century date. It probably took its name from the original tapestry hangings. The room was restored in Dean Stanley's time (1865–81), who uncovered the original roof and repanelled the walls with cedarwood brought from Lebanon. In this Chamber Henry IV died, and the traditional story, dramatized by Shakespeare in the play of *Henry IV*–which credits Henry V with putting on his

---

[1] *See page 80.*   [2] *See page 72.*

father's crown before his death–is connected with this room. The two modern busts of the King and his son were placed here by Dean Stanley. Henry IV was preparing an expedition to the Holy Land in 1413, and visited the Abbey on the eve of his departure. 'While he was making his prayers at St Edward's shrine to take there his leave and so speed him on his journey, he became so sick that such as were about him feared that he would have died right there. Wherefore they, for his comfort, bore him into the Abbot's place and laid him down before the fire in this chamber. On coming to himself and learning that he was in the chamber named Hierusalem, then said the King, "Laud be to the Father of Heaven! for now I know that I shall die in this chamber, according to the prophecy made of me beforesaid, that I should die in Hierusalem," and so he made himself ready, and died shortly after.'[1] The Chamber was redecorated by Lord Keeper Williams, Dean of Westminster in the reign of James I. His arms, combined with those of Westminster and Lincoln (he was also Bishop of Lincoln) may be seen on the carved cedarwood overmantel, which he erected to celebrate the betrothal of Charles I–then Prince of Wales–and the French Princess Henrietta Maria (1624), when he entertained the French Ambassador with a banquet in this room. The Chamber has been the scene of many gatherings. It was used by those engaged upon the Authorized Version of the Bible in 1611, on the Revised Version of 1885, and on the New English Bible (New Testament) of 1961. The Upper House of Convocation has frequently met there and in it many famous persons have lain in state.

The Tapestries[2] in the Jerusalem Chamber have been cleaned and repaired and the subjects identified. The Circumcision of Isaac and the fragments of the return of Sara from the Egyptians belong to the 'History of Abraham', which is in the great Hall at Hampton Court. The right-hand part of the Circumcision is now in St Faith's Chapel; the borders of all these pieces are missing except a strip from the Sara series which is hanging between the windows. The 'Rebekah at the Well',[3] opposite the Circumcision, belongs to a later and inferior set. The healing of the lame man by St Peter at the 'Beautiful Gate' of the Temple[4] is from a series called the Acts of the Apostles, apparently made in England by a weaver using a Flemish mark; these are distributed in different places, including Boughton and Haddon Hall, and have not all been found. Some of the subjects, like this one, are based upon Raphael's designs, but are very much simplified. In St Faith's Chapel, a piece of tapestry facing the entrance, similar to that near the High Altar, and also to another, which is in the Deanery, are thought to belong to a set at Holyrood of Flemish manufacture, sixteenth or seventeenth century.

---

[1] *Fabyan's* Chronicles.

[2] *Information supplied by Mr H. C. Marillier.*
[3] *Given by the Sub-Dean Lord John Thynne in 1871.*
[4] *Also given by Lord John Thynne.*

THE CLOISTERS

A GREAT FIRE IN 1298 probably destroyed or ruined most of the old Cloisters. The present Cloisters were not begun till the thirteenth century, when Henry III's church was building, and were finished in the late fourteenth century, towards the end of Richard II's reign. The difference in dates can be detected by a careful examination of the tracery and vaulting.

The first four bays nearest the church of the **Eastern Cloister,** including the entrance to the Chapter House, which was finished in 1253, were begun by Abbot Crokesley early in 1244, shortly before his death, and continued by Abbot Simon de Bircheston who died of the plague in 1349, and is buried in this walk. The East Cloister door and the first four bays of **The North Walk** coincide in date with the building of the Choir Aisle, in Abbot Ware's time. Notice the heads of Henry III and Queen Eleanor of Provence on either side of this door, and also the roses in the mouldings. The last two bays and the West Cloister door are of mid fourteenth-century date and were begun (1350) during the abbacy of Bircheston's successor, Langham (see page 54), and finished (1366) two years after he became Bishop of Ely, by the next Abbot, Nicholas de Litlyngton, who, when Prior, had superintended the work for many years before; his initials and arms are carved upon some of the bosses.

Langham gave generously to the building of the Cloisters, and bequeathed large sums to ensure the continuance of the Nave. **The South Walk** was rebuilt *c.* 1350–70 and **The West Walk** was rebuilt a few years later. The Cloisters unfortunately have been much spoilt by restorations at various times. Blore practically rebuilt much of the South Walk (1835) and Sir Gilbert Scott, in the later nineteenth century, refaced the stone work, and renewed much of the window tracery in the North Walk.

In these Cloisters the monks spent a great part of their time; at first only the upper half was glazed and the lower part was open to the wind and weather, but later on the whole was filled in with coloured glass. Carpets of hay and straw in winter, and rushes in summer covered the stone floor and benches, the walls·were decorated with paintings, and lamps were suspended here and there by chains from the roof.

On Thursday in Holy Week the Abbot held his Maundy in the East Cloister; thirteen aged men were seated on the broad stone bench against the west wall; some of the rings to which the mats for their feet were hooked are visible just below the bench. The Abbot himself washed their feet, which were carefully cleansed first, wiped them with a towel, and then kissed them; after which he gave each man 3*d.*, and seven red herrings, also some ale and three loaves apiece. The monks meantime washed the feet of children in the South Walk, where their Maundy seat, 'a faire, long bench of stone', still exists. Close to the Abbot's bench is a doorway which leads by a spiral staircase to the Triforium.

In the **South Cloister,** which belongs to the period of Langham and Litlyngton (1351–65), the Abbots were usually buried.[1] Eight Abbots lie in this Cloister. **Vitalis,** d. 1085, whose name was erroneously inscribed on Laurence's tombstone, lies at the feet of **Gervase de Blois.** Sulcard's history of the Abbey was written while Vitalis was Abbot and dedicated to him. **Gilbert Crispin's** (d. 1117) worn slab of black marble, the oldest sculptured

---

[1] *The three worn effigies beneath the seat are now known to be (from east to west) Abbots Laurence, Gilbert Crispin and William de Humez. See J. Armitage Robinson,* Flete's History of Westminster Abbey, *pages 22–4.*

effigy here, was moved beneath the bench in the eighteenth century to preserve it and is the central effigy. In Gilbert's time the Confessor's coffin was opened (1102) and the body found 'incorrupt, the sceptre, crown, and robes intact, the face, rosy and smiling'. Gilbert, a saintly man, was followed after a gap of three years by **Herbert,** d. 1136; he had a long dispute with the Prior, Osbert de Clare, about the ruinous state of the monastic buildings, a quarrel which embittered the first part of his time but was finally healed. His grave is nearer the Refectory door. His successor, **Gervase de Blois,** deposed 1157(?), died 1160, buried at the feet of Humez, was a natural son of King Stephen and 'a thoroughly bad abbot'. Nevertheless it

East Cloister

was by Gervase that the first attempt was made to persuade the Pope to canonize the Confessor. He sent the Prior, Osbert, who wrote a life of the Confessor, on an unsuccessful mission to Rome in 1139 for this purpose.

The easternmost effigy is of his successor, **Abbot Laurence**, d. 1173, a favourite of Henry II and the Empress Maud, who was successful in obtaining the long-promised canonization of the saintly King, 7 February 1161. Laurence was granted the favour of wearing the Mitre, Ring, and Gloves by Pope Alexander III, but died before they arrived. The next Abbot, **Walter of Winchester,** d. 1190, buried further west, was granted the additional privilege of the dalmatic, tunicle, and sandals, but was inhibited from wearing the mitre on account of the disgraceful quarrel for precedence between the two Archbishops in St Catherine's Chapel (see page 116). **William Postard** (d. 1200), described as *Pater et Pastor*, who followed Walter, was therefore the first Abbot who wore the mitre; he lies next to Walter. The westernmost slab with a worn effigy in full vestments belongs to **William de Humez** (d. 1222), who collected large sums of money for the building of the new Lady Chapel, but died two years after the young King, Henry III, had laid the foundation stone. Under a large blue stone are said to lie twenty-six monks who died (1349) of the same plague which carried off Abbot Bircheston.

At the west end of the South Cloister the early fourteenth-century doorway used to lead into the monks' Refectory; on one side are four recesses, which were originally closed with wooden doors and had hooks inside for hanging up the monks' towels. Round the corner in the West Cloister is a recess much modernized, where was formerly the trough at which the monks washed their hands before entering the Refectory. On some of the bosses in this Southern Cloister are Litlyngton's initials and arms, and it was he who rebuilt the great dining-hall more than half a century after the fire of 1298. Part of the Norman dividing wall remains along the lower part of this walk, but the upper part of the wall arcading dates from Litlyngton's time.

The two vaulted bays leading to the entrance into Dean's Yard used to be the monks' parlour, where they received guests, and were even allowed to entertain ladies of rank. The outer gateway itself belongs to Litlyngton's time; heads of Richard II and the Abbot are on either side of the outer arch. In the niches over the gate used to be figures of the Confessor and the Pilgrim.

We now enter the **West Walk**, where the novices were taught by a Brother, called the Master of the Novices, who had his seat close to the West Cloister door, above which was a picture of the Crucifixion, painted by order of Prior Merston (1376). Upon the sides of these Cloisters were paintings, with verses alluding to the history of the foundation. A favourite game of the period–'nine holes'– was evidently played by the novices in intervals of leisure, as traces of it are found both in this and in the first bay of the North Cloister close by, where the holes are clearly visible on the stone bench near the Prior's seat. The **North Walk** was the place where the monks read and studied. A special room called the 'Scriptorium' was set apart elsewhere in the monastery for the copying and illuminating of manuscripts. Bookcases 'wherein did lye as well the old auncyeint written Doctors of the Church as other profane Literature, with dyverse other holie men's workes', were pegged against the wall, or stood on the floor and wooden partitions divided the 'carrells' wherein the monks

sat and studied 'all the afternoone till evensong tyme; this was their exercise every day' (Rites of Durham). These little studies with wooden benches and tables were placed in the best lighted bays, and it has been pointed out that this walk was chosen because of the warm south sun, and also as the furthest from the smell of food, and the clatter of plates in the Refectory. The green or garth in the centre seems to have been used as a garden; the cemetery where the lesser brethren were buried was situated to the north-east, beyond where the Chapter House now stands. After the Dissolution the Westminster boys held their fights on this green, and even played racquets and football in the Cloisters. The walks also were haunted by beggars and all sorts of disorderly persons, 'idle boys playing cards and dice for money, cursing and swearing the while', until in the eighteenth century the Dean and Chapter appointed a constable to keep order. Amongst these 'miserable wretches' the Duke of Portland remembered seeing, in his school days, Sarah, Duchess of Marlborough, seated on the stone bench, dressed in rags, mourning the death of her only son (d. 1703).

Monuments in the Cloisters
West Walk

A tablet commemorates the **Civil Services of the Crown in India, 1858–1947.** Unveiled by Queen Elizabeth II on 7 March 1958. Designed by *S. E. Dykes Bower*.

On 21 May 1948, Mr Winston Churchill unveiled a War Memorial to commemorate respectively the **Commandos**, the officers and men of the Submarine Service of the Royal Navy, and all ranks of the Airborne Forces and Special Air Service who fell in the Second World War. The Memorial, designed by *Gilbert Ledward, R.A.*, consists of three bronze figures representing three types of fighting men–submarine seaman, commando man, and parachutist.

John Thomas Micklethwaite, b. 1843, d. 1906. Surveyor of the Abbey fabric, who devoted himself to the preservation of the church and buildings in the precincts.

Elizabeth Woodfall, b. 1768, d. 1862, daughter of the printer Henry Sampson Woodfall, who published the *Letters of Junius*.

John Broughton, b. 1703, d. 1789, the most famous pugilist of his day, called on his monument, in deference to the protest of the Dean and Chapter, only 'Yeoman of the Guard'. It was from Broughton's arms that Rysbrack modelled those of his statue of Hercules.

Tablets to four of the Abbey organists who are buried below: **Benjamin Cooke**, b. 1734, d. 1793. Cooke became deputy organist at the age of twelve and was afterwards the organist here for thirty years (1762–93), as well as Master of the Choristers and a lay vicar. He took part in the Handel Festival in the Abbey (1784) and received one of the royal medals. A large collection of his manuscript musical compositions is extant at the Royal College of Music. His son **Robert**, organist here 1802–14, lies near his father.

James Turle, b. 1802, d. 1882, organist and Master of the Choristers for fifty years.

Sir Frederick Bridge, C.V.O., b. 1844, d. 1924, succeeded Turle as organist, a post he held for nearly forty years. He retired in 1918, but continued to live in the old house, Litlyngton Tower. During this period he arranged and superintended the music at the coronation of King Edward VII and Queen Alexandra (1902), and of King George V and Queen Mary (1911), and composed many anthems and chants besides secular works. He was also Professor at the College of Music and Gresham Lecturer. Also buried in this Cloister, but without a tablet, is **Thomas Greatorex**, b. 1758, d. 1831. Organist of the Abbey, 1819–31.

Another musician is commemorated and buried in this walk: **Thomas Sanders Dupuis**, b. 1733, d. 1796, a member of an old Huguenot family, organist and composer to the Chapel Royal, where he had been educated as a chorister under Bernard Gates (see North Cloister), who left him in his will an estate in Oxfordshire – North Aston. Three volumes of Dupuis's cathedral music were published after his death.

Two eminent engravers have memorials in this walk: **George Vertue**, b. 1684, d. 1756, and **William Woollett**, b. 1735, d. 1785 – *Incisor Excellentissimus*. Vertue was a Roman Catholic; he lies in the North Cloister, near William Vertue, a monk of Westminster (1509/10–1535(?)) whom he claimed as a member of his family. He was official engraver to the Society of Antiquaries, and executed most of the plates in *Vetusta Monumenta*, and for the Oxford Almanacks, besides engraving many valuable portraits. For forty years Vertue collected materials for a history of the fine arts in England; these were purchased from his widow by Horace Walpole who compiled his *Anecdotes of Painting* from them. Woollett lies in Old St Pancras Churchyard; he was the most celebrated English engraver of his time, and had a great reputation abroad. His best known work was an engraving of 'West's Death of General Wolfe' (1776), which so pleased George III that he gave Woollett the title of 'Historical engraver to His Majesty'. *Tablet by Banks.*

A mural monument now without inscription, to **Sir Richard Jebb**, b. 1719, d. 1787, F.R.S., F.S.A., a distinguished physician, one of the staff at Westminster Hospital; later on he became physician to the royal family, and was a favourite of George III. Jebb's professional reputation was very high; in three years (1779–81) his fees amounted to 20,000 guineas. He died at his house in Great George Street close by, from a fever caught when attending one of the princesses. A profile bust gives his features, his portrait by Zoffany is in the College of Physicians. Farther on is a tablet to another physician, **William Buchan**, b. 1729, d. 1805 (buried below), best known as the author of *Domestic Medicine*, the first work of its kind in England; 80,000 copies were sold in the author's lifetime.

A memorial to **Charles Godolphin**, b. 1651, d. 1720, brother to Sidney, 1st Earl of Godolphin, M.P., and Commissioner of Customs, records the 'benefactions' of himself and his wife **Elizabeth** (d. 1726), daughter of Francis Godolphin of Coulston, Co. Wilts., to the education of 'young gentlewomen of small fortunes' in Wiltshire. The Godolphin School, near Salisbury, was started sixty years after the death of Mrs Godolphin, and still continues to flourish. On her anniversary, 24 June, the girls come and place flowers on the monument.

Edward Wortley Montagu, b. 1750, d. 1777, a son of the eccentric traveller, Edward Wortley Montagu, and a grandson of the famous Lady Mary Wortley Montagu, was shipwrecked on his voyage home from the East Indies. The tablet, which is of artificial stone by *Coade*,

was put up by Sir John English Dolben, Bt., a member of Archbishop Dolben's[1] family, in commemoration of a friendship, begun at Westminster School, 'continued at Oxford, not lessened by the barrier of half the world, a friendship unbroken by death, to be renewed in heaven, if God so will' (from the Latin inscription). Montagu left his friend Dolben heir to his books, and residuary legatee.

In the West Walk are commemorated three Clerks of the Works: **Thomas Wright**, d. 1906, aged eighty-three, who was Clerk of the Works here for thirty-seven years (1871–1906). Close by lies his son and successor, **Thomas James Wright**, b. 1851, d. 1928, who carried on the traditions of his father for fifty-five years. **William Bishop**, M.V.O. (d. 1962), Clerk of the Works, 1928–56.

Emily Tennyson Bradley (Mrs A. Murray Smith), b. 1862, d. 1946, a daughter of Dean Bradley, who by her books and devotion to the Abbey did much to elucidate its history. She, and her sister Lady Birchenough, were the original compilers of this Guide.

W. Richard Lethaby, b. 1850, d. 1931, architect, Surveyor of the Fabric, 1906–28. His scholarly books on the architecture of the Abbey first traced in detail the history of its building and the names of the craftsmen who built it. Under his personal superintendence the restoration of the exterior of the Chapel of Henry VII was begun, but not completed till 1932, a year after his death.

Close by is the grave of **Sir Walter Tapper, R.A.**, b. 1861, d. 1935, President of the Royal Institute of British Architects, 1927–8, and Surveyor of the Fabric, 1928–35. The important work of the cleaning and repair of the roof and interior of the Chapel of Henry VII, completed in 1935, was carried out under his direction. With a gift of £9,000 from the Pilgrim Trust, he designed and completed a successful improvement, by means of which the Chapter Library and Muniment Room were connected. This was done by raising the roof of the Cloister, inserting two dormer windows, and adding a panelled gallery, stretching the length of the Cloister, and connecting the Library with the Muniment Room by means of a spiral staircase. Besides his work at the Abbey, Tapper designed many churches and war memorials; he was also consultant architect to York Minster and Manchester Cathedral.

Sir Sydney Hugo Nicholson, M.V.O., Organist of Westminster Abbey, 1919–28. Founder and Director of Royal School of Church Music.

North Walk

The earliest memorial commemorates **Edward Bernard**, d. 1584, one of the Queen's Scholars on Elizabeth I's foundation. A master at the School **George Jewell**, d. 1725, is buried close by. His widow **Lucia** (d. 1767), who married Vincent Bourne, the well-known Latin poet, survived both her husbands, and lies in Jewell's vault.

The **Revd. Richard Gouland**, d. 1659, the first keeper of the Chapter Library (1626) after Dean Williams had reinstituted it in the Old Dormitory. His epitaph states that he was 'well skill'd in the languages, and otherwise very well furnished with the best and choicest learning'. A tablet to **John Stagg**, d. 1746, bookseller, is a reminder of the days when bookstalls filled Westminster Hall.

A somewhat mutilated tablet, removed from the South

---

[1] *Dolben was Dean of Westminster, 1662–82.*

Walk, commemorates **Ephraim Chambers**, b. 1686, d. 1740. He was the author of the second *English Encyclopaedia*, which was afterwards (in 1859) eclipsed by that of his namesake William Chambers. In the Latin epitaph Chambers described himself as a man whose name was 'familiar to many, himself known to a few; one who walked betwixt light and shade, neither erudite nor ignorant, who passed his life in devotion to letters'.

A gravestone to **Thomas Ravenscroft**, d. 1708, aged eighty, once bore the inscription: 'What I gave I have; what I spent I had; what I left I lost by not giving it.'

On a mural monument is a curious epitaph to **William Laurence**, d. 1621, aged twenty-seven, who was private secretary or steward to one of the prebendaries.

> With Diligence and Trust most exemplary
> Did WILLIAM LAVRENCE serve a Prebendary;
> And for his Paines now past, before not lost,
> Gain'd this Remembrance at his Master's cost.
> O reade these Lines againe: you seldome find
> A Servant faithfull and a Master kind.
> Short Hand he wrote: his Flowre in prime did fade
> And hasty Death Short Hand of him hath made.
> Well covth he Nv'bers, and well mesur'd Land;
> Thvs doth he now that Grovnd where on yov stand,
> Wherein he lyes so Geometricall;
> Art maketh some, but thvs will Nature all.

Bernard Gates, b. 1685(?), d. 1773, aged eighty-eight, musician, lies with his wife and family in this walk. He was master of the Children of the Chapel Royal for over forty years, and member of the Abbey choir in his young days. Three volumes of his musical compositions were published after his death. He married the adopted daughter and heiress of **Elizabeth Atkinson**, d. 1726, body laundress to Queen Anne, whose monument is close by; two of Gates's daughters were called Atkinson after their mother's benefactress.

Two authors are buried in this walk: **Dr William King**, b. 1663, d. 1712, under an unmarked stone, and **Sir John Hawkins**, b. 1719, d. 1789, who has only his initials, date of death, and age upon his grave. **King** had been a Westminster King's Scholar and was a miscellaneous writer of some merit, counting Swift and Pope amongst his friends. Swift calls him a 'poor starving wit'. Lord Burlington befriended him in his last days. **Hawkins**, the son of a carpenter, claimed descent from the noted Elizabethan navigator, John Hawkins, Drake's boon companion. His principal work, a *History of Music*, was suggested by Horace Walpole. An ardent fisherman himself, he published an edition of Izaak Walton's *Compleat Angler*, which went through five editions. Hawkins was an early friend of Dr Johnson and one of the original nine members of Johnson's famous club. He wrote a biography of the doctor, which was, however, eclipsed by Boswell's *Life*. The wits of the day composed an epitaph upon Hawkins in allusion to his drawling voice:

> Here lies Sir John Hawkins
> Without his shoes and stawkins.

Samuel Foote, b. 1720, d. 1777, actor and dramatist, who was buried by torchlight in the West Cloister in an unmarked grave. He was that witty comedian who made Johnson laugh against his will. 'The dog was so very comical, Sir, he was irresistible.' Foote was an actor and writer of excellent burlesques, specially notorious for his mimicry; by his cruel wit he made many enemies.

In the same year (1777) died **Spranger Barry**, b. 1719, actor. Garrick's successful rival, especially in the parts of King Lear and Hamlet. His triumph was short-lived. He lost his health, his looks, and his fortune, and ten years before his death was glad to accept small parts at Drury Lane and a salary from the generous Garrick. He was buried privately at night in the North Cloister. Twenty-five years later his grave was opened to receive the coffin of **Ann Crawford**, b. 1734, d. 1801, actress, his pupil and second wife, who was then the queen of comedy at Drury Lane. While professing that she only acted in tragedy 'to please the town', this versatile lady rivalled Mrs Cibber and Peg Woffington in tragic parts, and even when 'old, coarse, and ugly' her younger rival Mrs Siddons was unable to surpass her in certain roles, such as Cordelia and Desdemona. Her third husband, Crawford, spent the old actress's money and broke her heart. **Susannah Maria Cibber**, b. 1714, d. 1766, actress, wife of Theophilus Cibber, lies close by. 'Barry and I remain, but tragedy is dead on one side', exclaimed Garrick when he heard of her death.

In the North Walk is the grave of **General John Burgoyne**, b. 1722, d. 1792, Commander-in-Chief of the British forces in the American War of Independence. He was forced to surrender to Gates, the American general, early in the war, and returned to England in disgrace. Although restored to royal favour, he never fought again, but spent the remainder of his life in a house near the Abbey, surrounded by his books. In 1960 his gravestone was identified and his name and dates were cut upon it. A brass tablet to the **Most Revd. William Markham**, b. 1719, d. 1807. Head Master of Westminster School, 1753–64. Dean of Christ Church, Oxford, 1767–77; Bishop of Chester, 1771–7; Archbishop of York, 1777–1807, who is buried beneath with other members of the Markham family, including his brother **Enoch Markham** (d. 1801), who went to Canada as a volunteer and fought under Wolfe. He afterwards raised the 112th Foot (the Royal Musketeers) and fought throughout the American War. He was buried with the colours of his old regiment, which had long been disbanded, wrapped round his body.

Against the north wall is a tablet to the memory of seven of the **Queen's Westminster Volunteers** (13th Middlesex), who died in the Boer War of 1900. Unveiled 22 June 1901.

Also tablets to commemorate those who served in the **Sudan**, 1898–1955. Erected in 1960; and those who served in **Malaya**, 1786–1957. Unveiled by Queen Elizabeth the Queen Mother on 1 November 1962.

Below are the graves of:

Charles St Clair Bedford, b. 1810, d. 1900, Chapter Clerk for thirty years and Westminster Coroner for forty-three years.

Basil Wilberforce, b. 1841, d. 1916, Canon and Archdeacon of Westminster and Rector of St John's Church, Westminster; his wife, **Charlotte**, b. 1841, d. 1909.

William Boyd Carpenter, b. 1841, d. 1918, Bishop of Ripon, 1884–1911, Sub-Dean and Canon of Westminster, 1911; his second wife, **Ann**, b. 1854, d. 1915.

Robert Henry Charles, D.D., b. 1855, d. 1931, Canon (1913) and Archdeacon (1919) of Westminster. A learned scholar and author of Commentaries on the Apocalypse and on the book of Daniel; his wife, **Mary Lilian**, b. 1857, d. 1935.

Kenneth Augustus, 1st Baron Muir-Mackenzie, G.C.B., b. 1845, d. 1930, High Bailiff of Westminster, 1912–30.

Percy Dearmer, D.D., b. 1867, d. 1936, Professor of Ecclesiastical Art, King's College, 1919, Rector of Chelsea Parish Church, 1930, Canon of Westminster, 1931. During the First World War Dearmer was Chaplain to the British Red Cross in Serbia. Author of many books and pamphlets on Ecclesiastical Art and Church History, and editor of the hymn-book *Songs of Praise*, 1931.

Sir Edward Knapp-Fisher, C.V.O., b. 1864, d. 1940. Chapter Clerk, Receiver General and Custodian, 1917–40.

Vernon Faithfull Storr, b. 1869, d. 1940, Sub-Dean of Westminster and Rector of St Margaret's. Buried at Matfield, Kent.

East Walk

First of all is the unmarked stone of **Thomas Betterton**, b. 1635(?), d. 1710, actor, son of an under-cook in Charles I's kitchen, who was born, bred and buried in the shadow of the Abbey. He was considered the best tragedian of his day, and for fifty years no actor surpassed him in the public favour. His first great triumph was on 28 December 1661, when he acted Hamlet, and his future wife and pupil, **Bess Saunderson** (d. 1711) took the part of Ophelia; his last appearance (for his benefit) was on 15 April 1710, in Beaumont and Fletcher's *Maid's Tragedy*. A fortnight later he died in his wife's arms, and both are buried in the same grave. Steele pays a high tribute to Betterton's character in the *Tatler* (No. 167). A famous actress, **Mrs Anne Bracegirdle**, lies close by, d. 1748, aged eighty-five. She was brought up in Betterton's family, and began her career on the stage as a child of six. So popular was she that it is said of her that 'scarce an audience saw her that were less than half of them lovers, without a suspected favourite amongst them', but her career was comparatively short, for rather than be eclipsed by the young and rising favourite Ann Oldfield (page 26), Mrs Bracegirdle left the stage in 1707, only to appear once more at her adopted father Betterton's benefit. Near their graves is a stone with the name of **Aphara** or **Aphra Behn**, b. 1640, d. 1689, the only woman dramatist and novelist interred at Westminster. Charles II employed her as a political spy at Antwerp in 1666, whence she gave notice of the memorable raid up the Thames planned by De Ruyter and De Witt, which they actually carried out, for so bad was Aphara's reputation that nobody believed her warning. A few steps further lies her friend, the scandalous satirist and facetious essayist, **Thomas Brown**, b. 1663, d. 1704; it was said that he had less 'the spirit of a gentleman than the rest of the wits', but he was more of a scholar; the only specimen of his humour which remains is a witty epigram on the famous Dr Fell, Dean of Christ Church, ('I do not love thee Dr Fell' etc.), which saved him from rustication in his youth.

A tablet against the wall near by to **Bonnell Thornton**, b. 1724, d. 1768, author, and editor of the *Connoisseur*, which ran to 140 weekly papers and six editions. The poet Cowper, who was one of Thornton's schoolfellows at Westminster, contributed to this work; Dr Johnson was also a friend of Thornton and used to enjoy his witty sallies at the famous dining club. The Latin inscription was written by another friend, Dr Joseph Wharton, and is a contrast to the simple words on a tablet close by, 'Jane

Lister, deare child', d. 1688. She was the daughter of Dr Martin Lister, F.R.S., an eminent zoologist and physician of York. Her brother Michael Lister (d. 1676 and buried at York) is also commemorated on this tablet.

Under a defaced gravestone in the south-east Cloister, near Jane Lister's tablet, lies **Pelham Humfrey**, b. 1647, d. 1674, a musician of considerable repute. He was sent abroad by Charles II and studied at the University of Paris under the famous Lully. He was one of the first children of the Chapel Royal after the Restoration, and succeeded Dr Cooke as Master. In 1664, he and his fellow choristers, Blow (page 38) and Turner, composed the well-known 'Club' anthem, 'I will give thanks unto the Lord', and later on he and his former pupil Purcell (page 38) held the joint patent of Lutenist to the King. Pepys mentions Humfrey's proficiency on the lute in his *Diary*, and calls him a 'little Frenchman'. Besides composing many anthems and sacred chants Humfrey wrote secular songs, and showed his skill as a dramatic composer in the vocal music for Shadwell's (page 43) version of the masque in *The Tempest*. He died at Windsor.

Arthur Agard, b. 1540, d. 1615, a distinquished anti-quary, Deputy Chamberlain in the Exchequer, is buried close to the entrance to the Chapter House, where so much of his time had been passed in cataloguing State papers. He was one of the original members of the Society of Antiquaries, founded by Archbishop Parker. On the wall is the monument which he raised to his wife's memory in 1611, and near Agard's grave is buried the **Revd. Ambrose Fisher**, d. 1617, the blind scholar, author of the *Defence of the Liturgy*, who seems to have been a tutor in the family of Dr Grant, one of the Prebendaries.

Charles Wellington Furse, b. 1821, d. 1900, Canon and Archdeacon of Westminster, and Rector of St John's, formerly Principal of Cuddesdon College, Oxford.

John Troutbeck, b. 1832, d. 1899, Minor Canon (1869) and Precentor (1869), Chaplain in Ordinary to Queen Victoria, and his wife **Elizabeth**, b. 1832, d. 1923, sister of Canon, Duckworth. The last thirty years of Dr Troutbeck's life were devoted to the Abbey, where he personally superintended the arrangements for many special services, notably Queen Victoria's Diamond Jubilee. He translated much of Bach's Passion music, including the St John and St Matthew, and a number of Bach's cantatas; his English version of the *Redemption* was approved by Gounod himself. Editor of the *Westminster Abbey Hymn Book*.

Herbert Francis Westlake, b. 1879, d. 1925, Minor Canon, 1909; Custodian, and Keeper of the Muniments. Westlake's researches into the records resulted in the publication of *Westminster Abbey, a History of the Church and Monastery*, in two finely illustrated volumes, as well as of several smaller works, notably a history of St Margaret's Church, and a guide book to the Abbey monuments.

Amongst the soldiers and Old Westminsters commemorated or buried in the East Walk, the following names may be noticed:

Lieut.-General Henry Withers, d. 1729, lies below his monument in the same grave as his friend **Colonel Henry Disney**, d. 1731, familiarly called 'the Duke', from his habit of using that word as an ejaculation, who erected the memorial; the inscription was written by Pope, and condemned by Johnson as 'full of commonplaces with something of the common cant of a superficial satirist'.

A tablet to 'two affectionate brothers, valiant soldiers, and sincere Christians', both of whom were officers in the English Army, although of French birth. **Scipio Duroure** was Colonel of Wolfe's first regiment, the 12th Foot, and was killed at Fontenoy, 1745. His elder brother, **Alexander Duroure** (buried below), rose to the rank of Lieut.-General, and died in 1765. Close by is a tablet to **Colonel Richard Webb**, d. 1785, the great-grandfather of Thackeray, who gave his name to *Esmond*'s general, and thus immortalized Webb's memory.

Colonel Walter Hawkes, d. 1808, Judge Advocate in the West Indies, shipwrecked with his wife on their voyage home. This memorial, like that of Montagu, in the West Cloister, is a record of a Westminster School friendship continued in after life, for it was put up by William Franklin, formerly a King's Scholar, who had shared in Hawke's studies, and taken part with him in 'arduous warfare'.[1]

Sir John Kemp, Bt., b. 1754, d. 1771, who 'after passing through Westminster School with improvement and applause' is commemorated here by 'two young friends, who loved him'.

Albany Charles Wallis, who was drowned in the Thames in 1776, aged thirteen, 'being his father's only hope'. David Garrick, an intimate friend of the boy's father, erected this memorial, and the elder Wallis, who died in 1800 and lies near his son's grave in this Cloister, placed the statue of Garrick[2] in Poets' Corner.

Further on we find a large mural monument with the name of **Edward Godfrey**, who died in 1640, aged twelve, just after his election as a King's Scholar at Westminster School. This memorial was repaired fifty-six years later by Benjamin Godfrey, one of his many brothers (their father Thomas had twenty children in all, by two wives), who placed a tablet beneath it with a Latin inscription recording the murder of **Sir Edmond Berry Godfrey**, b. 1621, d. 1678, the best known of this large family. He was educated at Westminster School, became Justice of the Peace for Westminster, and was esteemed 'the best Justice in England' at that time. Godfrey was a zealous Protestant, but lived on such excellent terms with the Catholics that Titus Oates pretended to betray the Popish Plot to him. Three weeks later the Judge's body was found in a ditch on Primrose Hill transfixed by his own sword, but with marks of strangulation. A reward of £500 was offered for the discovery of the murderers, and three of the Queen's Catholic servants were arrested and hanged, notwithstanding their protestations of innocence. The probable assassin was an adventurer who took the name of Scott; he fled the country afterwards and could never be traced. King Charles II and Pepys were both very much harassed by the unfounded accusations made against the Queen's servants.

South Walk

A large monument to **Daniel Pulteney**,[3] b. *c.* 1683, d. 1731, politician, lauding his independence in politics, was placed at the east end of this walk in 1732; he, his wife (d. 1763), and daughter Frances (d. 1782), who succeeded to the Bath estates on the death of General Harry Pulteney,

are buried near. Daniel held various political posts, but the whole of the latter part of his life was absorbed in futile hatred of Robert Walpole; he gave up 'pleasures and comforts and every other consideration to his anger', and practically died of chagrin and disappointment. *G. Leoni sculpt.*

The large blue stone,[4] called 'Long Meg', was traditionally supposed to cover the remains of a famous virago and giantess, called 'Long Meg of Westminster', who lived in Henry VIII's reign, and is often referred to by the old dramatists. A monument with a portrait-bust commemorates **Edward Tufnell**, b. 1678, d. 1719, Master-mason to the Abbey, 1692–1719 under Sir Christopher Wren.

A curious epitaph, given by Camden, used to be inscribed over the grave of a centenarian, **Ann Birkhead**, who died in 1568, aged 102:

An auncient age of many yeeres,
Here liued *Anne* thou hast;
Pale death hath fixt his fatall force
Upon thy corps at last.

Pierre Courayer, b. 1681, d. 1776, the well-known French divine and writer, was buried here by his own request; a Latin inscription records the chief facts of his life and the virtues of his character. He had made friends with the exiled Dean Atterbury in Paris, and when threatened with excommunication fled, by Atterbury's advice, to England, in 1728, where he spent the rest of his life, and was very popular at Court and in learned society.

Three musicians and composers are buried in the same grave: **Johann Peter Salomon,** b. 1745, d. 1815, a distinguished violinist and composer, a native of Bonn, where in later years he won the affection of the young Beethoven. His name is inseparably connected with that of Haydn, whom he engaged to play at his concerts in London, for which Haydn composed his finest works, the twelve *Grand Symphonies*. Salomon took an active part in founding the Philharmonic Society, and led the orchestra at their first concert (1813). **William Shield,** b. 1748, d. 1829, and **Muzio Clementi,** b. 1752, d. 1832, an eminent Italian musical composer, called the father of the pianoforte. Shield was principal viola player at the Italian Opera for eighteen years, and composer at Covent Garden; he afterwards became master of the King's Musick. He was also an original member of the Philharmonic Society, and helped to found one of the two famous Glee Clubs. He left his favourite Stainer viola to King George IV, who generously paid his widow its full value.

Four **Wesley** children were buried here (1725–31); their father Samuel was a brother of the celebrated John and Charles Wesley,[5] and a master at Westminster School.

Samuel Flood Jones, b. 1826, d. 1895, Minor Canon for thirty-six and Precentor for twenty-five years, also Rector of St Botolph's, Aldersgate.

On the left-hand wall of the entrance to the Cloisters is a monument to **Captain James Cornewall,** b. 1699, killed 1744 in a victorious action against the French off Toulon. His monument, the first voted by Parliament to commemorate a naval hero, was removed here (1932) from the Nave. *R. Taylor sculpt.*

---

[1] *Moved to the Dark Cloister.*
[2] *See page 46.*
[3] *Cousin of the Earl of Bath, page 75.*

[4] *Marks the grave of twenty-six monks who died of the plague.*
[5] *See page 35.*

THE CHAPTER HOUSE AND ITS SURROUNDINGS [1]

IN THE EAST CLOISTER is the thirteenth-century entrance to the Chapter House. The carvings on the arch are sadly decayed–no traces remain of the brilliant colours, vermilion and gold on a blue background, which once made this doorway a 'gate beautiful'. The stone statues of the Virgin and Child over the arch crumbled away, and part only of one of the two angels is left. The vaulted passage within is very low, because the night path from the monks' dormitory to the South Transept was above it.

Here are buried **Edwin**, Abbot, 1049–71, the friend and adviser of Edward the Confessor, the first Abbot of his church, and **Hugolin**, the Confessor's Chaplain and Treasurer. When the Cloisters were rebuilt their bones were removed to this dark passage, and placed with those of the monastic historian, the monk **Sulcard** (d. 1075), under a marble tomb on the south side, of which no trace remains. Sulcard wrote a history of the monastery, which he dedicated to Abbot Vitalis; two copies of this manuscript are extant in the Cottonian MSS in the British Museum.

Further on is a Roman sarcophagus, with a cross on the lid (found on the north side of the Abbey), with an inscription to the effect that it was made by the sons of Valerius Amandinus in memory of their father. It dates probably from early in the third century, but seems to have been re-used in Saxon times for the burial of a Christian.

Two early doorways on either side of the vestibule lead into the Chapel of St Faith[2] on the left, and the monastic treasury (the Chapel of the Pyx) on the right. The latter entrance originally enclosed three doors, only one of which remains. The central door used to be covered with a human skin, tiny fragments of which can be detected at the back of the top hinge. This was probably the tanned skin of a thief, who had been caught robbing the treasury. Here are deposited the **R.A.M.C. Rolls of Honour** for the First and Second World Wars.

On the right of the Chapter House entrance is a window, with a portrait head beneath it, to **James Russell Lowell** (d. 1891), the American poet and prose writer, Minister of the United States in London, 1880–5. 'Placed here by his English friends.'

Below this is a white marble tablet to **Walter Hines Page**, b. 1855, d. 1918, Ambassador of the U.S.A. to the Court of St James, 1913–18, the 'friend of Great Britain in her sorest need' during the First World War.

We now enter the 'incomparable' **Chapter House**,[3] as Matthew of Westminster justly calls it. Begun in 1250, and finished in 1253, it belongs to the same time as the church of Henry III. The style is the traditional English form. The English mason was was employed by the King's chief mason, Master Henry, was probably Master Alberic. The shape is octagonal with a central pillar; in size it is one of the largest in England, 60 feet in diameter. In 1540, on the dissolution of the monastery, the Chapter House passed under the jurisdiction of the Crown, and was fitted up as a receptacle for State papers; the beautiful interior was practically concealed by wooden galleries and divided into two storeys by a wooden floor. The old roof, which was flat, had been taken down as ruinous in 1740. In 1865, Sir Gilbert Scott undertook a complete restoration of this unique building, as far as possible, to its original state, for which purpose a sum of money was granted in Parliament. The dividing column in the double archway of the entrance door was cut away at some period, and a tympanum, with a majesty, now replaces the ancient sculpture. But fortunately some of the original polished marble columns with sculptured foliage[4] round the arcading remain intact, also the beautiful figures of the Virgin and the Angel on either side of the tympanum.

Considerable traces remain of the mural paintings; until nearly the end of the nineteenth century these were visible but decayed in part, but since then many have been uncovered, and can be clearly seen and identified with their subjects. The earliest on the eastern wall, where the Abbot sat, represented the *Doom*, i.e., *The Last Judgment*, and dates from *c.* 1400. The western wall was decorated with scenes from the Apocalypse, which were executed by the order of John of Northampton, who was a monk here from 1372 to 1404. When the wooden flooring was removed early in the nineteenth century the original tiled pavement was found to be in an almost perfect state, the colours in many places as brilliant as when first laid down, about 1250. Amongst the varied subjects, which will be found south of the central pillar, are represented: the Confessor giving his ring to a beggar (i.e. to the disguised St John the Evangelist); a king on a throne (Henry III), playing with his hound; a queen (his wife, Eleanor of Provence) with a hawk on her hand; an abbot (Crokesley) with hand upraised in blessing. On some of the outer tiles are curious Eastern patterns, a fine rose window, and also the royal arms.

The unusual size of the Chapter House is accounted for by the fact that it was intended for secular as well as monastic assemblies, and was used for both from early times.

There was room for eighty monks on the stone benches round the walls, and on the east side were seats for the Abbot and four of the chief brethren. Every morning the whole convent passed in solemn procession from the church to the Chapter House after early Mass, about 9 a.m. Here all took their places, the Abbot beneath a great Crucifix on the east side, and prayers were read from a valuable lectern, presented by Henry III, which stood near the central pillar. All were then given their appointed tasks for the day, and the novices and some of

---

[1] *For windows, see page 120.*
[2] *See page 49.*
[3] *See J. G. Noppen and S. E. Rigold, The Chapter House, Westminster Abbey (Ministry of Works Official Guide, H.M. Stationery Office, 1961).*

[4] *On one of the eastern spandrels is a beautiful arcade of roses.*

the lesser monks retired. After this the affairs of the monastery were discussed in solemn conclave. The mutual improvement of the community was sought, not only by catechizing and reading, but also by penitential discipline; against the central pillar the elder monks were chastised for serious offences; the younger brethren and the novices were reprimanded and punished in the Cloisters.

In 1257 the King's Great Council assembled here, and from the reign of Edward I the Chapter House was used as a Parliament House for the Commons, and here they continued to sit until the end of Henry VIII's reign; in 1547 Edward VI granted them the use of St Stephen's Chapel in the old Palace of Westminster. Since the Dissolution the Dean and Chapter have had no rights over the Chapter House, which belongs to the Crown.[1]

Below the Chapter House, approached by a doorway and stone staircase in Poets' Corner, is a small crypt with a recess for an altar in the eastern bay and a thirteenth-century piscina and aumbry. This may have been intended for the Chapter House Revestry, but it has been found that the walls, originally 12 feet thick, were increased to 17 feet, and there seems no doubt that either Henry III or Edward I appropriated this strong-room for their private treasury: it is in fact described as the 'Treasury of the King's Wardrobe', about 1303. In that year, during Edward I's absence in Scotland, this treasury was broken into, the regalia and other crown jewels, as well as a large sum of money, were stolen, and strong suspicion fell on the monks. The Abbot and forty-eight brethren were sent to the Tower, but released after a long trial, two only of the lesser monastic officials having been proved guilty. Most of the valuables were found hidden round about the precincts, but the King afterwards removed his money chests from the Abbot's care. The regalia seem, however, to have been left in the precincts, but were probably removed to the monastic treasury in the Chapel of the Pyx, where they remained until the Commonwealth.

In this Crypt are kept, under the care of the sacrist, the vestments, copes, silk banners and the ornaments of the altars.

The Chapter Library and Muniment Room

Adjoining the Chapter House entrance is a doorway opening on to a stone stair (formerly the day stairs to the monks' dormitory), leading up to the Library. This room originally formed part of the great dormitory where all the brethren slept; later on, it may have been partitioned into cubicles, as at Durham. At the north end a stone gallery crossing St Faith's Chapel led by a staircase into the South Transept; by this way the monks used to descend into the church for the night offices. The staircase no longer exists and the entry to it from the gallery is now blocked by the monument of the Duke of Argyll (see page 44). The room itself is lofty, and has a fine roof, supported by massive beams. It probably dates from the end of the fifteenth century. Above the fireplace is a contemporary portrait of Dean Williams (appointed Dean in 1620) who entirely remodelled this room and

---

[1] For a description of the glass in the windows of the Chapter House see p. 120.

fitted it up as a library, furnishing it with valuable books and manuscripts at his own cost. Almost all these manuscripts were unfortunately destroyed by a fire in 1694. In the reign of Edward VI an order was published by Council for 'purging the library of all missals, legends, and other superstitious volumes'. Fortunately, however, a few are still extant. Among these is the famous *Liber Regalis*, which contains the recension used at the Coronation of Richard II, and followed in its main features at every coronation since–this is possibly the very copy used by the boy King himself.

The Litlyngton Missal, the Islip Roll, and the Indentures of the Foundation of Henry VII Chapel are kept in the Muniment Room.

The Muniment Room is on the west side of the South Transept, overlooking the Choir and Poets' Corner; within it is the vast collection of documents concerning the business life first of the medieval Abbey and later of the Collegiate Church. Here is a bronze tablet erected by the Dean and Chapter to **Dr Edward John Long Scott,** b. 1841, d. 1918, sometime Keeper of Manuscripts and Egerton Librarian at the British Museum and subsequently Keeper of the Abbey Muniments (1893–1918), whose labours in the arrangement and cataloguing of the Abbey documents are thus commemorated.

Next to the entrance to the Library and the Muniment Room in the East Cloister is the Pyx Chamber.

The Pyx Chamber

(*Open to the public on weekdays only from 10.30 a.m. to 6.30 p.m. March to October; from 10.30 a.m. to 4 p.m. October to March.*)

Next to the Library entrance a heavy oak doorway with six locks leads into the so-called 'Chapel of the Pyx'.

Within is a vaulted chamber, built between 1065 and 1090, which formed part of the early monastic buildings. An altar, the only stone altar left *in situ* at Westminster, with a thirteenth-century piscina on the column near by, shows that this must have been used as a chapel at some time before the fourteenth century, when it was no doubt the monastic treasury. The tiled floor dates from the thirteenth century and so does one of the large chests. The other chest is probably of late fifteenth-century date. After the Dissolution it passed into the possession of the Crown, and was never restored to the Abbey authorities.

In this chamber, was kept the 'pyx', or box containing the standard pieces of gold and silver, and here once a year took place the trial of the pyx–the testing of the current gold and silver coinage–which now takes place in the Mint.

The Undercroft and Abbey Museum

A wall divides the two and a half vaulted bays which form the Pyx Chapel from the five and a half bays of the so-called 'Undercroft', a name which applies to both of these substructures of the monks' dormitory. The Undercroft is approached from the East Cloister. It is about 110 feet long by 45 feet wide. On two of the pillars the original eleventh-century carving remains, the others have been modified by slightly later decorations.

In monastic times it was probably the common-room of the monks. In 1908 it was turned into a museum in memory of the late Mr John T. Micklethwaite who was for many years the Abbey Architect and Surveyor of the Fabric.

The Wax Effigies. These effigies are the remnants of an ancient custom: 'At the funeral of a great man his "lively effigy" or representation, dressed to imitate life, was carried before him to the grave. After the burial it was set up in the church under a hearse or temporary monument. It was then customary to affix short laudatory poems or epitaphs to the hearse with pins, wax, or paste.'[1] The well-known epitaph attributed by some to Ben Jonson, on the Countess of Pembroke:

Underneath this sable herse
Lies the subject of all verse,
Sidney's sister, Pembroke's mother, etc.

was probably one of this kind. The 'herse', which was a wooden platform decorated with black hangings, and containing the waxen effigy of the deceased, usually remained in the Abbey for about a month, in the case of sovereigns for a longer period. Mary I's hearse was 'adorned with angels of wax, the valence fringed, and adorned with escocheons'.[2]

The royal effigies can be traced back to the fourteenth century. Edward I's is the earliest of which there is any record; like most of the other early figures, it seems to have lain for a long while on the top of his tomb. Up to Henry V's time the embalmed bodies of the sovereigns and not the effigies, were carried on the funeral cars. The earlier effigies were made of wood, some with heads, hands, and feet of plaster, later on the heads were of wax. A few had wigs and the faces were painted. Dryden speaks of the open presses, where 'you may see them all a-row', when the figures of Edward I and Eleanor, Edward III and Philippa, Henry V and Catherine, Henry VII and Elizabeth of York, James I and Anne of Denmark, and Henry, Prince of Wales, were easily identified.

In the eighteenth century, Dart tells us, they were 'sadly mangled, some with their faces broke, others broken in sunder, and most of them stripped of their robes, I suppose by the late rebels. I observe the ancientist have escaped best, I suppose by reason that their cloaths were too old for booty. There is, as I take it, Edward III, with a large robe once of crimson velvet, but now appears like leather. There is Henry V, but I can't suppose it is that that was carried at his funeral, for that was made of tann'd leather, but this is of wood, as are all the old ones. The later are of stuff, having the heads only of wood, as Queen Elizabeth, who is entirely stripp'd, and James I.' Walpole, who was well acquainted with the figures, mentions that the face of Elizabeth of York was still perfect in his time. 'You will smile,' he says, 'when I tell you that t'other day a party went to Westminster Abbey, and among the rest saw the ragged regiment. They inquired the names of the figures. "I don't know them," said the man; "but if Mr Walpole were here he could tell you every one."'[3] No record was kept of the name attached to each figure, but the existing ones have been identified by antiquaries, and placed in glass cases, which are arranged in the Norman Undercroft Museum.

There are two full-length wooden effigies–those of Edward III and Catherine of Valois, wife of Henry V. The face of Edward III is very probably a death-mask; the slight droop at the corner of the mouth suggests a facial paralysis, which would have resulted from the stroke

[1] *Cunningham's* Handbook, *page 16.*
[2] *Sandford, page 480.*   [3] *Walpole's* Letters, *vol. ii, page 252.*

Hearse of Abbot Islip from his Mortuary Roll

which the King suffered shortly before his death. The other four effigies are only of the head and shoulders of the subject. These were mounted on wooden frames covered with padding to which appropriate robes were attached for their part in the funeral rites. The head of Henry VII is also a death-mask; the right eyebrow shows clotting of the hair by the grease applied to the face to prevent the plaster from sticking. The nose of this effigy has been restored, using as a model a terra-cotta bust of the King in the Victoria and Albert Museum. The unusual long face of Anne of Bohemia, wife of Richard II, shows a marked similarity to the pictures of the Queen in the illustrations of the *Liber Regalis*, an illuminated manuscript of the Order of Service believed to have been prepared for her coronation. The wig on Elizabeth of York is a modern one, but the effigy is known to have had a similar wig at the time of the funeral.

An eighteenth-century drawing by John Carter, hanging in the museum, shows these wooden effigies as they were, lying in the Chantry Chapel of Henry V.

There are eleven wax effigies which were cleaned and restored 1932–5. Their clothes were found to be in a remarkably good state of preservation and are of considerable interest for the history of costume.

King Charles II (d. 1685). This figure is contemporary although it was not actually carried at the funeral. The modelling of the face is most remarkable. As a contemporary wrote in 1695, ''tis to ye life, and truly to admiration'. The King is dressed in his Garter robes–the earliest which have survived in England. His doublet and breeches are of cloth of silver and his cravat and sleeve ruffles are of Venetian 'gros point' lace. Notice

Wax Effigy of Charles II

Wax Effigy of Lord Nelson

particularly the Garter hat with its plume of ostrich and heron feathers.

William Pitt, Earl of Chatham (d. 1778). This figure was placed in the Abbey very shortly after Pitt's death. It was not carried at the funeral. It was made by an American, Mrs Patience Wright, to whom Pitt is known to have sat. The head (now, owing to damage, shown separately) is astonishingly lifelike and impressive. The great statesman is represented in his parliamentary robes.

Edmund Sheffield, Duke of Buckingham (d. 1735). He was a son of the 1st Duke by his wife, Catherine, whose effigy is in the next case. This figure is exactly as it was carried at his funeral. The face is a death-mask. He is dressed in his robes, with his ducal coronet, and wears a magnificent red silk coat embroidered with floral patterns

in silk and metal thread. His feet rest on a roughly carved wild boar, one of the supporters of the family coat of arms. He died at the age of nineteen.

Catherine, Duchess of Buckingham (d. 1743). She was a natural daughter of King James II by Catherine Sedley. She married, as her second husband, John Sheffield, 1st Duke of Buckingham, the builder of the original Buckingham Palace. The effigy was made during the life-time of the Duchess and under her personal supervision. It was the last actually carried at a funeral. She is dressed in her coronation robes and wears her coronet. The skirt is French brocade and beneath it are two quilted petti-coats. Her shoes are of green satin. Her point lace ruffles date from about 1700. When the figure was cleaned it was found that the paste jewellery had been mounted on black

Undercroft Museum

velvet stiffened with bits of old playing cards. These have been framed and now hang in the case.

By her side is the figure of her eldest son, **Robert, Marquess of Normanby,** who died at the age of three in 1715. He wears a long undercoat of yellow figured silk brocaded with silk and silver gilt thread on a blue satin ground. Beneath this is a corset, and over all a frogged robe of crimson coloured velvet. At the back of this are slits for leading strings. His cravat is of Valenciennes bobbin lace and he wears an elaborate turned-up cap. At his feet is a painted wooden unicorn, one of the supporters of the family coat of arms. He was the elder brother of Edmund, Duke of Buckingham.

Frances, Duchess of Richmond and Lennox (d. 1702). She was a granddaughter of Walter Stuart, 1st Lord Blantyre, and she married Charles Stuart, 6th and last Duke of Richmond and Lennox of that line. She was a great beauty and sat for the original figure of Britannia on the coinage.

The effigy was made immediately after her death at a cost of £260 by Mrs Goldsmith. She is dressed in her robes which she wore at the coronation of Queen Anne. Her skirt is of late seventeenth-century French brocade and her sleeve ruffles are of bobbin lace (point de Paris). Her shoes are of white kid with gilt braid. She has an elaborate headdress (fontange), behind which, originally, her coronet was placed at an awkward angle. Her fan, which formerly hung from her waist, is now displayed in the case, and another fan has been substituted in its place. By her side is her favourite parrot. It died a few days after the Duchess. It is a West African grey parrot, and is, perhaps, the oldest stuffed bird which has survived in England.

Queen Elizabeth I (d. 1603). This effigy was entirely remade in 1760 to replace an earlier figure. The head is modelled from the effigy on her tomb in the Abbey. The dress is an attempt to represent the dress worn by the Queen at the thanksgiving service for the defeat of the Spanish Armada in 1588.

King William III (d. 1702) and **Queen Mary II** (d. 1694). These are contemporary figures modelled by Mrs Goldsmith, who made the effigy of the Duchess of Richmond. They were not carried at the funerals. The face of the King, with his nose 'curved like the beak of an eagle', closely resembles his portraits. He is placed on a footstool to make him nearer to the height of the Queen. The robes are contemporary and were made for the effigies. The Queen has a brocaded skirt probably of French weaving (c. 1700). Her ruffles are gros point de Venise, and the clasps on her bodice are silver set with pastes.

Queen Anne (d. 1714). The effigy was made after her death. The skirt is of French Louis XV yellow brocade. The Star of the Order of the Garter on her robes is a genuine contemporary one. The wig was added in 1768 and should have been dark brown and not black.

Horatio, Viscount Nelson (d. 1805). This effigy was bought early in 1806 in the hope that it would attract people back to the Abbey and away from his tomb in St Paul's. It was modelled by Catherine Andras to whom Nelson is known to have sat. The face is extraordinarily life-like and attractive and a remarkable likeness. The contemporary Duchess of Devonshire, who knew Nelson well, said of the whole figure that it 'is as if he was standing there'. There is very little doubt that the whole of the clothes belonged to him. The Orders are the Bath, St Ferdinand (The Two Sicilies), the Crescent (Turkey) and St Joachim. The medal is that of the Battle of the Nile. The cocked hat (now shown in one of the central cases)

also belonged to him and has the green shade which he wore after the loss of his eye.[1]

In the Museum is the Chair made for the Coronation of King William III and Queen Mary II who were recognized as joint sovereigns. Queen Mary II was crowned in this Chair, but it has not since been used at Coronations. We may note, also, the armour of 'General Monck' (George Monck, Duke of Albemarle) which was carried at his funeral in 1670. Here also are displayed the replicas of the Regalia (used at the Rehearsals for the Coronation of Queen Elizabeth II, the Essex Ring (see p. 74) and a collection of tiles, pottery, and other objects which have been found from time to time in and about the Abbey. There is a fine medieval cope-chest (fifteenth century) and the early fourteenth-century chest with ornamental ironwork formerly used for keeping some of the Abbey Charters and other documents. Here also is the Bell which formerly hung in the South Transept and later in the Belfry Tower. It was cast by Thomas Lester in 1742, and was used for the last time on the first Armistice Day. A smaller medieval bell is probably the bell which hung outside the Refectory door in the South Cloister and was struck with a staff by a monk to summon the brethren to meals.

The Little Cloister

South of the East Cloister a dark arch and vaulted passage to the left formed part of the Confessor's monastic buildings, and led to the monks' infirmary; it is now the approach to the courtyard called Little Cloister. On the right an old house, 'Litlyngton's Tower', is at present the dwelling of the Abbey organist. A door in one of the rooms in the first floor used to lead into the Westminster 'School', which was the monks' dormitory. Passing into Little Cloisters, on the left is the School Armoury, with a room used as a classroom above it. These rooms formerly belonged to one of the Canonical houses, and were given to the School in 1861, when a covered playroom, now the gymnasium, was built for the boys. The Armoury appears to have been a chapel dedicated to St Dunstan in Norman times; later on, in the fifteenth century, it was rebuilt and a decorated niche, which may have held the statue of St Dunstan, and a piscina near the site of the altar still remain. The modern gymnasium, which is on part of the monk's cemetery, is bounded on the west by the Norman wall of the Pyx Chapel, the barred and blocked up windows of which can be seen below. The Tudor windows above them formerly belonged to the Canon's house. The original entrance to these rooms was from the Dark Cloister, but when Dean Robinson turned the vaults below the old dormitory into the 'Undercroft', a new entrance was made. The present Little Cloister and the surrounding houses, of various dates, stand on the site of the monks' infirmary, which seems in early times to have consisted of one large room, with smaller houses round it for the sick, infirm, and aged monks. After the great fire of 1298, which destroyed most of the monastic houses, or at any rate rendered them uninhabitable for a time, more temporary accommodation had to be found,

[1] For the history etc. of the effigies see W. H. St J. Hope, 'On the Funeral Effigies of the Kings and Queens of England' (Archaeologia, vol. lx (1907)); L. E. Tanner and J. L. Nevinson, 'On some later Funeral Effigies' (Archaeologia, vol. lxxxv (1936)); R. P. Howgrave-Graham, 'The Earlier Royal Funeral Effigies' (Archaeologia, vol. xcviii (1961)).

but the new buildings were not added till later in the fourteenth century. Portions of these and of the earlier work are built into the modern dwellings, and in one a vestibule with fine oak beams in the roof was probably the Infirmarer's private dining-hall. The herb garden led out of this, but does not appear to have been on the site of the present 'College' garden, which is entered by a door in the south-west corner. In the Southern Walk a beautiful fourteenth-century doorway led into the ancient **Chapel of St Catherine.**

The original Chapel was built in the twelfth century; the part which survived the fire of 1298 was rebuilt in the fourteenth century. In 1578, when a prebendal house was placed on the site, most of the Chapel was destroyed, but a few arches remain in the Canon's garden. The Chapel was a large building with aisles and a nave; it was used for many important assemblies, both secular and clerical, including the consecration of various prelates. Here took place the quarrel (1176) for precedence between the Archbishops of Canterbury and York, which resulted in the one receiving the title of Primate of '*all* England', the other 'of England'. Fuller thus describes the dispute: 'A Synod was called at Westminster, the Pope's Legat being threat; on whose right hand sat, as in his proper place, Richard of Canterburie, which in springs Roger of York and finding Canterburie so seated fairly sits him down in Canterburie's lap (a baby too big to be dandled thereon), yea Canterburie his servants dandled this lap-childe with a witness, who plucked him thence and buffeted him to purpose.' Roger of York then rushed into the Abbey, where King Henry II was hearing Mass, and (showing his torn cope) demanded reparation, but only got laughed at. In this Chapel Henry III, with a lighted candle in one hand and the Gospel in the other, swore to maintain the Magna Charta, surrounded by the archbishops and bishops, also holding lighted candles. After the King's oath the candles were extinguished and cast smoking to the ground, typifying the fate of the souls of those 'who violate or wrongly interpret this injunction'.

Close to the entrance door a gravestone marks the resting-place of **John Wilson,** b. 1595, d. 1674, a distinguished lutenist, chamber musician to Charles I. Wilson is said to have been 'the best at the lute in all England'.

Henry Lawes, b. 1595, d. 1662, musician, lies somewhere in the Cloisters. He was a member of the King's Band in the reigns of both Charles I and Charles II, and 'betook himself to the teaching of ladies to sing' during the Commonwealth. He was a friend of Milton, and is believed to have recommended him to the Earl of Bridgwater for the composition of the words in the masque of *Comus,* for which he himself wrote the music. Lawes is best known as a composer of the airs of many well-known songs by Herrick, Lovelace and other poets; several books of his collections exist in manuscript as well as in print. He also wrote anthems, notably the music for 'Zadok the Priest' for Charles II's Coronation.

A tablet on the wall of the house where he used to live commemorates **John Charles Thynne,** b. 1838, d. 1918, younger son of Lord John Thynne,[1] Sub-Dean. He was Receiver-General from 1865 to 1908.

A tablet on the eastern wall is noticeable for the curious inscription to **Thomas Smith,** d. 1664, who 'through the spotted veil of the smallpox, render'd a pure and unspotted soul to God'.

---

[1] *See page 37.*

THE COMMUNION, ALTAR PLATE AND PROCESSIONAL BANNERS

None of the present plate in the possession of the Dean and Chapter dates from monastic times; such pieces as still existed after the Dissolution were broken up or sold under the Commonwealth, and new vessels and ornaments were presented after the Restoration.

Among the more important pieces of plate are:

A chalice and paten presented to the Dean and Chapter (1918) in memory of Cyril Dupe, an Oxford undergraduate, killed in the First World War. They were found in the river near Oxford, and are thought to have originally formed part of the plate belonging to one of the college chapels, date about 1550.

A pair of large plain chalices, with covers forming patens, and a pair of similar flagons, all London made; initials of maker R.A., date 1660.

A pair of chased chalices, no maker's name or hallmarks, given by Prebendary John Sudbury, afterwards Dean of Durham, date 1671.

A pair of tripod candlesticks and a pair of embossed flagons, London made; an embossed centre salver and alms-dish, combined, London made; two smaller alms-dishes, one dated 1684, the other about the same period.

A straining spoon, date 1697.

Two silver-gilt alms-dishes inscribed 'given to Westminster Abbey by Their Royal Highnesses Princess Elizabeth and the Duke of Edinburgh to mark the occasion of their wedding on 20th November 1947'.

Two pairs of modern chalices and various ornaments have been presented to the altars of St Faith and St Edward at different times. A silver-gilt cross and a pair of vases were given by Lord Rosebery for the High Altar in 1899, after his elder daughter's marriage in the Abbey.

A silver-gilt alms-dish was presented by Col. Sir Charles Wyndham Murray, K.C.B., Gentleman Usher of the Scarlet Rod at the second Installation of the Knights of the Bath in Henry VII's Chapel, 18 May 1920.

In 1928 the citizens of Westminster, in recognition of Dean Ryle's constant efforts to bring the City and the Abbey together, presented two richly carved alms-dishes in his memory. An official stall with the arms of the City of Westminster above it has been since assigned to the Mayor 'in perpetuity'.

On the Altar in St Edward's Chapel are a pair of silver candlesticks, seventeenth-century Italian work, presented by the Duke and Duchess of York (afterwards King George VI and Queen Elizabeth) in commemoration of their marriage, 26 April 1923. On either side of this Altar are tall standard candlesticks of sheeted silver, given in 1924 by the Order of Crusaders.

In St Faith's Chapel is a lamp of silvered copper. A

silver-gilt chalice and paten, given by the Society of St Faith; a parcel-gilt chalice and paten given by Lady Hudson in memory of the late Sir Robert Hudson.

To be used in this Chapel: two silver chalices and patens, given by the Girls' Friendly Society and the late Admiral Sir Austem Moore.

The Processional Banners

These are displayed in the Sanctuary on great festivals of the Church and festivals of the Abbey.

The Banner of Our Lady – Presented by the Girls' Friendly Society, 1922. The Banner of St Martin – Presented by the Church Lads' Brigade after the First World War. The Banner of St Peter – Presented by the Mothers' Union, 1926. The Banner of St Oswald – Presented by the Church of England Men's Society, 1938. The Banner of St Edward – Presented in 1942 by Miss Eulalie Buckmaster in memory of her father, Walter Selby Buckmaster. The Banner of St George – Presented by Mrs Louis Beatrix Itterson-Pronk in 1948.

THE PAINTED GLASS

THERE IS VERY LITTLE LEFT of the ancient glass except the east windows in the Clerestory, two windows at the east and west ends of the Nave, and the plain glass with the initials H.R. in Henry VII Chapel. In the Jerusalem Chamber, Jericho Parlour, and Vestibule are collected fragments of the early thirteenth-, fourteenth-, and fifteenth-century glass which filled the windows of the church before the Reformation; those which remained intact after the fifteenth century were no doubt destroyed by the Puritans two centuries later. In the north window, below Dean Williams's arms, are six small panes of thirteenth-century glass of special interest; the scenes depicted include the Massacre of the Innocents, the Stoning of St Stephen, the Martyrdom of St Alban, the Pentecost, St Nicholas and the false pilgrim, and the beheading of St John the Baptist.

The East Windows

These are a collection of ancient and modern glass. The older parts were probably pieced together in the seventeenth century when the blank spaces were filled up with glass of that period. Early in the eighteenth century the whole window was repaired by Wren, when Surveyor of the Fabric, and the glaziers scratched their names with the dates of their work (1702 and 1706) upon the modern pieces. There is some pot metal in this window, which includes thirteenth-, fourteenth-, and fifteenth-century fragments. The central figures of St Edward holding out the ring to his patron saint, St John the Evangelist, who is in pilgrim's dress, date from about 1490, with the exception of the King's head which is later. Several early coats of arms are intact. These include the three leopards of Henry III, the arms of his father-in-law Raymond, Count of Provence, and of his brother-in-law Richard, Earl of Cornwall.[1]

The window below this in the Triforium shows Queen Eleanor of Castile, the wife of Edward I, and Lady Margaret Beaufort, with their coats of arms above them. This window was designed by *Sir Ninian Comper*.

The four-light window immediately above the Henry V Chantry Chapel is filled with glass salvaged from a window in the South Transept made by Messrs. Burlison and Grylls, which was severely damaged in the Second World War. There are four kings shown, Henry III, Edward III, Henry V, and Henry VII with their coats of arms, which were made by *Edward Moore*, who designed the window.

At the **west end of the Nave,** the figure in fifteenth-century glass under the South Tower is traditionally supposed to represent the Black Prince. The corresponding figure under the North Tower is made up of fragments of various dates, and represents an unidentified bearded saint. In 1922–3 the glass from all these windows was releaded, repaired and cleaned under the auspices of the Victoria and Albert Museum.

The Rose Windows and the West Window

In 1722 the **Rose Window in the North Transept** was remodelled and new glass inserted under Dean Atterbury's directions a few months before he was arrested for treason and sent to the Tower. The previous year (1721) the artist, *Sir James Thornhill* (d. 1734), who had already been employed on the paintings inside the Dome of St Paul's, received £100, by Atterbury's orders, for designing '16 large figures 7 feet high of the Apostles and Evangelists on Canvasses and Frames in proper Colours for the glass painter to work by. Also the Glory in the middle and Cherubim Heads, etc.,' for the great North Window. It may be noted that Judas Iscariot is omitted and only eleven Apostles are shown. *Joshua Price*, the glass-painter, was paid £44 16s. for carrying out this design, and in December 1733, received another sum of £400 from the Dean and Chapter, on commission for his work on the **great West Window** at the end of the Nave, the design for which was in all probability sketched out by Thornhill the year before his death. This window, created in 1735, has the figures of Abraham, Isaac, and Jacob together with those of fourteen prophets. Beneath these are the arms of George II flanked by those of King Sebert, Queen Elizabeth I, Dean Willcocks, and the Collegiate Church.

Both these windows were put up at the time when Sir Christopher Wren and his successor, Nicholas Hawksmoor, were restoring the stone work on the north front and completing the west end with the new Towers.

In the late nineteenth century, the Abbey architect, Pearson, completely remodelled the tracery of the Rose Window on the north front, and subsequently the old glass was cleaned and put back as far as possible in its original place.

During the Second World War the glass in the six lancet windows below the North Rose Window, which commemorated seven officers who gave their lives in the Indian Mutiny, was destroyed. In 1958 these windows were

---

[1] *These coats of arms are now moved to St Edmund's Chapel.*

replaced by a series, designed by *Brian Thomas*, representing the Six Acts of Mercy.

The **Rose or Wheel Window in the South Transept** is the largest of this type, the stone work outside was remodelled under Sir Gilbert Scott in 1849–50, having been filled with stained glass by *Messrs. Ward and Nixon* in the taste of that period. The whole of this glass was removed in 1901, and the present window substituted for it in September 1902. The money was raised, by public subscription, as a memorial to **Hugh Lupus Grosvenor, 1st Duke of Westminster** (b. 1825, d. 1899). G. F. Bodley, R.A., superintended the work of the glass-painters, Messrs. Burlison and Grylls, and Dr M. R. James, Provost of Eton, drew up the scheme of subjects.

Thirty-two figures in the outer circle were chosen to represent the Preparation of the World for Christ. In the upper half are sixteen Jewish prophets. In the lower half: (from left to right) Enoch, Abraham, Moses, David, Solomon, Job, Ezra, Sirach–representing the Chosen People. Plato, Aristotle, Æschylus, the Sibyl, Zoroaster, One of the Magi, Virgil, Seneca represent these Seekers for the Truth in the heathen world.

In the inner circle, round the central figure of Christ, are sixteen figures, symbolical of the Virtues and the Orders of Angels. In the lower spandrels is the Annunciation, represented by St Gabriel and the Blessed Virgin. Adam and St John the Baptist are in the upper spandrels. The twelve trefoiled lights below contain great representative teachers of the Greek and Latin Church; in the upper range: St Clement of Alexandria, St Athanasius, St Chrysostom, St Jerome, St Augustine of Hippo, St Gregory the Great. In the lower range the Christian teachers of our own islands: St Alban, St Ninian, St Patrick, St David, St Augustine of Canterbury, St Aidan. In the upper range of lights are the emblems of St Peter and St Paul on either side of the royal arms. The shields above the figures in the lower range are those of St Edward the Confessor, the Abbey of Westminster, the City of Westminster, and the Royal Arms.

During the nineteenth and twentieth centuries various memorial windows were presented to the Dean and Chapter or put up by them.

In the wall of the **west aisle of the North Transept** is a window to the memory of the officers and men who were drowned in the shipwreck of H.M.S. Captain, off Cape Finisterre, 7 September 1870.

Next to this is a window dedicated, 25 January 1915, to the memory of **John Bunyan**, b. 1628, d. 1688, designed by *Sir Ninian Comper*. The subjects were taken from the first part of the *Pilgrim's Progress*.

In the **North Choir Aisle** is a window in memory of **James Turle,** b. 1802, d. 1882, organist at the Abbey for fifty years, with portraits of himself and his wife, put up by his son.[1]

In **St Benedict's Chapel** was a window commemorating officers and men of the Queen's Westminster Rifles who fell in the First World War. This window was destroyed by blast in 1940, and has been replaced by a window to the memory of those citizens of Westminster who gave their lives in the Second World War. It was designed by *Hugh Easton* and was unveiled by H.R.H. Princess Margaret on 7 November 1948. The window depicts St George and St Michael with the arms of the City of Westminster and various badges and emblems representing the armed forces and other organizations in which the citizens of Westminster served during the war.

The Nave

On the **north side of the Nave** is a series of windows, designed and carried out by *Sir Ninian Comper* (see also the Bunyan Window) after a scheme drawn up by Dr J. Armitage Robinson, when Dean of Westminster (1902–11), which embodies the kings and abbots, in whose time the present Nave was gradually built, with their coats of arms and badges.

Sir Charles Parsons, O.M., K.C.B., b. 1854, d. 1931, marine engineer. The figures represent King Henry III and Abbot Richard de Ware (d. 1283) in whose time the eastern half of the present Abbey Church was built. This window was dedicated in 1950.

William Thomson, 1st Baron Kelvin, b. 1824, d. 1907, whose grave is below.[2] The figures represent King Henry V, a generous contributor to the western bays of the Nave, and William of Colchester (d. 1420), the Abbot in whose time the work was carried out.

Donald Alexander Smith, 1st Baron Strathcona and Mount Royal, b. 1820, d. 1914, a great Canadian imperialist and philanthropist; the king in this window is Richard II and Abbot Litlyngton (d. 1386), who devoted the whole of his time at Westminster, first as Prior then as Abbot, to continuing the rebuilding of the monastery and church begun by his predecessor, Langham.

Sir Benjamin Baker, b. 1840, d. 1907, a distinguished engineer, the builder of the Forth Bridge, a small picture of which is on the glass. The figures represent King Edward III, and Archbishop Langham (d. 1376), Litlyngton's predecessor as Abbot, whose munificent bequest enabled his successor to carry on the building of the Nave and the Cloisters.

Sir John Wolfe Barry, K.C.B., b. 1836, d. 1918, Past-President of the Institute of Civil Engineers. The figures represent King Edward I, in whose time the new building begun by his father, Henry III, was carried on as far as the second bay of the Nave, and the contemporary Abbot, Walter de Wenlock (d. 1307). Within the canopy above there is a statuette of the Abbot giving the heart of Henry III to the Abbess of Fontevrault, a scene which took place in the presence of Edmund Crouchback, the King's brother, and of William de Valence, his uncle, whose statuettes are in the niches below, both of whom are buried in the Abbey.

Sir Henry Royce, Bt., O.B.E. The first aero-engineer to be commemorated in the Abbey. The window shows King Edgar the Peaceful and St Dunstan (d. 938). Under these figures are the arms of Sir Henry Royce and the City of Derby. In the canopy above the figure of King Edgar is a scene from a drawing by St Dunstan himself, of Our Lord enthroned and St Dunstan kneeling before him. In the right-hand window St Dunstan reads the Scriptures, while an angel plays his harp which hangs on the wall of his cell. The scene in the tracery quatrefoil shows King Edgar sailing into Chester with six kings, with whom he had made peace.

Two windows complete the series, and commemorate

---

[1] *See page 106.*

[2] *See page 32.*

the **Royal Army Medical Corps** (presented in 1927), and the **Prisoners of War** (presented in 1926), who died in Germany, 1914–18. The **R.A.M.C.** window has for its subject King Edward the Confessor and Abbot Edwin (d. 1071). Upon the other window King Henry VI stands beside Abbot Harweden (d. 1441). In both, the patron saints of these kings are represented, and various scenes from their lives. A panel has been added commemorating those who fell in the Second World War.

Two eminent civil engineers of high repute are commemorated in two nineteenth-century windows, which contain small pictures of their various works. **Isambard Kingdom Brunel**, b. 1806, d. 1859. He assisted his father, Sir Marc I. Brunel on the Thames tunnel and designed the Clifton suspension bridge. He also designed the Great Eastern steamship.

Richard Trevithick, b. 1771, d. 1833, the father of the steam locomotive engine. In 1801 he completed the first steam carriage to convey passengers at Redruth, Cornwall.

A window in the **North Choir Aisle** commemorates **Robert Stephenson**, b. 1803, d. 1859, engineer, and his father **George Stephenson**, b. 1781, d. 1848, inventor and founder of railways.

On the south side, above the **Warriors'** or **St George's Chapel**, is a memorial window to **George W. Childs**, d. 1875, citizen of the U.S.A., erected in recognition of his generous benefactions to our country. It commemorates **George Herbert** and **William Cowper**, 'both religious poets, both Westminster scholars, and representing two opposite poles of the English Church',[1] the ecclesiastical and evangelical.

Above the Abbot's Pew is a window unveiled 26 May 1922, in memory of the officers and men of the **British Flying Corps** who fell in the First World War. The design is by *Harry Grylls*, carried out by the firm of Burlison and Grylls; the theme is Flying Men and Wings, illustrated by passages from the prophets Isaiah and Ezekiel. The armour and weapons borne by them are: the Breastplate of Righteousness, the Shield of Faith, the Helmet of Salvation, the Sword of the Spirit (Ephesians vi. 13, 17). In the tracery above is the Archangel Michael, the patron saint of airmen. The window was presented by Mrs Louis Bennett, of West Virginia, whose son, a pilot of the R.F.C., was killed in France.

West of the Cloister door is a window, dedicated 14 November 1921, which was presented by an anonymous donor as a memorial to the services rendered through the **Young Men's Christian Association** during the First World War, and in memory of its founder, **Sir George Williams**, b. 1821, d. 1905, knighted by Queen Victoria in 1894, two portraits of whom as a young and older man appear at the base of the glass. The design is by *Dudley Forsyth*. The subjects are the Sermon on the Mount and the Transfiguration of Our Lord; above are the saints, St Michael, the 'Protector of Souls', and St George, the Patron Saint of England; below these are the royal coat of arms, and the Collegiate arms. In the quatrefoil above is Our Lord in Glory, and surrounding this are types of the soldiers from all parts of the empire who served their country during the First World War, with the shields and arms of various British Dependencies.

In the **Islip Chapel** there is a window, executed by *Hugh Easton*, which was presented by Dr Alan Don, the then Dean, as a thankoffering for the deliverance of

Westminster Abbey and St Margaret's Church from the perils of the Second World War and in remembrance of John Islip, sometime Abbot, and of Paul de Labilliere, sometime Dean.

It depicts Abbot Islip (d. 1532) kneeling in prayer, holding in his hand a model of the Islip rooms which survived the destruction of the greater part of the Deanery by enemy action. Above is inserted a diamond-shaped piece of medieval glass with the Abbot's rebus – an eye and a slip. In the panel to the left is a cherub holding a model of the Abbey from which flames ascend to commemorate the fire that destroyed the roof of the Lantern Tower in May 1941. Above are the arms of Dean de Labilliere, who was Dean throughout the war. The other central figure represents St Margaret of Antioch. In the panel to the right is a cherub holding a model of St Margaret's Church, Westminster, the chancel of which was rebuilt by Abbot Islip. Above are the arms of Dr Don, who was Rector of St Margaret's from 1941 to 1946. In the lights at the head of the window are (1) the Cross Keys of St Peter with the ring of Edward the Confessor, (2) the arms of Abbot Islip, (3) the emblem of St Margaret, (4) the arms of the Abbey of Westminster.

In the **upper chantry of the Islip Chapel** is a window designed by *Hugh Easton*, in memory of the nurses who gave their lives in the Second World War. It shows a nurse with her arms outstretched to the Holy Family. The lower part of the window is filled with the emblems of the nursing organizations and the countries from which they came. The window was unveiled by H.M. Queen Elizabeth the Queen Mother on 2 November 1950.

At the east end of Henry VII Chapel is a chapel dedicated to the memory of the men of the Royal Air Force who died in the Battle of Britain. The principal part of the memorial is the stained and painted glass window designed by *Hugh Easton*. This was unveiled by H.M. King George VI on 10 July 1947. In the lower lights are the badges of the sixty-three squadrons that took part in the battle. In the centre of the window, between the royal arms and the badge of the Royal Air Force, are the flags of the countries from which the men who died came. Grouped around these are four panels showing figures in the uniforms of the Royal Air Force, representing Dedication, Sacrifice, and Triumph through Resurrection. In the upper part of the window winged Seraphim raise their hands to Heaven.

The following windows were either destroyed or seriously damaged by bombing in the Second World War:

Henry VII's Chapel. South Apse Chapel, commemorating Lady Augusta Stanley, d. 1876 (see page 70).

East end of Choir, commemorating Archdeacon Bentinck, b. 1784, d. 1868.

Henry V's Chantry Chapel, commemorating John Ireland, Dean of Westminster, b. 1761, d. 1842.

St Michael's Chapel, commemorating officers and men who died in the Ashanti War, 1873–4.

Six Lancet Windows below the North Transept Rose Window, commemorating seven officers who lost their lives in the Indian Mutiny.

St Andrew's Chapel, commemorating Vincent Novello (b. 1781, d. 1861), musician.

East wall, South Transept, commemorating Geoffrey Chaucer and Edward the Confessor.

Nave (removed), commemorating Sir William Siemens, b. 1828, d. 1883, electrician, and Joseph Locke, b. 1805, d. 1860, engineer.

---

[1] *Stanley, page 282.*

The Chapter House Windows

The Windows of the Chapter House were largely re-glazed by *Miss Joan Howson* after they had been extensively damaged by air-raids in the Second World War.

The previous glass in the windows was by Messrs. Clayton and Bell, and was given as a memorial to Dean Stanley in 1882. It was found possible to incorporate some undamaged panels of this glass, which are easily recognizable, in the new windows, but the opportunity was taken to fill some of the windows with coats of arms set in clear glass, thus reverting to what is known to have been the way these windows were originally glazed.

The arms include those of sovereigns, other royal personages, and great feudal lords who were benefactors of the Abbey, as well as those of abbots who added to the fabric. Among the abbots thus commemorated are Langham, later Cardinal and Archbishop of Canterbury, Litlyngton, Islip, and Feckenham.

In the south-west and south-east windows are the devices of the medieval master-masons, Henry de Reyns who designed the present Abbey Church, and Henry Yevele who rebuilt the Nave. Other eminent architects and officials connected with the Abbey and Palace of Westminster are also commemorated. These include William of Wykeham, Bishop of Winchester and sometime Surveyor of the King's Buildings, Geoffrey Chaucer, Poet and Clerk of the King's Works, and Richard Whittington, Mayor of London and Treasurer, during the reign of Henry V, for the rebuilding of the Nave.

The arms of later architects include those of Sir Christopher Wren, Surveyor of the Fabric, Sir John Vanbrugh, and Sir Gilbert Scott, Surveyor of the Fabric, who restored the Chapter House in 1865.

There are also the arms of three First Commissioners of Works: Lord Mount Temple, who held office at the time of Scott's restoration; Lord Eversley, who was First Commissioner when the previous windows were inserted; and Lord Llanover (Sir Benjamin Hall), after whom 'Big Ben' is named. His arms are encircled with a clock-dial.

THE BELLS

THE ABBEY BELLS are eight in number; two new bells were added and the peal re-hung in 1919. The 'sermon-bell', technically called 'the tenor bell', strikes forty times after the sixth and seventh bells whenever a sermon is to be delivered. A small bell, called the 'Saints' Bell', cast by Thomas Lester in 1739, is rung before early celebrations for fifteen minutes on Sundays and five minutes on weekdays. On the occasion of a death within the precincts the sixth bell rings every half minute for half an hour; at the death of a member of the royal family, or of the Dean the tenor bell is sounded every minute for one hour. A muffled peal is rung after every funeral service.

THE ABBEY FLAGS

The following flags are flown on certain days on the North West Tower.

The Flag of St Peter (A pair of golden crossed keys surmounted by the ring of Edward the Confessor, on a red ground) is flown on all Church Festivals.

The Collegiate Flag (Azure, a Cross patonce between 5 martlers or; on a chief or France and England (old) quarterly on a pale between 2 double roses argent on gules seeded and barbed proper). This is flown on all occasions of local importance and significance. As the Sovereign is the Visitor of the Collegiate Church it is flown on Accession Day, Coronation Day, the Sovereign's Birthday, the Birthdays of the Royal Family, and the Queen's Wedding Day.

It is also flown on days associated with St Edward the Confessor (5 January and 15 October), Foundation Day (17 November), the Feast of the Dedication of the Church (28 December), Westminster School Election, the Election of the Mayor of Westminster, Civic Sunday, and the annual service attended by the Lord Chancellor and the Judges.

The Royal Standard is flown whenever the Sovereign is within the Abbey or its Precinct, and also whenever the Sovereign opens Parliament in person (a privilege specially granted by King Edward VII).

The Union Flag is flown on Commonwealth Day and Remembrance Sunday.

The Flags of the National Saints are flown on the following days: St George (23 April), St Andrew (30 November), St David (1 March) and St Patrick (17 March).

The Dominion Flags are flown on their Foundation Days: Australia (26 January), New Zealand (6 February), Canada (1 July).

The Royal Air Force Flag is flown on the Commemoration of the Battle of Britain.

N.B. At a Funeral or Memorial Service, or on the occasion of a death, the Collegiate Flag is flown at half-mast.

INDEX

The reference in heavy type is to the principal entry or entries.
An asterisk indicates more than one entry on the same page.
Italic figures indicate that the name only occurs on a plan.